THROUGH THE YEAR WITH DAVID WATSON

THROUGH THE YEAR WITH DAVID WATSON

Devotional readings for every day

edited by

JEAN WATSON

HODDER AND STOUGHTON
LONDON SYDNEY AUCKLAND TORONTO

British Library Cataloguing in Publication Data

Watson, David
  Through the Year with David Watson
  1. Devotional calendars
  I. Title   II. Watson, Jean
  242'.2   BV4810

ISBN 0-340-52076-0

First published in Great Britain 1982. This edition 1989.
Third impression 1991.

Published by Hodder and Stoughton
a division of Hodder and Stoughton Ltd,
Mill Road, Dunton Green, Sevenoaks, Kent TN13 2YA
Editorial Office: 47 Bedford Square, London WC1B 3DP

Printed in England by Clays Ltd, St Ives plc

CONTENTS

ACKNOWLEDGEMENTS

Key to acknowledgements in the text

K   — Key Cassettes, Scripture Union, 130 City Rd.,
             London EC1V 2NJ
AR   — Anchor Recordings, 72 The Street,
             Kennington, Ashford, Kent TN24 9HS
YTL   — York Tape Library, 36 Fellbrook Ave.,
             York YO2 5PS
CFP   — Christian Foundation Publications,
             45 Appleton Rd., Hale, Altrincham, Cheshire
C/LANL   — Cassette: Live a New Life
LANL   — Live a New Life, Inter-Varsity Press
IBIE   — I Believe in Evangelism, H & S*
IBITC   — I Believe in the Church, H & S*
OITS   — One in the Spirit, H & S*
HW   — Hidden Warfare, Send the Light Trust
IAT   — Is Anyone There? H & S*
ISOG   — In Search of God, Falcon Books
MGIR   — My God is Real, Falcon Books
D   — Discipleship, H & S*
PL   — Pastoral Letters
STD   — Start the Day Cassette, Scripture Union
TLR   — Talk for Local Radio
BRN   — Bible Reading Notes, Scripture Union

We are grateful for permission to use copyright material
*H & S — Hodder & Stoughton

INTRODUCTION

Over the years I have often been encouraged by extracts from the writings and sermons of others. These readings have not always been profound — far from it. But the brevity and simplicity of them have sometimes touched a personal need, strengthened faith in God, or stimulated me to further thought, study or prayer. It is with this in mind that, hesitatingly, I offer these simple and fallible words of mine.

I am enormously grateful to Jean Watson (no relation, except in Christ) for her painstaking patience and skill. How she ever studied so many of my books and listened to so many of my recorded sermons, I cannot imagine! Truly a feat of human endurance! What she has prepared for the reader is like a buffet which offers a wide variety of light dishes. My prayer is that some, at any rate, will suit your taste and that all will be nourishing. If, through these readings, your appetite is whetted for a more substantial meal from Christ himself as you feed on his word, we shall be well pleased.

In the words of the invitation of our Lord and Saviour, 'Come, everything is ready!'

David Watson

About this book . . .

Compiling these readings has been anything but a gruelling slog: I count it all joy — so great has been my excitement at discovering so many truths and insights towards which, I now realise, I have been groping for some time, but which I have never before heard or read so consistently or clearly expressed. I feel as though shuttered windows have been suddenly thrown open to let in more light and give access to fresh views.

I am very eager that many others should, through this book, gain inspiration from David Watson's ministry. His style is challenging but friendly, clear but not simplistic, and his many humorous touches and apt illustrations make his teaching the more memorable.

The material has been gathered from more than two hundred of David Watson's talks and sermons on cassette and from his books and pastoral letters. They cover a wide range of topics — thirty-four of which are listed in the index so that people can follow each theme through if they so wish.

For the first week in each month, the readings are geared to one of twelve major themes: worship and praise; new birth— new life; the Scriptures; Christian basics; committed discipleship; renewal; the Church worldwide; spiritual war; mission; prayer; life's experiences; Church fellowships. On the first day of each month there is a Bible study idea, with suggested references, on some aspect of the appropriate theme. Other Bible study ideas occur in the readings and for these suitable references can be found with the help of a concordance.

After the first week, readings range over various topics, but they have been arranged with an eye to balance and continuity where possible.

Throughout the book each reading is headed by a verse or verses of Scripture and is followed by a prayer and an idea for action or meditation, or a question. The New International Version has been the basis for all Scriptural quotations.

We hope that the book will be useful for individual prayer-times and for those responsible for family prayers, talks or epilogues, in homes, clubs, houseparties and other situations. Though primarily intended for devotional use, its Bible study ideas and index open up other possibilities. We have tried to bear in mind, as potential readers, both new Christians and the more spiritually mature.

Jean Watson

JANUARY
Worship and Praise

January 1   **Look ahead**

Forget the former things; do not dwell on the past. See, I am doing a new thing! Now it springs up; do you not perceive it? I am making a way in the desert and streams in the wasteland.
Isaiah 43:18,19

The journey of the children of Israel from Egypt to Jordan began with great joy and worship, many miracles and the tangible presence of God. However, instead of reaching the promised land in about a year, as they should have done, the Israelites took forty years — by which time many of the original group had died. What went wrong and what can we learn for ourselves?

Don't cling to the past. Under trial, the Israelites began to think they would have been better off if they had stayed in Egypt. Some Christians are always looking back to the 'good old days' too, but God has something *new* for us and we must follow the Spirit's leading today.

Don't grumble about the present. As God tested the Israelites, they responded with grumbling and complaints against God and their leaders. Criticism, gossip, resentment, grumbling, bitterness — these things quench the Holy Spirit and can keep us in the spiritual desert for years. When the pressure is on, often we look for someone on whom to offload our frustration and anger. This scapegoat may be someone we have never truly forgiven for some past hurt. But God forgives

11

and forgets, and we must do the same if we want to experience his blessings.

Be full of faith for the future. God is able to do new things, unless our unbelief prevents him. He wants to change the moral and spiritual wilderness into a land filled with the fruit of his Spirit. Do you believe this? Then worship and praise the Lord for it! (PL)

Father, help me to look ahead into this new year with confident faith.

Have I put the past year happily to rest?

Bible study: How and for what should God's people worship him? *Starters:* Exodus 20:1-3; Psalms 29;116;136; Acts 2:42-47; I Corinthians 14:26-39; Ephesians 5:18-20; Colossians 3:16; Revelation 4 and see under 'worship and praise' in index.

January 2   How do we worship?

The true worshippers will worship the Father in spirit and truth.   John 4:23

In many Christian circles today we have neglected, to our cost, the priority of worship. The church has two basic functions: first to worship, secondly to witness. It is to offer 'spiritual sacrifices acceptable to God through Jesus Christ' before it declares to others 'the praises of him who called you out of darkness into his wonderful light' (1 Peter 2:5,9). Unfortunately, worship for many has come to mean a few hymns and prayers arranged in some liturgical or non-liturgical pattern; whereas 'the true worshippers will worship the Father in spirit and truth,' Jesus said.

Here the combination is important. It is not only a question of *what* we say or sing. It is a question of *how* we say or sing it. It must be from the heart — from our inmost being. Just as the Spirit witnesses with our spirit that we are children of God,

12

prompting us to cry, 'Abba! Father!' (Galatians 4:6) — so all true worship should have this communication between Spirit and spirit, so that we worship the Father in spirit as well as in truth. Not spirit alone, for that could be purely emotional; nor truth alone, for that could be purely intellectual. But 'all my inmost being' should 'praise his holy name' (Psalm 103:1) (OITS)

Lord, I ask for a new spirit of worship for myself and for my church fellowship in this coming year.

Do we need to spend more time preparing for worship? If so, how?

January 3   Why worship God?

Holy, holy, holy is the Lord God Almighty, who was, and is, and is to come.   **Revelation 4:8**

In this verse we are given three reasons for worshipping God.

First, he is worshipped for his holiness. The word 'holy' repeated three times emphasises God's exceeding, unimaginable holiness. When the sun shines in great strength, plants with their roots deep in the soil grow, but those whose roots are not in the soil wither up. Similarly, if we are rooted and grounded in the soil of God's love, we can blossom and flourish and not be shrivelled up by his burning holiness. Once we understand the utter holiness of God, we will worship him more fervently for his incredible mercy in Jesus. The fact that he is so holy makes his forgiveness all the more amazing and calls forth our deepest worship.

Secondly, God is worshipped for his omnipotence: 'the Lord God Almighty'. The first Christians in the midst of their sufferings needed to know this truth, and so do we. A vicar friend of mine, while preaching on suffering, said, 'What would you say if I dropped down dead?' Not long afterwards he did just that.

One of the things I wrote in my letter to his widow was this: 'The Lord reigns.'

Thirdly, God is worshipped for his changelessness: 'who was, and is, and is to come'. This is a fantastic truth in this world of change. He is the eternal one, the great I AM who is always present and sees into our innermost being.

When we realise all this we will take care to draw near to worship God 'having our hearts sprinkled to cleanse us from a guilty conscience' (Hebrews 10:22). (YTL)

When I come to worship is my conscience quickened by the holiness of God?

'Hallelujah! For our Lord God Almighty reigns' (Revelation 19:6).

January 4   Worship means sacrifice

Through Jesus, therefore, let us continually offer to God a sacrifice of praise — the fruit of lips that confess his name. And do not forget to do good and to share with others, for with such sacrifices God is pleased.   Hebrews 13:15,16

'We take a convert and immediately make a worker out of him,' wrote Dr. A. W. Tozer. 'God never meant it to be so. God meant that a convert should learn to be a worshipper, and after that he can learn to be a worker. The work done by a worshipper will have eternity in it.'

The Bible is shot through with examples and expressions of worship, and here are three sacrifices by which we can worship God today.

First, there is the sacrifice of praise. 'He who sacrifices thank-offerings honours me' (Psalm 50:23). Singing and music play a very important part here, so let's encourage our singers and musicians to sing, to play and to compose for God's glory and the enrichment of our worship.

Secondly, there is the sacrifice of possessions. This was a

14

major secret of spiritual power in the early church, quite apart from the fact that God was glorified (Acts 4:32).

Thirdly, there is the sacrifice of persons. The vitality and power of the Body of Christ will depend on the extent to which our bodies become living sacrifices (Romans 12:1). (PL)

How sacrificial is our worship?

Lord, we do not naturally welcome the idea of sacrifice. Please may your Holy Spirit fill us with such love for you that we will not even want to hold anything back from you.

January 5   Joyful worship

Praise the Lord, O my soul: all my inmost being, praise his holy name.   Psalm 103:1

There are seven different words used for worship in the New Testament and the one used far more often than the rest could be translated literally, 'I come towards to kiss.' In other words, in worship, I come as a son or daughter towards my loving Father, to love and adore him, and he embraces me with his love. Don't be afraid of sometimes being a bit emotional when you catch a glimpse of God's love and glory as you worship him. If you're not emotional then, when *will* you get emotional?

One of the chief elements in worship is praise (Hebrews 13:15). In Hebrew there are three main words for praise. The first means *making a noise* — and quite a loud noise at that! The second means *playing an instrument* and the third means *moving the body*. The psalms speak of clapping hands and also of lifting hands. When I used to return home after being away, my children — then small — would call, 'Daddy, Daddy!' and run towards me with their arms outstretched. So there's nothing strange about raising our hands to our heavenly Father and calling out, 'Abba, Father.' Dancing is also mentioned in the psalms. Many people are word-resistant

15

today, but these same people may well be touched with God's presence when they see God's people filled with joy as they worship him. (AR)

Set me free, Lord, to praise you with my inmost being and to let the joy I feel find its natural expression.

How can I show God and others that I'm glad to come into his presence?

January 6   Worship nourished by truth

Worthy is the Lamb who was slain, to receive power and wealth and wisdom and strength and honour and glory and praise.   Revelation 5:12

The worship of heaven is based on truth (Revelation 4 and 5).

First of all, worship in heaven arises from *the truth of God's character*. He is holy, changeless, almighty. The more we learn of the truth of his character, the more truly can we worship him.

Secondly, worship in heaven is occasioned by *the truth of God's creation*. 'You are worthy, our Lord and God, to receive glory and honour and power, for you created all things, and by your will they were created and have their being' (Revelation 4:11). Because we know that God created all things, we worship the Creator, in contrast to the many who exchange 'the truth of God for a lie, and worship and serve created things rather than the Creator' (Romans 1:25).

Thirdly, worship in heaven and on earth springs from *the truth of God's redemption*. The Archbishop of Milan tells a story about a gang leader who was dared to go into the Cathedral, make up the most startling confessions, and take whatever penance the priest suggested. The lad took on the dare, and the old priest told him to kneel before a crucifix and say, 'You died for me and I don't care a damn.' So he knelt down and said, 'You died for me and —' but he couldn't look into the model of the face of Christ and end the sentence in that way. The Archbishop of Milan ends the account like this: 'I know the story's true, because I was that gang leader.' (YTL)

Father, I worship you for who you are and what you have given us in creation and done for us in redemption.

Do I turn truth into worship?

January 7   **Praise and you will find**

Be joyful always; pray continually; give thanks in all circumstances, for this is God's will for you in Christ Jesus.
                                                    1 Thessalonians 5:16-18

Christians all over the world are experiencing great things when they praise God. As they praise the Lord for his love, they find themselves abiding in his love. As they praise the Lord that his grace is sufficient, they experience that it is sufficient. As they praise the Lord for his control over their lives, they see his control in different parts of their lives. As they praise the Lord for his gentleness and tenderness, they sense his gentleness and tenderness. As they praise the Lord for setting them free, they find new freedom.

Whatever you praise the Lord for, that will increasingly become your living experience, because the more we focus on God, the more he meets our needs.

So often it's our attitude, rather than our work, that robs us of our strength. The joy of the Lord is our strength (Nehemiah 8:10), and so when we praise the Lord, even when we find it a costly sacrifice to do so, we are likely to discover fresh springs welling up within us, refreshing and strengthening us.

But be prepared for things to go wrong at times. We may be experiencing great things through the power of praise, and then something happens and we are brought low and wonder what God is doing. In that situation we must simply press on and one day we will come out into the brightness again — and

17

know the joy of his presence with us once more. (YTL)

Lord, I offer you now a sacrifice of praise for ...

Am I prepared to obey this verse, literally, starting today?

January 8   Joyful awe

So all Israel brought up the ark of the covenant of the Lord with shouts, with the sounding of rams' horns and trumpets, and of cymbals, and the playing of lyres and harps.

1 Chronicles 15:28

When David and the people first tried to bring the ark of God back to Jerusalem, their exuberant joy turned quickly to grief, when God had to give them a sharp reminder of his utter holiness. Humbled and chastened, they tried again; this time there was awe as well as joy, and the ceremony went off smoothly.

Right through the Bible, those who encountered God were filled with awe and a sense of their own unworthiness (see Exodus 3:6; Isaiah 6:5; Daniel 8:27; Luke 5:8; Revelation 1:17; 6:16).

Nations today need to rediscover the holiness of God. So do many Christians, who rightly teach the friendship of Jesus but omit to emphasise God's holiness. We misunderstand and misuse prayer if we think that we can breeze into God's presence with a string of requests. We misunderstand and misuse God's forgiveness if we sin lightly, thinking, 'Of course, God will forgive.'

At the outset of any revival, usually a small group of people have seen afresh the utter purity and holiness of God. The king of glory can come in only when his people have seen his holiness and have 'clean hands and a pure heart', as David wrote in the psalm (24) composed for this special occasion in the nation's life.

But God's presence doesn't only cause awe; it also — if things are right — produces overflowing joy (Psalm 16:11). There's no

18

joy on earth compared to that of knowing that God, the holy God, is with you, protecting, caring for and loving you. (YTL)

Is lack of joy or lack of awe my point of spiritual weakness?

Lord, I need a fresh vision and experience of you so that I will worship you with joyful awe.

The heart is deceitful above all things and beyond cure. Who can understand it?   **Jeremiah 17:9**

There was a famous correspondence in *The Times* on 'What's wrong with the world?' Probably the most penetrating of all the letters was from G.K. Chesterton: 'Dear Sir, I am. Yours sincerely.' That is precisely the answer. The heart of the human problem is the problem of the human heart.

Once you step out of an intellectual greenhouse into the fierce storms of everyday life, you are forced to be realistic about human nature. You cannot be blind to the sin which exists in the heart of man. Dr C.E.M. Joad, who for many years embraced a 'rational-optimist philosophy', found his idealistic beliefs shattered in the last world war. He came to see that 'evil is endemic in man, and that the Christian doctrine of original sin expresses a deep and essential insight into human nature'.

Christ taught a good deal about sin. He saw it as man's number one need for God. He saw it as corrupting and spoiling the life of every person born into the world. That is why he came: to 'save his people from their sins' (Matthew 1:21). He knew that unless the diagnosis of man was known and accepted, and unless the surgeon's knife could do its work, this cancer of sin would spread and kill.

What's wrong with the world is that it's full of people like me but without my Saviour. Do you believe that? (MGIR)

If I'm obsessed with the sin in the world, I could be 'anti' everything and become an angry bore; if I'm obsessed with my own sin, I could be a joyless depressive. How can I avoid these extremes and yet treat sin, wherever I see it, with due seriousness?

Lord, I don't want to be bogged down by sin, nor do I want to gloss over it. Help me to have, more and more, the mind of Christ in this matter.

January 10   It's *good* news!

Jesus went throughout Galilee, teaching in their synagogues, preaching the good news of the kingdom, and healing every disease and sickness among the people.   Matthew 4:23

Essentially the gospel is good news for sinners. Everywhere Jesus went, people were healed, forgiven, set free, filled with joy and life. The disciples didn't fully grasp this. When some Samaritans didn't welcome Jesus they asked, 'Shall we call down fire from heaven? Do you want to judge them?' But Jesus rebuked them (Luke 9:51-56). He had come to save. True, there were severe warnings about judgment for those who refused the good news, but Jesus proclaimed the good news first of all. The kingdom of heaven he likened to a wedding feast — a very happy occasion.

We must not only *tell* people the news is good; we must *show* them that it is, too. A circus clown was sent to a town to warn the people that the big tent was on fire and that the fire might easily spread to the town. He went about in his clown's outfit, shouting, 'There's fire! There's fire!' but the people roared with laughter, thinking he was being funny. The fire *did* spread and the town was burnt down. The people hadn't taken any notice of the clown's words because his image cancelled out his message. Does our image cancel out our message?

We tell people the message is about life and joy, but unless our lives are full of life and joy, they won't believe us. If we present an old-fashioned image, whatever our lips are saying, the message we are conveying is that our God is a God of yesterday only. As someone has said, 'The brand image of the church is meaningless, old-fashioned, opinionated, way behind the times, incomprehensible, irrelevant. Where are your consumer benefits?' (YTL)

Is the image which we are presenting to the world in keeping with the good news we're talking about?

Father, thank you that the gospel is good news. Thank you for the good it has brought into my life . . .

January 11   **The rule of the king**

Do not be afraid, little flock, for your Father has been pleased to give you the kingdom.   Luke 12:32

In normal use, a kingdom means a realm ruled by a king, but in the Bible, the kingdom of God means the rule of the king, so that we are in the kingdom when God is king of our lives. This means repentance, or an about-turn, laying down our arms of rebellion and putting ourselves and our lives at God's disposal. As members of his kingdom we are to submit to God and depend on his sovereign control in every part of our lives (Luke 12:27-34).

The *message* of the kingdom is God's message —not ours. When Jesus sent out the seventy, he gave them their message (Luke 10:8-12). The gospel of the kingdom is still God's message which is entrusted to his people (2 Corinthians 5:19). If I lent you my car, I would expect you to return it intact, not with bits knocked off or added on. It's the same with the message God has entrusted to us: we are not to take anything away from it or add anything to it; we are simply to be faithful in passing it on intact.

The *methods* of the kingdom are to be God's methods —not

ours. We see the priorities of the early Christians (Acts 2:42-47). They were people profoundly conscious of their own weakness and inadequacy for the task ahead, and so totally dependent on God to show them his methods. They concentrated on fellowship, teaching, worship and prayer — making sure that their relationship with the Lord and with one another was absolutely right.

Jesus proclaimed the kingdom of God and what came was the church. The kingdom has all the basic principles which were found later in the church. (YTL)

Is God honestly ruling in every part of my life?

Father, may your kingdom come in me.

January 12   **What does repentance mean?**

The kingdom of heaven is near. Repent and believe the good news.   **Mark 1:15**

If someone asked you to explain what repentance means — would you be able to do it?

Repentance means a change of mind, leading to a change of heart, resulting in a change of direction.

With the mind we must acknowledge our sin and guilt before God: 'There is no-one who does good, not even one' (Romans 3:12).

However, mental assent to that is not enough; the heart must feel some sorrow and deep-seated regret that, by our sin, we have offended God and crucified his Son. Simon Peter, when he knew what he had done in denying Jesus, went out and wept bitterly. In practice, the degree of sorrow may vary considerably.

Yet even the change of mind and heart is not enough. There must also be a change of direction. Repentance means an about-turn. It means being willing, with the help of Christ, to turn away from all that is wrong in our lives, and to go with

Jesus instead. No man can knowingly remain disobedient to God and receive Christ at the same time. No man can hold on to sin with one hand, and try to take Jesus with the other. It simply does not work.

It is seldom possible, or even wise, to spell out the full implications of discipleship, beyond the acceptance of Jesus Christ as Lord, but often certain practical consequences of repentance will have to be faced: a young couple sleeping together must either separate or get married; dishonest business deals or fiddling the income tax returns will have to be put right as soon as possible; resentment and bitterness must be handed over immediately to Christ; racial prejudice must be confessed; pornographic literature or occult books must be destroyed. There is nothing airy-fairy about repentance, nor is it simply a turning away from what is wrong. It is turning towards a life of sacrificial love, as a true follower of Jesus Christ. (IBIE)

Finish this sentence in your own words, as though explaining to a friend: 'Repentance is . . .'

Lord, show me if there's anything I need to turn from now.

January 13   **No Spirit — no life**

Unless a man is born again, he cannot see the kingdom of God. . . Flesh gives birth to flesh, but the Spirit gives birth to Spirit.   **John 3:3,6**

Only the Holy Spirit can cause spiritual birth to take place. People can be church-going, God-fearing, and yet spiritually unborn. I had the joy of leading one such person to a personal faith in Jesus, but it was the Holy Spirit who brought about the inner change which is called *being born again* or *receiving the new birth*. Afterwards that person wrote; 'All I can say now is that I was completely blind and could not see what God was offering me all the time. Consequently I went on being hungry and thirsty. I am so glad that now I know Christ is real and alive and I want you to share this joy with me.'

It is the Holy Spirit who confirms our salvation (Romans 8:16). One of the first cries of a child is 'dadda'. And one of the first cries from the heart of someone spiritually born is, 'Abba, Father.' Deep inside us, he makes us sure of our relationship with God.

The Holy Spirit is vital to the Christian's growth. He helps us to worship and to praise (Philippians 3:3). The English word *praise* comes from an old Latin word meaning *prize*. The Holy Spirit helps us to see and to prize our riches in Jesus. Spiritual birth, life and growth — all these come from the Holy Spirit. (AR)

Lord, may your Holy Spirit teach me to prize and value what you give to me in Jesus, and to praise and worship you with my whole heart.

How much time do I spend in worship each day, each week? Is it enough?

January 14   **Putting things right**

Forgive, and you will be forgiven.   **Luke 6:37**

A little girl is said to have remarked to a Scotsman playing the bagpipes, 'If you let it go, it'll stop screaming.' In fairness my family comes from Scotland and I love the bagpipes, but adapting that comment I would say that unless we let go of our hurts, they will go on screaming inside us. Equally, unless we learn to forgive and love, we will never be able to convince others of the Christian message. An American professor of theology said this: 'We want none of your talk of forgiveness: we want to see a community where forgiving, accepting love is happening and changing personal behaviour.'

Bishop Festo Kivengere had an argument with his wife one evening. Afterwards he had to go out and preach, so he said goodbye and went off. But as he walked down the drive, God spoke to him — and this is how Bishop Festo described the ensuing dialogue between himself and his Lord.

'Festo,' said the Lord, 'you go back and apologise to your wife.'

'But Lord, I've got a very important sermon to preach.'

'You go and apologise to your wife.'

'But Lord, there are hundreds of people waiting for me and we're going to have a good time tonight.'

'You go and apologise to your wife.'

'But Lord, I'm almost late and someone's waiting to collect me.'

'All right,' the Lord said, 'you go and preach your sermon and I'm going to stay with your wife in the kitchen.'

Bishop Festo ended the story with these words: 'I went back into the kitchen and apologised. So there was revival in the kitchen before there was revival in the church.'

God has forgiven us a million times more than we shall have to forgive anyone else, so let's make sure that we are not holding anyone in the prison of our unforgiveness, whether the fault was ours or the other person's. (AR)

I release from my resentment . . . and pray for your love for him/her.

Is our home and our church family a place where Christian forgiveness is constantly practised?

January 15   Can I be sure that I am forgiven?

If we confess our sins, he is faithful and just and will forgive us our sins and purify us from all unrighteousness.   1 John 1:9

The head of a large mental hospital said that he would be able to send *half* his patients home *cured*, if only they could be assured of forgiveness.

We are assured that the blood of Jesus purifies us from every

25

sin (1 John 1:7). The verb is in the present tense so the verse is really saying that the blood of Jesus goes on and on cleansing and purifying us from all sin. The Bible is full of magnificent promises about forgiveness (e.g. Isaiah 1:18; Jeremiah 31:34: Psalm 103:12; Micah 7:19). But there are conditions.

We need to confess our sins to God. Walking in the light involves honestly facing up to the fact of our sins and confessing them before God without making any excuses for ourselves.

We may also need to confess our sins to one another (James 5:16). James links this kind of confession with healing and this certainly includes the healing of the mind, the memories, the personality and relationships.

We must forgive those who have wronged us (Matthew 6:14; 18:15-20; Mark 11:25). In practice, it may not be enough for us to forgive the person in our hearts, nor even to *tell* him of our forgiveness for him. Often, we need to *show*, through practical acts of love, our changed attitude. It is the loving action which demonstrates to ourselves, as well as to the person concerned, that we really have forgiven him completely. (YTL)

Is there anyone who needs to be assured of my forgiveness for him or her? What can I do about it?

Father, as I obey you, by putting relationships right with others, please assure me of your forgiveness.

January 16   Building a relationship

Grow in the grace and knowledge of our Lord and Saviour Jesus Christ.   2 Peter 3:18

Starting a relationship with Jesus is rather like starting a marriage relationship. At our wedding service, the minister asked me, 'David, will you have Anne as your wife?' and I replied, 'I will.' Then he turned to Anne, saying, 'Anne, will you have

David as your husband?' and she replied, 'I will.' At that moment a new relationship was established. Similarly God asks, 'Saviour, will you have this sinner?' and Jesus *always* answers, 'I will.' Then God turns to us saying, 'Sinner, will you have this Saviour?' and when we answer, individually, 'I will,' a new relationship begins.

But just as we have to work at our marriage relationships, so we need to build on our relationship with Jesus. Becoming a Christian can be summarised in three words: *knowing Jesus personally*. Living and growing as a Christian can be summed up as *getting to know Jesus better and better*.

If someone were to come to you and say, 'I'm a Christian, but I seem to be standing still, I don't seem to be making any progress,' what would you answer? Take time to work out in your own mind and perhaps on paper, too, how Christians can build on their relationship with Jesus, or grow as Christians. Try to avoid theological jargon and have references to back up your points. (AR)

Lord, if there is anyone who needs to hear what I have discovered from your word today, bring us together, and may your spirit give me humility and courage to share it.

How can I grow as a Christian, and how are we encouraging spiritual maturity in our church?

January 17   One sacrifice

When this priest [Jesus] had offered for all time one sacrifice for sins, he sat down at the right hand of God.   Hebrews 10:12

Under the old covenant there was no assurance of forgiveness because there were endless sacrifices for sin. Every year 113 bullocks, thirty-seven rams, thirty goats and 1,093 lambs were sacrificed. Christ went to the cross as our one perfect sacrifice, and because of that, in the new covenant, God is able to say to us, 'I will forgive their wickedness and will remember their sins no more' (Jeremiah 31:34).

There are Christians who are still living under the old covenant. Some still have no assurance of forgiveness and peace of mind. They cannot see that when Christ cried out on the cross, 'Finished!' he meant that he had done everything necessary to give us peace with God and a conscience freed from guilt.

Others still firmly believe that they are right with God and have a place in heaven because they are doing their best and leading a decent, religious life. But this is a delusion. We have to come humbly to Jesus, take him as our personal Saviour and put our trust in him alone and not in anything we might or might not have done. Only then can God remember our sins no more.

Under the old covenant, God says, in effect: 'If you keep my laws, I will bless you;' under the new covenant: 'You can't keep my laws, therefore I offer you salvation as a free gift.' There are some people who are too proud to accept charity — even from God — and who say, 'I can get on very well by myself, thank you,' instead of, 'Lord Jesus, I need you and I take you.' (YTL)

What's the difference between Christ's one sacrifice and any sacrifices which a Christian is expected to make?

Father, thank you that Jesus was a full, perfect and sufficient sacrifice for the sins of the whole world, including mine.

January 18   **The prayer priority**

Lord, teach us to pray.   **Luke 11:1**

Prayer has always been a primary mark of the saints of God in every generation of the church. George Whitefield, who retired punctually at 10 pm every night, rose equally promptly at 4 am in order to pray. John Wesley spent two hours daily in prayer, and commonly said that 'God does nothing but in answer to prayer'. Martin Luther commented, 'If I fail to spend two hours in prayer each morning, the devil gets the victory through the day. I have so much business I cannot get on without spending three hours daily in prayer.'

The leaders of the Clapham Sect, such as William Wilberforce, who initiated enormous social reforms in England, habitually gave themselves to three hours of prayer each day. They organised Christians throughout the country to unite in special prayer before critical debates in Parliament. They knew, and persistently proved, the power of prayer. William Temple replied to his critics who regarded answered prayer as no more than coincidences, 'When I pray, coincidences happen; when I don't, they don't.'

With such examples of the heroes of faith, it is hard not to feel a crushing failure! I suspect that most of us are ashamed of the poverty of our prayer life. In Western society in particular, we are consumed by activism and have lost the prayerful meditation of our Eastern brethren.

The prayer of those first disciples, then, is highly relevant for us. (D)

Lord, teach me to pray.

How can I rearrange my life so that I can spend more time in prayer daily?

January 19   The helper

The Spirit intercedes for the saints in accordance with God's will.   Romans 8:27

We know that the Holy Spirit makes Christians, but what does he do for them afterwards?

He helps us to pray. If you are finding prayer hard, ask specifically and definitely for the help of the Holy Spirit in this area *before* you begin praying. Time and again I have done this and have received help.

He helps us to overcome sin (Romans 8:2). Hold a Bible up

on the palm of your hand and it'll be subject to two forces: the force of gravity wanting to pull it down and the force of your hand holding it up. Remove your hand and the Bible would fall. The law of sin and death is like gravity, wanting to pull us down, but the law of the Spirit of life, like our hand, can hold us up and set us free from all that would drag us down or chain us.

He helps us to serve (1 Corinthians 12:5). God's grace shines into his people and is expressed in a whole range of gifts by which we can serve each other.

He helps us to become more like Jesus (2 Corinthians 3:18). One woman changed so much through knowing Jesus that when she sent in her passport with a new photograph of herself, asking if that could be substituted for the old one, the officials wrote back saying, 'We cannot believe the two photographs are of the same person.' So she had to sign a form and buy a new passport! We might not change so dramatically or quickly, but change we most certainly will and should if the Holy Spirit is in control of our lives. (AR)

Father, I ask for the help of the Holy Spirit in praying day by day.

What has the Holy Spirit been doing in and for me during the past weeks and months?

January 20   **Prayer must be real**

Listen to my prayer, O God, do not ignore my plea; hear me and answer me ... My heart is in anguish within me; the terrors of death assail me.   **Psalm 55:1,2,4**

The glorious fact about prayer is that we do not have to pretend with God. He knows all about us, anyway. He simply wants us to share every part of our lives with him, and that includes our fears and failings, our moods and emotions, our thoughts and anxieties — everything, even those things of which we are deeply ashamed. Read the Psalms and see the total honesty of the psalmist. Constantly he told God all about his doubts and difficulties, his anger and despair, his confusion, pain and joy. His prayer was real.

So it was with Jesus. We see no stoicism in the Garden of Gethsemane: 'Father, if it is possible, may this cup be taken from me' (Matthew 26.39). Three times he prayed the same prayer with his sweat like great drops of blood falling on the ground. He shrank from the appalling ordeal of the cross, even though he submitted himself perfectly to his Father's will.

Again, look at the transparent honesty of the apostle Paul. In his letters he wrote specifically about his own weaknesses no less than twenty-two times. He admitted that at Corinth he was 'nervous and shaking with fear'. At times he even despaired of life itself. His whole life, including his prayer life, had this refreshing touch of reality about it.

Do not be afraid of bringing your most secret thoughts and desires to God: all he looks for in us is honesty. As soon as we are open with him, he will work gently in our lives to mould us more into the likeness of Christ. (D)

Lord, help me to be utterly honest with you.

Buy a notebook and start writing down exactly what you share with God and what you ask of him each day in prayer.

January 21   God's word

In the past God spoke to our forefathers through the prophets at many times and in various ways.   **Hebrews 1:1**

Having sent his messages through the prophets, God spoke a *personal* word when 'the Word became flesh and lived for a while among us' (John 1:14). Jesus was God's personal word for all people and all time. When he spoke 'the crowds were amazed at his teaching, because he taught as one who had authority' (Matthew 7:28,29).

The personal word is not with us today as he was two thousand years ago, but we have instead God's *written* word, the Scriptures. The Bible is not an easy book to understand and so some have leant on one kind of authority or another to help them interpret it.

Tradition, or what the church says, is one authority some have chosen to rely on, but Jesus showed that this was not reliable (Mark 7:8-13). Others rely on reason to interpret the Scriptures but Jesus rejected this rationalist approach (Matthew 22:23-33). Others still rely on a leader — this is dangerous and, taken to extremes, produces cults in which leaders become the word of God to their followers.

The only major authority for judging Scripture is by Scripture itself; it is its own authority. Jesus saw the Scriptures as God's word which could not be broken (John 10:35), from which nothing could be taken away and to which nothing should be added (Matthew 5:17-19), and which he came to fulfil by all he said and did (Matthew 26:53,54).

God also uses the *spoken* word — which comes through preaching, witness, sharing, prophecy — but this must always be in accordance with the *written* word, the Scriptures, and glorifying to the *personal* word, Jesus. (YTL)

Thank you, Father, for your personal word and your written word. Keep me ready to obey him and it.

Do some Bible study, linking passages which expand or interpret one another.

January 22   **Keep listening**

Man does not live on bread alone, but on every word that comes from the mouth of God.   **Matthew 4:4**

We need sensitive spiritual ears to hear God speaking to us. He speaks through his world, through people and events and through other means but, most of all, he speaks through the

Bible, his word. It is not enough to read books about God's word, or even books of readings such as this one! These may be helpful and inspiring 'extras', but they cannot take the place of daily Bible reading.

Notes are helpful in keeping us regular and in explaining difficult verses, but we shouldn't depend on them too much. It is the Holy Spirit who is our teacher, so we need to pray before we read that he will open our spiritual ears to God's voice, and then expect him to answer that prayer.

Our lives are frequently too busy for us to find time to read the Bible every day; we have to *make* time for it and be disciplined about keeping to it.

As we read, the question in our minds should be: 'What is God saying to me through this?'

And when we understand what God is saying, we must act upon it. God doesn't speak to us to satisfy our curiosity. He speaks so that we will act. Hearing and obeying must go hand in hand. (C/LANL)

Am I really reading the Bible each morning, expecting God to teach me something or to say something to me?

Lord, I am listening. Speak to me, for your words are life.

January 23   The secrets we know, we must share

The secret things belong to the Lord our God, but the things revealed belong to us and to our children for ever, that we may follow all the words of this law.   Deuteronomy 29:29

If God has shared his secrets with us, we have a great responsibility to share them with others. Thousands of people are thirsty for a satisfying life and are trying to find it through drink, sex, money, marriage, and so on. If we know that those who drink of the water Jesus gives will never thirst again (John 4:14), we must tell them this. Thousands are anxious and dependent on pills to keep them calm. If we know that Jesus

33

brings peace (Matthew 11:28-30), we have a responsibility to share this. Thousands are lost and confused. If we know that Jesus brings light (John: 8:12), we must pass it on.

In sharing what God has revealed to us, our first responsibility is to our own families and our own circle of friends. No one else has the same family and friends that you have — and so 'there's a work for Jesus none but you can do.' If God has shown us that he's loving and holy, that there's salvation and judgment, that Christ is the only way to God — then we must surely do everything we can to let the people round us, close to us, know these things.

If you have a Christian home, why not invite in friends and neighbours and tell them, through tapes, through a speaker, or in any other way, the secrets which God has shown to you? If everyone did this, the impact would be tremendous. (YTL)

God forbid that any of my family or friends should miss salvation through my fault.

Am I really sharing with those closest to me what God is teaching me of himself?

January 24   This word changes lives

Let the word of Christ dwell in you richly as you teach and admonish one another with all wisdom, and as you sing psalms, hymns and spiritual songs with gratitude in your hearts to God. And whatever you do, whether in word or deed, do it all in the name of the Lord Jesus, giving thanks to God the Father through him.   **Colossians 3:16,17**

When we went to St. Cuthbert's York, in 1965, we longed to preach Christ crucified. At the age of twenty-one Jesus became real to me, and ever since then I have wanted others to know his reality too. Within a week of our first day of prayer and fasting, I was able to lead four people to Christ. It was as though God was saying, 'This is the right priority. You concentrate on prayer, then I will work through you.'

At the same time, I preached simple Biblical sermons, based on a Bible book or character or theme. My first series was on Abraham, a man of faith, and since I was preaching to an almost empty church, I needed to hear my own sermon week by week, in order to be able to hold on by faith! At first I realised that the moment I started to preach, people automatically switched off. But over a period of time and with patient persistence, lives began to open to God's truths and then to be changed by them. As I have found since, you need to say something incessantly for about a year before anyone notices that you're saying anything different. But at last, God's truths were heard with people's ears and then received into their minds and finally into their hearts and out into their lives. (AR)

Lord, make my heart and life really receptive to your word.

Does the word preached each Sunday actually affect and change the day-to-day lives of those of us who hear it? If not, why not?

January 25   The dramatic word

He [Jesus] got up from the meal, took off his outer clothing, and wrapped a towel round his waist. After that, he poured water into a basin and began to wash his disciples' feet, drying them with the towel that was wrapped around him.

John 13:4,5

We have found that drama is a very powerful way of reaching those right outside the Christian church. God is a God of drama. What could be more dramatic than the incarnation, when the Word of God became a human being? What could be more dramatic than when Jesus washed the feet of his own disciples, instead of just telling them to serve one another? What could be more dramatic than some of Ezekiel's prophecies or those of Agabus in the New Testament?

35

We have been able to go into a prison in Belfast where many terrorists are detained. When we go there, we sing and do short pieces of drama followed by a short talk. The response from the prisoners has been tremendous. The first time we went, the commander of one of the leading terrorist groups in Northern Ireland was converted. He wrote to me afterwards like this: 'I had been considering for some time becoming a Christian, but after seeing your team (and I noticed that he did *not* say, "after hearing your sermon") I no longer had any doubts, and have now been saved by the blood of Christ.' Later on, he told his prison chaplain: 'For the first time in my life, I feel free.' Although a man convicted of violence, he is free in Christ.

We have found that simple dramatised versions of the parables and other teachings of Jesus can be very powerful indeed. (AR)

What did people see when they worshipped at our church last Sunday?

Lord, if there are those in our fellowship with dramatic or other visual gifts, please make it possible for them to use them for your glory and the enrichment of our worship.

January 26   God's Law

Where there is no revelation, the people cast off restraint.
Proverbs 29:18

All over the world today people are rebelling against authority, law and order. When moral justice breaks down the basis of a free society also collapses. Richard Wurmbrand has written, 'When man has no faith in the reward of good or the punishment of evil, there is no reason to be human, there is no restraint on the depth of evil which is in man.' And after his experiences in Communist prisons, he knows what he is talking about.

Our nation is not atheistic, but we are suffering from a lack of God-consciousness and moral restraint, which shows in street violence, stealing, sexual licence and many other ways. In every area there is little or no God-framework and many feel they can do as they wish.

Someone has said, 'Society has significantly changed in history only as a result of either revival from within the church, or revolution from without.' To put it another way, we can have God's rule or mob rule.

It's important to remember that God's commands are not arbitrary — they are the maker's instructions for our good. Their purpose is threefold: to express God's love for us, to expose our sin, and to drive us to Christ (Galatians 3:24).

I believe we're heading for revival or revolution. As Christians we must seek to bring the presence of God wherever we go — in homes, schools, colleges and places of work, in streets and shops, so that it will be God's rule and not mob rule that will prevail. (YTL)

Father, as I walk along the streets, help me to pray for the people I meet who seem to be worn or worried.

Am I doing anything other than grumbling about the state of the country? Should I act in some way?

January 27   **God's will in God's way**

David was angry because the Lord's wrath had broken out against Uzzah. . . David was afraid of the Lord that day.
                                                   2 Samuel 6:8,9

David knew that he needed God's presence with him to help him rule wisely and well. So he arranged for the ark, the symbol of God's presence, to be brought back to Jerusalem on a cart pulled by oxen. As the cart rumbled along, David and the people celebrated with all their might, singing and playing musical instruments.

Suddenly, disaster struck. A man put out his hand to steady

the ark. The next moment he was dead. The music stopped and the body was carried out. Angry and then afraid, David and the people went home. What was God doing? David had wanted the right thing — God's presence in the centre of his kingdom. So what had he done wrong? Undoubtedly, he searched the Scriptures for the answer.

There he discovered that he had made two important mistakes. First, the ark should never have been dumped on a cart drawn by oxen. The ark had been made with four rings in it, and two poles for slotting through these rings. God's instructions were that the poles should *always* be in the rings so that the ark could be carried by this means (Exodus 25:12-15).

Secondly, the ark of God was to be carried only by the Levites and even they were strictly forbidden ever to touch the gold-covered box (Numbers 4:15).

Three months later, David had another big, joyful celebration as the ark was brought into Jerusalem, but this time he made sure everything was done according to God's word (1 Chronicles 15). God had had to teach David and the people, at a crucial time in their history, that he was utterly holy and that his word was sacred and must not be flouted. (YTL)

Father, please show me if in any area I'm doing wrong even for right reasons.

Why is it so important that God's will must be done in God's way?

January 28   **I know better**

Jesus told them [his disciples], 'This very night you will all fall away on account of me, for it is written: "I will strike the shepherd, and the sheep of the flock will be scattered."'

Matthew 26:31

Jesus said that all his disciples would desert him but warm-hearted, impulsive Peter knew better. 'Oh, no, Lord!' he protested. 'The others may fall away but not me' (see Matthew 26:33). He had made an almost identical mistake when Jesus had said he *must* suffer and be killed. Then Peter had exclaimed, 'Never, Lord! This shall never happen to you' (Matthew 16:22).

On both occasions, he doubted Christ's word, and this is a symptom of that deadly sin — spiritual pride. The serpent asked Eve, 'Did God really say. . .?' (Genesis 3:1) — and this temptation to doubt or distrust God's word has been one of the devil's most successful tactics ever since.

As Christians, we often doubt God's word. In spite of God's warning about sex, many play about with sex. A friend of mine who counsels large numbers of young people says that the vast majority of them have problems in this area: they have doubted God's word in this matter and gone their own way. In spite of repeated warnings in the Bible against spiritism, many dabble in the occult. In these and many other ways, we say to God, in effect, 'You have said this, but we know better: we'll do that.'

Perhaps there's a warning here to Christians of longer standing, who might doubt some part of God's word on the grounds that it's never happened to them and therefore it couldn't happen at all!

We must all beware of the spiritual pride that doubts *any* word that comes from God's mouth. (YTL)

Lord, I admit that I do not know better than you in this matter . . .

What is the remedy for spiritual pride?

Brothers loved by God, we know that he has chosen you, because our gospel came to you not simply with words, but also with power, with the Holy Spirit and with deep conviction.   1 Thessalonians 1:4,5

What is the word of God? Answer: Anything by which God communicates himself to man. There are five important ways in which God expresses himself to people today.

First, and supremely, Christ himself is the word of God (John 1:1,14). He was able to say, 'Anyone who has seen me has seen the Father' (John 14:9).

Secondly, there is the word of the gospel which, in its broadest sense, is the good news of Jesus Christ as revealed in the Scriptures. We need to soak ourselves in this book and let its words permeate our lives at all levels.

Thirdly, the Body of Christ ought to be the word of the Lord. Paul was able to write to the Thessalonians: 'The Lord's message rang out from you' (Thessalonians 1:8) and to the Corinthians: 'You know that you are a letter from Christ. . . written not with ink but with the Spirit of the living God' (2 Corinthians 3:3). It is through our transformed lives together that God can and does speak to the world.

Fourthly, God speaks through the gifts of the Spirit, so don't quench the Spirit or despise prophecy or any other gift (1 Thessalonians 5:19,20).

Fifthly, creation, God's handiwork, also declares the word of God (Psalm 19), and so can creative artistic gifts, such as singing, music, dancing, drama, art and architecture, if they are inspired by the Holy Spirit.

These are some ways in which God expresses himself to man but any so-called word from the Lord must be tested against the written word, the Scriptures. (YTL)

Am I eager every day for God's word?

I pray that the Lord's message may ring out from us.

To all who are loved by God and called to be saints.
Romans 1:7

It's a tremendous privilege to be the people of God but all privileges bring responsibilities.

God's call to his people is for *holiness*. We are to be saints, meaning 'set apart for God'. This will affect all our lives including our relationships (2 Corinthians 6:14).

God's call to his people is for *everyone*. In the New Testament there's no basic distinction between clergy and laity. All Christians are both priests (1 Peter 2:9) and laity. In many places today, only the ordained clergyman can pronounce forgiveness or celebrate communion. In the New Testament, however, we are told to confess our faults to one another, and we read that the early Christians broke bread from house to house. What happens when we think in terms of leaving everything to the paid professional is that we are asking the impossible and ignoring the potential of the laity. A passive, untrained laity is *not* the New Testament ideal. The ministry and gifts of the Spirit are for everyone in the church.

God's call to his people is to *a corporate life*. God's people are to worship together, work together, put on the whole armour of God together, and generally share their lives. We are saints. The New Testament writer does not speak of the solitary saint.

God's call to his people is to *sinners*. The church is Christ's hospital. When I see foolish, sinful things happening in the church, I have to remember that the church is for foolish, sinful people, just like myself! We should never be shocked by one another, since we all need God's mercy and renewal (Galatians 6:1). (YTL)

How impressive are we as saints?

Lord, thank you for calling us to be the people of God. Help us to use the gifts you have given us so that you can give us more

*of your many kinds of blessings for the benefit of your people
and those as yet outside.*

January 31   Eager hospitality

**Do not forget to entertain strangers, for by so doing some
people have entertained angels without knowing it.**
Hebrews 13:2

Abraham is an example of eager hospitality (Genesis 18:1-8).
He hastened to meet the three men, pressed them to take
refreshment from him, hurried to tell Sarah to bake bread,
rushed to the herd to get a tender calf and give it to the servant
to cook, and finally brought the food to his visitors.

If we claim to follow the Lord, we should show the same
eager hospitality. You might say that Abraham was merely
showing typical eastern hospitality, but even so his example is
a good one to follow. We do not readily open our doors, let
alone our hearts, to other people, except perhaps to our
families and our immediate circle of friends. But the Christian
should be very different in these matters. Our hearts should be
large towards other people; we should be ready to open our
doors to anyone in need, including those in need of the gospel.
If the good news is to spread in our land, home meetings will
play a vital part in such a programme.

In the story, Abraham did not just entertain angels — he
entertained the Lord himself. We need to show eager
hospitality to Jesus, because he will not force himself on us. On
the road to Emmaus, 'Jesus acted as if he were going further'
and the two disciples had to 'urge him strongly' to stay with
them, rather like Abraham who said, 'Do not pass your
servant by' (Genesis 18:3). (YTL)

*How eagerly hospitable are we to one another in our church
fellowship?*

*Lord, you are so welcome in our home. Thank you for your
presence with us. Stay with us always.*

42

FEBRUARY
New birth — new life

February 1   **What is life?**

Do not worry about your life, what you will eat; or about your body, what you will wear. . . But seek his kingdom, and these things will be given to you as well.   **Luke 12:22,31**

What is life? People have given some very depressing answers to that question down the years. Shakespeare wrote:

> it is a tale
> Told by an idiot, full of sound and fury,
> Signifying nothing.

Longfellow said that life was 'but an empty dream', Thomas Browne that it was 'but the shadow of death,' and O'Henry that it was 'made up of sobs, sniffles and smiles — sniffles predominating'. According to Samuel Butler, 'Life is one long process of getting tired,' and Ernest Hemingway, who was both rich and famous, wrote, 'I live in a vacuum that is as lonely as a radio when the batteries are dead.'

Contrast these views with what Jesus and one of his followers said about life. Meditate on each passage.

'This is eternal life: that they might know you, the only true God, and Jesus Christ, whom you sent' (John 17:3).

'He who has the Son has life; he who does not have the Son of God does not have life' (1 John 5:12).

'I have come that they may have life, and have it to the full' (John 10:10).

43

'I am the resurrection and the life. He who believes in me will live, even though he dies; and whoever lives and believes in me will never die' (John 11:25). (AR)

Lord Jesus, I believe that you are 'the life' (John 14:6). May your life control my life more and more fully.

Bible study: What, according to St. John's Gospel is the definition (what?), source (where from?), purpose (what for?), and outcome (what next?) *of life.* See under 'new birth — new life' in index.

February 2   Spirit and Person

While they were worshipping the Lord and fasting, the Holy Spirit said, 'Set apart for me Barnabas and Saul . . .' The two of them, sent on their way by the Holy Spirit, went down to Seleucia and sailed from there to Cyprus.   Acts 13:2,4

The Holy Spirit is a person, with all the marks of a person. He thinks, speaks, acts, feels. He is the counsellor — the one called alongside to help. We all need counsellors from time to time but sometimes human counsel is not available or possible. This is often so for people in positions of leadership. I asked one leader, 'How do you deal with the loneliness of leadership?' and he said, 'I can talk to people sometimes, but when that isn't possible, I've learned to share with God and allow the Holy Spirit to teach and counsel me.'

The Holy Spirit is a wonderful teacher; he can make things clear to us. God has revealed himself in many ways: through creation, conscience, his word, his people, and, supremely, his Son. But it is the Holy Spirit who shows us what these all mean. He helps us to look at creation and see the power of God, to listen to conscience and hear the voice of God, to join a church fellowship and know in it the presence of God, to read the Bible and receive it as the word of God, to look at Jesus and see the Son of God. (AR)

O Lord, the Holy Spirit, thank you that you deal with me person to person. Help me to know you better.

What is my relationship with the person of the Holy Spirit?

February 3   **Yes, my sins are gone!**

As far as the east is from the west, so far has he removed our transgressions from us.   **Psalm 103:12**
You will tread our sins underfoot and hurl all our iniquities into the depths of the sea.   **Micah 7:19**
For I will forgive their wickedness, and will remember their sins no more.   **Jeremiah 31:34**

A little girl once broke a vase.

'Mummy, I've broken your precious vase—I'm so sorry,' she said, taking the bits to her mother.

'It's all right, my dear,' her mother replied. 'It was an accident. I forgive you. Put it in the dustbin.'

The next day the girl retrieved the broken pieces, took them to her mother and said, 'Mummy — look, here's your vase. I broke it and I'm very sorry.'

'I forgave you yesterday,' said her mother. 'Put it in the dustbin.' The girl obeyed, but again and again she returned with the pieces, asking for forgiveness. At last the mother said, 'Look — you must trust me. I told you that I forgave you — and I meant it. Now don't think about it any more.'

Sometimes God has to say to us, 'I have forgiven you. Why do you keep coming back to me with this problem? It's forgotten. I will remember it no more. So don't keep bringing it up again.'

God not only forgives — he forgets our sins. He casts our sins into the depths of the sea and puts up a notice saying, 'No fishing.' (YTL)

Thank you that you have turned your back on my sins, and that I can therefore do the same.

Stop fishing in forbidden waters!

I have come that they may have life, and have it to the full.
John 10:10

Do you sometimes wonder whether you really are spiritually alive? Here are some signs of spiritual life.

A new obedience (1 John 2:3): When we start wanting to do God's will, that's a healthy sign.

A new love for God (1 John 2:15): The Holy Spirit gives us such a love for God that 'the world' (meaning everything that does not come under the lordship of Christ) takes second place.

A new hatred for sin (1 John 3:9): It's a bad sign if we go on and on deliberately sinning, because those who are spiritually alive begin to hate what God hates and love what he loves.

A new love for other Christians (1 John 3:14): This love is not primarily an emotion, but is expressed in practical service.

A new peace (1 John 3:21): Many Christians can echo David's feelings of relief after his sins were confessed and forgiven in Psalm 51.

A new enemy ('the evil one' — 1 John 5:18,19): If you find yourself fighting against temptation and battling with problems harder than ever before — that's a good sign!

A new power over evil (1 John 5:4): We experience this as we trust Christ more and more. (C/LANL)

Are there signs of life in my life?

Praise and worship God for these and pray for more life.

No-one pours new wine into old wineskins. If he does, the wine will burst the skins, and both the wine and the wineskins will be ruined. No, he pours new wine into new wineskins.
Mark 2:22

Someone in Christ is a new creation! I talked to a man who had only been 'in Christ' a very short time and he was saying, 'I'm in a new world — everything's new: my eyes, my home, my wife, my job is new!' Another man, also soon after his conversion, said, 'The sense of newness is simply delicious. It makes new the Bible and friends and all mankind and love and spiritual things and Sunday and church and God himself.'

Since Christ makes us new creations, we need to relate to Christians as they are in Christ, not as they are in the world. 'From now on we regard no-one from a worldly point of view. Though we once regarded Christ in this way, we do so no longer' (2 Corinthians 5:16). We can see Christ as he was in the world — a carpenter's son, or itinerant preacher — but when we are a new creation, we see him as the Son of God. When we look at other Christians, we should see them first and foremost as our brothers and sisters in Christ. So often we relate to people as they are in the world: she's a professor, he's a student, and so on. But it's what they are in Christ that matters.

Also, we need to relate to non-Christians not simply as they are, but as they could be — in Christ. We should love people as they are, but see them as they could be — in Christ.

Jesus picked the oddest bunch of disciples you could ever imagine! We wouldn't have chosen them to be foundation apostles in the church; we'd have gone out and handpicked some nice, religious, well-connected people, perhaps. But Jesus saw what this strange assortment of people could become in him — and that's how we need to see people. (YTL)

Practise seeing people either as they are in Christ or as they could be if they were in Christ, as you meet and pray for them.

Lord, I see ... (a non-Christian) as ransomed, healed, restored, forgiven — a new person in you. May what I see by faith become a reality, in your name and for your glory.

February 6   I want to be free!

'I tell you the truth, everyone who sins is a slave to sin. . . If the Son sets you free, you will be free indeed.'   John 8:34,36

The prodigal son thought that freedom meant doing what he liked. He had money and went off to live his own life in his own way. But it wasn't long before he found that he was far from free. In fact, he was trapped by his selfishness, by his desires, by his circle of friends and, finally, by his loneliness. His father described him at that time as 'lost' and 'dead'. And that's how our Heavenly Father sees every one of us in our natural state, while we are going our own way. We may imagine we're free but we're dead and lost.

A trendy young person said: 'I've taken the pill, hoisted my skirts to my thighs, dropped them to my ankles, rebelled at university, abused the American embassy, lived with two men, married one, kept my identity — and, frankly, I'm lost.'

Freedom does not mean doing as you please. What sort of freedom would there be in a football match if every player 'did his own thing' regardless of the rules of the game? God's laws are rather like those rules; they're not designed to stop us having fun, but rather to set us free from the traps of our own sinfulness, to enjoy the best possible life. (AR)

Do I need to be set free by Jesus from some habit or sin?

Lord Jesus, I admit that I cannot free myself of . . . I ask you to set me free and keep me free of it, for your glory.

February 7   The lure of independence

Remain in me, and I will remain in you. . . Apart from me you can do nothing.   John 15:4,5
The eye cannot say to the hand, 'I don't need you!' And the head cannot say to the feet, 'I don't need you!'. . . You are the body of Christ and each one of you is a part of it.

1 Corinthians 12:21,27

Most of us have a deep inner desire for independence. But God made us in such a way that we can know the best in life only when we are fully and humbly dependent on him and also, in the right sense, on others.

The first recorded sin in the Bible is that of independence. Satan tempted Adam and Eve by suggesting that they could be 'like God, knowing good and evil' (Genesis 3:5). Innocent as this seemed, he was tempting them to live their lives without God.

The tragedy is that independence brings alienation. The appalling loneliness in the world results from the fact that many have separated themselves from God and from other people. If we pursue our wish to be on our own — then we may well achieve what we want and find ourselves trapped in lonely isolation.

The good news of God is that Jesus came to set us free from all that binds or traps us. He wants people to share their lives with him first of all, so that he can share his life with them. He wants them to know the depths of his love, and this is only possible when they are fully dependent on him.

Secondly, he wants them to share their lives with others and let others share their lives with them. Christian fellowship in the early church, as Ronald Sider points out in 'Rich Christians in an Age of Hunger,' meant 'unconditional availability to and unlimited liability for the other brothers and sisters — emotionally, financially and spiritually'. (PL)

Lord, I am available to you for anyone who needs me and whom you want me to serve in any way today.

Expect that prayer to be answered and take action when it is.

February 8   **Learning to listen**

I wait for the Lord, my soul waits, and in his word I put my hope.   **Psalm 130:5**
Speak, Lord, for your servant is listening.   **1 Samuel 3:9**

Today, the majority of Christians find it extremely hard — almost impossibly so — to hear the voice of God. The problem is that we have forgotten to be still before him, and we give little (if any) time for Christian meditation.

We need to use God's word to bring us consciously into God's presence. Let God's word speak to us, drawing us to the Father and glorifying the Son. By letting our whole mind and being dwell on one of the names of God or on one aspect of his character, the Spirit will help us to 'see God'. Words, phrases or even whole passages of Scripture are invaluable for this fresh encounter with God. For some, praying or praising in tongues may also be extremely refreshing. The purpose is not to empty the mind of everything, but to detach the mind from worldly cares in order to attach them to Jesus and his word.

To begin with, start with five or ten minutes in silent meditation. As you continue, you will be able slowly to increase the length of time, and, more important, you will begin to hear God speak to you through his written word or by his Spirit in your heart. Soon you will be able to enjoy an increasing sense of the presence of the living God, and better able to hear him as he speaks to you each day.

Dietrich Bonhoeffer writes: 'Silence is the simple stillness of the individual under the word of God. . . But everybody knows that this is something that needs to be practised and learned, in these days when talkativeness prevails. Real silence, real stillness, really holding one's tongue, comes only as the sober consequence of spiritual stillness. . . The silence of the Christian is listening silence, humble stillness. . . Silence before the word leads to right hearing and thus also to right speaking of the word of God at the right time.' (D)

Lord, teach me to listen and may I be willing to take time to do this.

Begin to meditate today, spending five minutes dwelling on a name of God or a verse from the Bible.

This is how you should pray: 'Our Father in heaven, hallowed be your name, your kingdom come, your will be done on earth as it is in heaven.'   Matthew 6:9,10

The most important reason for praying is Christ's example and teaching. Whether we understand how prayer works or not, that ought to be enough to get us and keep us praying. But there are other reasons for praying if we need them.

When we pray, we are fulfilling the purpose of our creation, which is to know God. Jesus said in his great prayer, 'Now this is eternal life: that they may know you, the only true God, and Jesus Christ, whom you have sent' (John 17:3).

Prayer helps to make us more like Jesus. People who spend much time in his company grow more like him. There is a different quality about the life of an individual or a church that makes prayer its highest priority.

Through prayer God releases his power in our lives and in the lives of others. We may not understand this, but it happens.

Looking at Jesus' life of prayer, we see that he prayed early in the morning, at the end of a busy day, when he was tired and busy (we usually give tiredness and busyness as an excuse for *not* praying!), when he was tempted, when he needed guidance and when he was dying.

There are many different times for and forms of prayer, but it should always be in the Spirit and, whenever possible, include a time of worship, stillness and quietness before God. George Muller, who fed 5,000 orphans simply in answer to prayer, said that he never came to requests or petitions in prayer until he had an active and living realisation of the presence of God. (YTL)

For meditation: 'Prayer has one function and that is to answer, "Yes," when Christ knocks' (O. Hallesby).

Do I answer 'Yes' to God as consistently as he answers my prayers?

As they began to sing and praise, the Lord set ambushes against the men of Ammon and Moab and Mount Seir who were invading Judah, and they were defeated.   2 Chronicles 20:22

It is interesting to see the prominence given to worship and praise in the Bible. Certainly, there must be a balance, but praise, more than anything else, will lead to a gracious sense of the presence of God. At the dedication of the temple, when the people began to praise the Lord, 'the glory of the Lord filled the temple of God' (2 Chronicles 5:14). Later, when God's people were faced with a tremendous battle, 'as they began to sing and praise,' God came down in power and gave victory (2 Chronicles 20).

The psalms are full of praise. Indeed, it was 'when our mouths were filled with laughter, our tongues with songs of joy' that they said among the nations, "The Lord has done great things for them"' (Psalm 126:2,3).

The New Testament also refers frequently to thanksgiving and praise (see Revelation chapters 4,5,7,15 and 19 for instance). Praise is the language of faith now, and the language of heaven later. In one sense, therefore, it is the meeting-place of heaven on earth; it brings a breath of heaven into our own lives and fellowships.

It is possible, of course, to swing to extremes and to neglect other vital forms of prayer: confession of sin and interceding for the needs of others, for example. Praise is no substitute for repentance; and all too often 'you do not have, because you do not ask God' (James 4:2). Nevertheless faith depends on our vision of God. As we therefore begin by praise and worship our vision of God grows, our expectancy grows, and intercessory prayer becomes more powerful. (OITS)

Is praise given sufficient priority in my life?

Lord, help my vision of you to grow and become clearer as I praise you more and more.

He [Abraham] did not waver through unbelief regarding the promise of God, but was strengthened in his faith and gave glory to God, being fully persuaded that God had power to do what he had promised. Romans 4:20,21

Faith means taking God's word as literally true. How do we become Christians? By claiming a promise of the Lord Jesus. How are we filled with the Holy Spirit? By claiming Jesus' promise that God would give the Holy Spirit to those who ask him. How do we find victory over sin and temptation? By believing in the promise of God. In other words, faith is trusting the faithfulness of God.

Faith is also a living thing which God wants to strengthen and therefore tests. Richard Wurmbrand, whose faith was tested for fourteen years in a communist prison, said that faith could be expressed in two words: *though* and *yet*. Job was able to say, '*Though* he slay me, *yet* will I hope in him' (Job 13:15). Can you say about your life and your relationship with God: '*Though* this may happen, *yet* I will trust him'; '*Though* my prayer seems unanswered, *yet* I will trust him'; '*Though* I may face huge disappointments, *yet* I will trust him'?

Abraham and Sarah's *though* and *yet* were quite staggering when we consider that God promised them a son when he was seventy-six years old and she sixty-six, and they had to wait twenty-four years for God's promise to come true! (YTL)

Is there a situation in my life for which I could claim a promise of God?

Lord, help me to hold on to what I have claimed from you in faith.

The Lord reigns, let the earth be glad; let the distant shores rejoice. Psalm 97:1

During a meeting I attended, a clergyman asked the Archbishop of York, 'What would you say is the main thing that God is saying to his church today?' The Archbishop, Dr. Stuart Blanch, paused for quite a long time before replying, 'I think it is this: the Lord is sovereign in everything.'

The Spirit is saying other things to the church today. He is, I believe, saying, 'Return to your first love for Jesus. Renew your commitment to one another in Jesus. Adopt a simpler lifestyle, sharing more freely with one another. Learn the lessons of spiritual warfare.'

But perhaps what individuals, churches and the world need to know at this moment more than anything else is the fact that the Lord reigns.

We must proclaim this with boldness and confidence in our worship and witness, personal and corporate. It needs to be heard as a great festal shout over and over again: 'The Lord reigns.' (AR)

Praise and glory and wisdom and thanks and honour and power and strength be to our God for ever and ever. Amen.

Focus on a person or need you are anxious about at the moment. Then shout out loud with glad certainty about that person or need, 'The Lord reigns!'

February 13   **All I need**

I shall lack nothing.   **Psalm 23:1**

'The Lord is my shepherd, I shall lack nothing.' How few people today display the spirit of contentment suggested by this verse! Instead, strikes, protests about wages, and many other forms of greed illustrate the truth of the words: 'For the love of money is a root of all kinds of evil' (1 Timothy 6:10). Christians are told: 'Keep your lives free from the love of money and be content with what you have, because God has said, "Never will I leave you, never will I forsake you." So we say with confidence, "The Lord is my helper; I will not be afraid"' (Hebrews 13:5,6).

Who will be content? Who will lack nothing? Those who can say, 'The Lord is my helper,' or, 'The Lord is my shepherd.' And if the Lord is my shepherd, he provides all I need. He leads and feeds me, he comforts, restores and protects me.

He meets my *spiritual* needs. Only the Lord Jesus can meet our need for God's love and forgiveness, for assurance about the future in the face of death. God has 'blessed us with every spiritual blessing in Christ' (Ephesians 1:3).

He also meets my *material* needs, so that I have enough for myself and to give to God's work. Over and over again people have proved that God is no man's debtor. I heard of a farmer who gave away large sums of money and yet remained prosperous. People couldn't understand how this could happen, but the farmer said to them, 'It's like this. I keep shovelling into God's bin and God keeps shovelling into my bin — but God has a greater shovel.'

If I am at the centre of my life, and God is only around to help me from time to time, then I may well lack all kinds of things. But if the Lord is *my* Lord and *my* shepherd — then how can I possibly doubt his provision for all my needs? (YTL)

Father, thank you for everything you give me and for so generously meeting my needs.

If there is anything I am doing simply and solely 'for the money' — am I happy about it? What action can I take?

February 14   **The mirage of money**

People who want to get rich fall into temptation and a trap and into many foolish and harmful desires that plunge men into ruin and destruction.   **1 Timothy 6:9**

Once we accept the biblical view of man, we should cease to be surprised by the covetousness which dominates our society today and the constant pursuit of money and possessions even when this denies human values and destroys personal relationships. Politicians promise monotonously to 'raise the standard of living', but the implicit assumption is that 'living' is synonymous with 'earning'. It is what *I* get out of it, in terms of hard cash, that determines the value of many a job.

Every now and then, of course, the materialist's dream comes true. . . There are a sufficient number of fulfilled dreams to encourage the materialist to go on dreaming, the gambler to go on gambling, the wage-earner to go on filling in those pools coupons. Money is seen to be the ultimate in self-fulfilment.

Any analysis of today's moods which does not focus on the basic selfishness and covetousness of man misses the heart of it all. (IBIE)

Do I, in my heart of hearts, and perhaps for very good reasons, such as wanting to share and to give, 'want to get rich'?

Lord, lead me not into temptation and deliver me from evil in the matter of covetousness.

February 15   **Living simply**

If we have food and clothing, we will be content with that.
1 Timothy 6:8

For countless Christians in the West, 'discipleship' means little more than going to church regularly, giving a proportion of one's income — usually at best one tenth, and often far below that figure — and getting involved in a limited number of church activities. Consequently, the lifestyle of most western Christians and churches has no prophetic challenge at all to the affluent society all around. In fact it is scarcely distinguishable from it. We have, quite unconsciously, adopted the values and standards of the world; and as the standard of living has risen considerably over the last thirty years, so we Christians, along with our neighbours, spend that much more on our cars and carpets, TV sets and washing machines, furniture and hi-fi equipment, until we regard most of these things as necessities for 'modern life'.

Where is there any serious attempt to live on 'enough', to be content with food and clothing, and to give the rest away for every good work? Where is there that commitment to one another in love, so that we really share our possessions, reduce our standard of living — despite inflation — and express the love of Christ in costly, tangible, sacrificial terms?

Ron Sider writes: 'The *evangelistic* impact of the first Christians' financial sharing was just astounding.' (D)

Am I really content now, or do I keep thinking I will be content if only . . .?

Lord, help me to be content with whatever you provide at each stage of my life.

February 16   It's not fair!

The older brother . . . answered his father, 'Look! All these years I've been slaving for you and never disobeyed your orders. Yet you never gave me even a young goat so I could celebrate with my friends. But when this son of yours who has squandered your property with prostitutes comes home, you kill the fatted calf for him!'   Luke 15:28,29-30

Although respectable and perhaps even religious, the older brother in Jesus' story was no better than the prodigal — in fact, he was probably worse in some ways.

First, he was *self-righteous*. This is an attitude none of us can adopt before God. Compared with each other, we may or may not look quite good. But compared with Jesus, God's standard, we fall very far short. Jesus once told a very good, respectable, religious man: 'You must be born again.' Even he could not earn a place in God's kingdom.

Secondly, the older brother was *resentful*. 'What have you

given me?' he asked, when the truth was that he could have enjoyed everything his father had. God gives us life, love, friendship, countless blessings, his Son to be our Saviour and his Spirit to live in us; but so often when something happens, we cry out, 'Why has God allowed this to happen to me? It isn't fair!'

Was it fair that Jesus should die in our place on the cross, so that we might know God's love and forgiveness for ever?

Thirdly he was *critical*. But he had no right to be, because however different he was outwardly from his brother, inwardly he was the same. John Lennon wrote, 'One thing you can't hide is when you're crippled inside.' We're all crippled inside, and we cannot hide that fact from God. (AR)

Lord, I'm so glad that you do not give me what I deserve. Thank you.

Is there someone I need to be more welcoming towards in our church fellowship?

February 17   Angry with God

This is what the wicked are like — always carefree, they increase in wealth. Surely in vain have I kept my heart pure; in vain have I washed my hands in innocence. All day long I have been plagued; I have been punished every morning.

Psalm 73:12-14

I talked with a young girl who had recently watched her mother die tragically and horrifically of cancer. She was very angry with God about what had happened and I understood her reaction completely. At last I said to her gently, 'Will you tell God what you have told me?' She wasn't sure about that, so I said, 'He's been listening to our conversation anyway, so just tell him how you feel.' She did this, and it was a time of release for her.

The psalmist is often very angry with God—and tells him so.

He doesn't use pious phrases because he feels he ought to. Here in this psalm he complains bitterly about life's injustice. The wicked go scot-free while he suffers day after day!

But as he talks to God about how he feels, he comes to see two things clearly.

First, he has been exaggerating. It isn't true that the wicked suffer no pain. It's easy to exaggerate, but when we do this — we often fall into the trap of self-pity.

Secondly, he has been judging at a superficial human level. For the moment he's forgotten the eternal realities — that God reigns; that God works for good in everything; that God will judge with justice; that there is a future life where right will be vindicated.

If we take our anger to God and let him deal with us and with it, our perspectives will be clear and true again. St. Paul had every right to be angry with God (2 Corinthians 11:24-27) but just look at his reactions (2 Corinthians 4:17; Romans 8:18)! (CFP)

Lord, I am puzzled and angry about . . .

What can I learn from this psalm and others about how to handle anger and cope with life in an unjust world?

February 18   **What's wrong with this country?**

My people have committed two sins: they have forsaken me, the spring of living water, and have dug their own cisterns, broken cisterns that cannot hold water.   **Jeremiah 2:13**

Jeremiah saw very clearly that there were three things seriously wrong with his country. First, the people had turned away from the living God to worship idols. Today people have done the same thing: they worship sex, money, the TV, the car, and so on. I'm told that the annual turn-over on gambling alone is two thousand million pounds and that total annual giving to missionaries is less than what is spent to buy food for budgerigars. People say, 'I can't come to church because Sunday is the only day of the week in which I can do my garden (wash my car, paint my house, and so on).' God says to such, 'Make those things your gods if you wish but in the time of trouble, which is surely coming, whether in the form of suffering, bereavement or death and judgment, don't call on me, the God you have forsaken; call on your gods and see whether they can save you.'

Secondly, Jeremiah saw very clearly that the religious leaders were no longer preaching God's word. 'They dress the wound of my people as though it were not serious. "Peace, peace," they say, when there is no peace' (Jeremiah 6:14). Today the same thing is happening. Many preachers are saying, in effect, 'God is a loving God. Just do your best. He'll understand. It'll be all right in the end.' They make a mockery of Christ's sufferings and work.

Thirdly, Jeremiah saw that the people had lost all sense of shame. He tells them: 'You say, "I am innocent; he is not angry with me,"' and God says about them: 'They have no shame at all; they do not even know how to blush' (Jeremiah 2:35;6:15). This could be applied with frightening accuracy to our country today. People sin and boast about it.

They needed to repent — and so do we. Then we must stand firm for God's truths and standards and pray with all our hearts. The future of this country is largely in the hands of Christians. (YTL)

Should we be praying more for our country?

Almighty God, help us as Christians not to fail our country, but to be salt and light so that people will turn back to you.

February 19   A spiritual house

You also, like living stones, are being built into a spiritual house to be a holy priesthood, offering spiritual sacrifices acceptable to God through Jesus Christ.   1 Peter 2:5

Peter describes the church as a collection of living stones, not left lying round in a pile, but built into a spiritual house. If you arrived at your church building and found a gaping hole in one wall and a heap of stones under it, you would know not only that the stones were in the wrong place but also that the building had been weakened by their absence. We are not to be like stones lying around, but stones built into one another, committed to one another, otherwise we will be useless and cause others to be less effective than they could be.

The unity of this spiritual building is vitally important. Party spirit, or some other sin can destroy it. Paul rebukes divisions in the church and issues a stern warning about those who destroy God's temple (1 Corinthians 3:16). In the letters to the seven churches (Revelation 2 and 3), God said by his Spirit that unless relationships were sorted out within the churches, he would remove the very light of Christ from their midst.

Home-groups can have a very important part to play in the matter of relationships and spiritual health and growth. These groups must be small. (Sociologists have found that twelve is the ideal optimum number in a group!) In a larger group people can hide behind others, be uncommitted, or, more important-ly, get hurt without it being noticed. Members must be real with one another, whether this brings conflict and pain or not. In our church we asked people what they most needed from a group, and the majority of those who replied said they wanted a place where they could be honest about themselves without fear of rejection. (YTL)

Father, whatever our church building looks like, make your people inside it into a truly spiritual house fit for you to live in.

Are the conflicts in our family (church family) swept under the carpet, faced and dealt with, or allowed to rage on and on?

February 20   Leaders' qualifications

Now the overseer must be above reproach, the husband of but one wife, temperate, self-controlled, respectable, hospitable,

able to teach, not given to much wine, not violent but gentle, not quarrelsome, not a lover of money.　1 Timothy 3:2,3

Any church leader should display personal holiness; his home should be ordered and disciplined; he should have a good knowledge of God's word and a good reputation in the community (1 Timothy 3; Titus 1:7-9).

Additional qualifications for deacons are made clear (1 Timothy 3:8-12).

Elsewhere in the New Testament further qualifications for elders are spelt out. They are to be the leaders with, in some cases, preaching and teaching responsibilities (1 Timothy 5:17) and to work hard (Acts 20:19; 1 Thessalonians 2:9), following the example of the 'Good Shepherd' who 'lays down his life for the sheep' (John 10:11). They are to 'guard' themselves, because they cannot begin to help another person unless their own personal lives are under control, to 'guard ... all the flock', 'be shepherds of the church of God' and feed them with God's word which is both milk and solid food (Hebrews 5:13,14). They are to admonish (1 Thessalonians 5:12), keep watch (Hebrews 13:17) and pray for the sick when called to do so (James 5:14,15). (YTL)

What is my attitude towards my leaders?

Father, show me how to encourage my leaders.

February 21　　　　　　　　　　　　　　　　**Super-love**

Love is patient, love is kind. It does not envy, it does not boast, it is not proud. It is not rude, it is not self-seeking, it is not easily angered, it keeps no record of wrongs. Love does not delight in evil but rejoices with the truth. It always protects, always trusts, always hopes, always perseveres. Love never fails.　　　　　　　　　　　　　　　　1 Corinthians 13:4-8

God's kind of love was so different from other kinds that a new

Greek word had to be invented for it: *agape.*

Meditate on the phrases above and the paraphrase or expansion of them below.

Love is inexhaustibly patient.

Love anticipates a person's needs and meets them.

Love doesn't mind when someone else has the limelight, responsibilities, popularity or privileges.

Love is not anxious to impress.

Love does not blow its own trumpet.

Love is not aggressive, but courteous.

Love does not insist on its own way.

Love is not touchy, or easily rubbed up the wrong way.

Love keeps no list of the faults and failings of others.

Love doesn't gloat over the mistakes of others in order to put itself in a better light; instead it is glad when others are right.

Love throws a cloak of silence over what is displeasing in other people.

Love trusts that in everything God works for good.

Love looks forward to the future glory promised by God.

Love is not shaken even by the worst of storms.

Love is eternal. (CFP)

Lord Jesus, the picture of love in this passage is a picture of you. Fill me with love like that, I pray, for your glory.

How can the cross of Christ and the Holy Spirit help me to be filled with agape *love?*

February 22   **A kingdom on the move**

The kingdom of God is within you.   Luke 17:21
I will not drink again of the fruit of the vine until the kingdom of God comes.   Luke 22:18

Talking to the Pharisees Jesus spoke as though the kingdom had come and to the disciples as if it was to come in the future. This is because the kingdom is both present and future. It is here and now because the king reigns in many hearts, but it is also in the future because the king will not reign in all his power and glory until the second coming of Jesus. Sometimes we sing, 'For the Lamb who was slain has begun to reign,' because we recognise that his reign is moving to completion, and we must move with it. We mustn't cling to the past. We must be on the move with God and his people. Only then will we see the power of the Spirit.

It's the responsibility of the leaders in our churches to try to understand where God is leading. When they communicate the vision they have caught, it is important that we accept what they say and submit to their leadership. I believe that renewal has leapt forward in some sections of the Roman Catholic church, because the principle of obedience to leaders is built into the structure of the church. Where leaders are Spirit-led, this leads to rapid spiritual progress. We must be prepared for change and movement because the kingdom of God and individuals and churches within it are not yet complete and perfect and the Holy Spirit still has to shape and change it and us. (YTL)

Am I resisting certain changes in the church? If so, what and why?

Lord, may I be secure enough to change and compassionate towards those who do not see eye-to-eye with me.

February 23   **Don't fear the Spirit**

For God did not give us a spirit of timidity, but a spirit of power, of love and of self-discipline.   **2 Timothy 1:7**

One woman said anxiously to her minister, 'I hope that nothing supernatural will happen in our church!' The trouble is, that through fear, it may not! Some are frightened of the dangers involved when the Holy Spirit is allowed full control. In our fears, we tend to box God up in the narrow limits of our own understanding. We tell him what we want, and what we don't want. We define the ways in which we are prepared for him to work — ways that are safe and respectable, that will not disturb or confuse, ways that we can easily grasp and keep firmly within our control.

But God's ways are not our ways, and his thoughts are not our thoughts. Sometimes the Spirit is a most uncomfortable Comforter! Often he cuts right across our preconceived patterns of thought. Cardinal Suenens has said, 'The Spirit of God can breathe through what is predicted at a human level with a sunshine of surprises.'

Never be afraid of the Spirit's renewing power. God is the giver of all good gifts. Moreover he gives, not a spirit of fear, but a spirit of power, love and a sound mind. (D)

I release to you the fears in my life. . . I am ready to receive your freedom from these fears and your love to flood all those dark secret corners in my life.

List your fears and continue to name them before God and receive his deliverance and love, day by day, or as often as you need them.

February 24   **How can I be filled with the Holy Spirit?**

If you then, though you are evil, know how to give good gifts to your children, how much more will your Father in heaven give the Holy Spirit to those who ask him!   Luke 11:13

A woodpecker sat on a large tree pecking away at the bark. Suddenly there was a flash of lightning and the tree fell over.

'My!' said the woodpecker, 'I never knew there was such power in my beak!' We are as foolish as the woodpecker unless we understand that we can do nothing without God's mighty power within us.

How can we really receive that mighty power? Basically, we need to ask for it. But there are barriers which prevent us from asking or, if we ask, from receiving.

One of the most common barriers today is confusion. People are confused about the work and person of the Holy Spirit because of some of the sad, extreme things which are happening. But the answer to *abuse* is not *disuse* but *right use*. A friend said this: 'Whenever a stream flows swiftly, it throws debris on to its banks. Let us not become so occupied with the debris that we fail to see the power of the stream itself and rejoice that the river-bed is no longer dry.'

Another barrier is lack of commitment. It's only when we hand over every part of our lives to God that he can fill them completely with his power and presence in the person of the Holy Spirit. (AR)

Show me, Lord, any barriers which are hindering me from asking for or receiving the filling of your Holy Spirit.

What does my use of time, money, gifts and possessions indicate about my degree of commitment to God?

February 25   **The witnessing Spirit**

We are witnesses of these things and so is the Holy Spirit, whom God has given to those who obey him.   **Acts 5:32**

Once we are filled with the Holy Spirit, we are inevitably involved in witness and evangelism. Nowhere do we read that the disciples had to exhort and remind one another to witness — it just happened. As someone has said, 'Evangelism never seemed to be an issue in the New Testament; that is to say, one does not find the apostles urging, exhorting, scolding, planning and organising for evangelistic programmes. In the apostolic church, evangelism was somehow assumed and it functioned without special techniques or special programmes. Evangelism happened, issuing effortlessly from the community of believers as light from the sun. It was automatic, spontaneous, continuous, contagious.'

Acts chapter 1 verse 8 is the spiritual equivalent of Genesis chapter 1 verse 28. We are, spiritually, to be fruitful and increase in number; to fill the earth and subdue it. If the Holy Spirit is really amongst us and in us, this will mean doing what comes naturally, just as having children is a natural happening, given the right conditions. It's only when we are 'off beam' that we have to study God's basic commands and see whether we are fulfilling them. We will obey the great commission, quite naturally, if we are filled with the Spirit. Those who bump into us, so to speak, will find out what we're full of. If we're full of self, that will spill out. If we're full of the Holy Spirit, he will flow out of us — and he is the witnessing Spirit whose chief aim is to glorify Christ. (YTL)

Does evangelism happen naturally in our church or are we constantly planning for it with very little result?

Lord, I want to spend time before you today, opening my life completely to you for cleansing and for filling brimful with your Spirit.

February 26   Start where you are

Respect those who work hard among you, who are over you in the Lord and who admonish you. Hold them in the highest regard in love because of their work. Live in peace with each other ... Do not put out the Spirit's fire; do not treat prophecies with contempt. Test everything. Hold on to the good. Avoid every kind of evil. 1 Thessalonians 5:12,13,19-22

A woman who had attended a mission wrote afterwards to the missioner saying: 'Dear Sir, I have come to know Jesus Christ during the mission. I feel he is calling me to preach the gospel. The trouble is, I have twelve children. What shall I do?' The missioner wrote back: 'Dear Madam, I'm delighted to hear that God has called you to preach the gospel. I'm even more delighted that he's provided you with a congregation!'

God wants us to start where we are. If God blesses you,

plough that blessing into the life and work of your local church. If you want to see more life in your church, give your life. If you want to see more love, give your love. If you want to see more prayer, give your prayer. If you want to see more commitment, give your commitment. If you want to see more service, give your service. Whatever you do, don't stand on the touchline, criticising and judging others.

Pray for your vicar, or minister, and your leaders. If we prayed for these people as much as we criticised them, we might have a revival on our doorsteps almost at once!

Don't split off from your present church fellowship and don't — this applies especially perhaps to leaders — quench the Spirit in the lives of those who have been blessed. Be willing for change; be prepared for new structures, new songs of praise, new methods of communication, new patterns of ministry with every member playing his or her part. (AR)

Lord, keep me faithful in praying for my leaders.

How can I plough back into the life and work of my church fellowship God's blessings and gifts to me?

February 27   The word demonstrated

Whatever you have learned or received or heard from me, or seen in me — put it into practice. And the God of peace will be with you.   **Philippians 4:9**
Follow my example, as I follow the example of Christ.
                          1 Corinthians 11:1

In every generation, and in every part of the world, the word has to become flesh before people can see the truth and reality of God. In this word-resistant age, it is not enough to throw biblical statements to the outsider. For most folk, God-words are empty words. But when the word can be demonstrated in our lives, relationships, lifestyle and love, the *presence* of the living Christ will be clearly manifested and perceived.

Calling for radical discipleship, some of the church leaders from Latin America at the Lausanne Congress affirmed that 'there is no biblical dichotomy between the word spoken and the word made visible in the lives of God's people. Men will *look* as they *listen*, and what they *see* must be one with what they *hear*.'

Although evangelism and social action are distinct, both are vitally and equally important in the total mission of the church. It is inadequate to call only for repentance from personal sins, and salvation for individuals; and it is nonsense to talk about 'evangelising' social structures. The Great Commission calls Christians to preach the gospel *and* to teach new converts to observe all Christ's instructions, many of which had strong social implications. Likewise the Great Commandment tells us to love our neighbour, and we cannot do this in the fullest sense unless we care about both his spiritual and social needs. (IBITC)

Do people look at me (our church) and see Jesus?

Lord may people not only hear what I believe, but see it too.

February 28   Dialogue is two-way

And the Lord's servant must not quarrel; instead, he must be kind to everyone, able to teach, not resentful. Those who oppose him he must gently instruct, in the hope that God will grant them repentance leading them to a knowledge of the truth.   **2 Timothy 2:24,25**

Engaging in dialogue does not automatically mean being willing to embrace the other man's religious beliefs; rather it means a willingness to *listen*, in a spirit of genuine love and humility, and to try to understand what the other man's religious beliefs really are. So often Christians fail miserably at this point, and are therefore accused of being narrow and intolerant. The answer to such accusations is not to retreat from the absolute truths of the gospel, as centred in Jesus Christ, nor to waver from the uniqueness of his person, his death and his resurrection; but to show the other man the love and respect he deserves because of the common humanity that we share. The aim of the dialogue will still ultimately be to win that person to Christ; but we cannot communicate the One who was full of grace and truth until wrong attitudes and prejudices have been cleared from our own lives. So often we hear only what we *expect* to hear, and maybe *want* to hear. Most of the tensions of life are ultimately due to a lack of communication or understanding.

When an atheist says to me, 'I don't believe in God,' I often reply, 'Tell me what sort of a God you do not believe in.' As often as not, I find that he has a strange and twisted caricature of God in his mind. So I comment, 'Well, I don't believe in that sort of a God either!' In this way, we find common ground; and after that, communication can be much more meaningful. If we cannot listen graciously and sensitively to someone who does not share our beliefs, we have absolutely no right to impose those beliefs on him. (IBITC)

Lord, may I learn to listen without speaking when that is right.

Are there opportunities in our church meetings for people to ask questions about the sermons and talks or to put their points of view without fear of being judged?

February 29   **No evangelism without opposition**

The seventy-two returned with joy and said, 'Lord, even the demons submit to us in your name.'   Luke 10:17

In virtually every evangelistic activity I have ever taken part in, I have sooner or later been forcibly reminded of the spiritual battle, if I have not given it due consideration from the start. Frequently God has brought us to our knees in more fervent and urgent prayer half-way through a mission because nothing seems to be happening. Sometimes there have been specific attacks on the home during evangelistic work. Over the course of a year or more I became increasingly aware of the fact that our special guest services were almost always accompanied by domestic disturbances or sickness. Then, when this had been made a matter for specific prayer, many of these disruptions ceased.

Certainly there will be battles, but we need to understand that these will be essentially spiritual conflicts, and God has given us the information and resources we need to resist the devil until he flees from us.

When the seventy reported back to their Master, jubilant as they were after a thrilling mission when they had seen 'even the demons' subject to them in Christ's name, Jesus replied, 'I saw Satan fall like lightning from heaven. I have given you authority to trample on snakes and scorpions, and to overcome all the power of the enemy' (Luke 10:18,19). (IBIE)

Lord, when disruptions occur, help me to see the hand behind them.

Having laid the blame where it belongs — what's the next step?

MARCH
The Scriptures

March 1   **This book needs obeying**

When your words came, I ate them; they were my joy and my heart's delight.   **Jeremiah 15:16**

God speaks to us, not primarily to impart information, but to guide our feet, to re-direct our lives, to change us continually into the likeness of Christ. 'Do not merely listen to the word, and so deceive yourselves. Do what it says' (James 1:22). As J. Aitken Taylor has expressed it well: 'One does not pray, "God, help me to resolve the seeming contradictions I have found in the Bible." One rather prays, "God, help me to receive thy word wholly, unquestioningly, obediently. Let me make it indeed and altogether *the* lamp unto my feet and the light unto my pathway." ' We must let God's word address us, challenge us, transform us.

And we must use it to shape our lives. If the world is not to squeeze us into its own mould, we must let God re-mould our minds from within. God's values are totally different from the world's. If we are to stand against the steady pressure of the world coming from advertising and the events of every day, we need to saturate our minds and hearts in the word of God. (D)

Lord, I want to obey your word. I want to delight in it more and more.

Am I really noting (perhaps in a book) what God's word is saying each day, and then letting it shape what I do, say and think?

Bible Study: See John 5:38,39 and link up Old Testament prophecies of Christ with their New Testament fulfilment.
Starters: Psalm 34:20, Exodus 12:46 and John 19:33; Psalm 22:15 and John 19:28; Zechariah 12:10 and John 19:34.

March 2   **Is the Bible reliable?**

All scripture is God-breathed.   **2 Timothy 3:16**

We have some 5,000 Greek manuscripts of the Bible, some of which go back to the second century AD and a few fragments even to the first century AD. And among all the different readings there isn't a single point of dispute over any *essential* doctrine.

The oldest surviving manuscript we have of Tacitus' dates from eight hundred years after the original, and yet most people would accept it as historically accurate and reliable.

Where the historical details of the Bible can be verified, they have been confirmed as accurate over and over again. Luke, who wrote the Gospel of Luke and Acts, has been called 'one of the finest and ablest historians in the ancient world', and the incidental political, geographical and nautical details he gives have been found to be accurate. If he takes such pains over these details, what reason do we have for distrusting him on other matters?

It's true that the first Gospel was written about thirty years after Jesus' death, but it's very likely that Jesus, in true rabbinic tradition, encouraged his disciples to learn his teaching by heart. In any case, in those days people were in the habit of remembering events and conversations in detail and passing them on with extreme accuracy.

Many of Jesus' contemporaries were still alive when the Gospels were written, and they, surely, would have pointed out any inaccuracies in them. But there is no evidence that anyone disputed anything in them.

There is so much evidence for the accuracy and reliability of the Bible that, had it been any other book, it would be accepted without the shadow of doubt.

Voltaire predicted that within a hundred years the Bible would simply be a museum piece. A hundred years later, the house in which Voltaire wrote those words was a Bible society printing press, producing approximately a Bible a minute! (CFP)

If someone who really wanted to look into the reliability of the Bible were to come to me, would I know what to say, or what book to lend him/her?

Lord, I pray for a Christian today who is hungry for your word but who is not allowed to read it. . .

March 3   The test of truth

Sanctify them by the truth; your word is truth.   John 17:17

We must be concerned with the truth, the whole truth and nothing but the truth.

Paul once made the same point emphatically to Timothy who was called to lead one of the most influential churches of the first century: 'What you heard from me, keep as the pattern of sound teaching, with faith and love in Christ Jesus. Guard the good deposit that was entrusted to you — guard it with the help of the Holy Spirit who lives in us' (2 Timothy 1:13,14).

Many of the great revivals of the past have begun with deep repentance, great joy, fresh love and spontaneous praise, but have withered away due to the neglect of God's word. The roots have not gone deep enough. Perhaps even worse, movements which began with the Spirit, went off at a tangent and later proved disastrous. This was certainly true of the Montanist movement in the second century, which began as a genuine work of God, but which became unscriptural and the leaders further refused to have their teaching tested by the Scriptures. In other words, they did not 'keep God's word', and from that moment onwards the whole thing went sour on them.

It is the church which bases its life upon obedience to God's word, especially the written word in the Scriptures, that is likely to see the power of God at work, provided that church is also dependent on the power of the Spirit. (IBITC)

I open my life today to the truth of your word, O God.

Do my life and words have about them the ring of truth?

March 4   **This word needs studying**

You are in error because you do not know the Scriptures or the power of God.   **Matthew 22:29**

Today a growing number of Christians are spiritually alive and enthusiastic but alarmingly ignorant of Scriptural truth beyond the purely superficial.

In the West we have almost an embarrassment of riches, so the culpability of ignorance is even greater. Nevertheless Biblical scholarship is one of the gifts of the Spirit for the benefit of the whole body of Christ, and is not to be neglected or despised. It is helpful to have more than one translation, if possible, perhaps one that is known for its accuracy of translation and another that is more of a stimulating paraphrase.

Also use a good concordance in order to follow through a word in different parts of Scripture. Several valuable handbooks and dictionaries are available today, too, and a Bible atlas can provide useful background information.

Commentaries, too, can be immensely helpful as we try to grapple with the meaning of the original text. . . However, use all this equipment to *supplement* your own study of the Bible and to check your understanding of certain words and phrases. . . In other words, first do your own study, with prayer and dependence on the Spirit of truth; and only then draw from the other resources at hand.

Variety is the key word as far as method is concerned. I have found these stimulating: rapid reading (four or more chapters a day), verse by verse, a book at a time, topical studies (theme by theme) and character studies. (D)

Lord, help me to want to examine your word daily and to do it even when I don't want to.

Should I take up one of the suggested methods of Bible study?

March 5   This book is dynamite

Now the Bereans were of more noble character than the Thessalonians, for they received the message with great eagerness, and examined the Scriptures every day to see if what Paul said was true. Many of the Jews believed.   Acts 17:11,12

The Bible is still the world's bestseller. Societies and nations have been transformed through its influence.

It is a spiritual book. Its many writers, spanning at least 1600 years, were inspired by the Spirit of God to give us his word — a word for all people everywhere through all time. And because it's a spiritual book, we need the Holy Spirit to help us understand it. But we have a part to play — and the people of Berea set us a good example here.

They were *willing to learn*: they received the message. Clearly they were open to God. Before we read the Bible, we need to be quiet in God's presence and ask him to speak to us.

Secondly, they were *disciplined*: they examined the Scriptures every day. This is where Bible study reading notes can be so helpful. According to your age, ability and appetite — there are notes to guide you wisely through the whole Bible in the course of a period of time.

Thirdly, they were *obedient*: many of them believed. This

book is not for the merely curious. It's out to change lives. We must act when God speaks.

Make every effort to set aside time for God each day. Ask him to speak to you, read part of his word, expect him to speak to you and act on what you learn. (BRN)

Lord, may your word shape my life as I read it day by day.

What can I learn from the Bereans?

March 6   This book is unique

I want you to know, brothers, that the gospel I preached is not something that man made up. I did not receive it from any man, nor was I taught it; rather, I received it by revelation from Jesus Christ.   **Galatians 1:11,12**

The argument is sometimes raised that, since the Scriptures were written by sinful men, they must be fallible. This does not follow. If the Scriptures are God-breathed, as was Paul's claim (2 Timothy 3:16), God is well able to speak by his Spirit through sinful men, accurately and infallibly, just as the Holy Spirit through Mary gave birth to God's perfect Son. God will not use those sinful men as dictating machines for his word; rather, by the breath of his Spirit, he breathes through their backgrounds, personalities, experiences and understandings which have been shaped by the culture of their day. The result is still God's inspired word, brought to us through human beings.

The Bible's own claim for divine authority can be tested only by its own consistency, reliability, and by the personal experience of all those who seek to live by it. Therefore, from the self-authenticating testimony of Jesus and the apostles, we must accept the Scriptures as the inspired word of God, *as originally given.* Certainly we are not to despise good biblical scholarship as we try to determine both the original text and the cultural and historical context of that text. But having

77

questioned the text, we must then allow the text to question us. Our conscience must become captive to the word of God. (D)

Lord, I accept the Bible as your inspired word. Speak to me through it today.

Think before reading: The words I am about to look at are God-breathed. What difference should that make?

March 7   Is God's word changing lives?

The message they heard was of no value to them, because those who heard it did not combine it with faith.   Hebrews 4:2

The danger in many biblically-based churches is that of developing a congregation of sermon-tasters. People listen to a stirring message on prayer on Sunday morning; they are challenged by a call to repentance on Sunday evening; they study the complexities of personal witness in a discipleship group on Tuesday; they are stimulated by an exposition from Isaiah on Thursday; and they are enthused by a spiritual renewal rally on Saturday. And all this on top of their own personal study of the Scriptures, which happens to be in Leviticus that week!

At the end of all that, how much of God's word has effectively taken root in their hearts? When most of that Bible teaching will be 'one-way' (preacher to a passive congregation), how much has really been assimilated? Is there really any chance for it to be lived out in the lives of God's people? The steward of God's word will need to think carefully about the diet and menu if he is to serve the household of God.

In a radical reappraisal of the preaching ministry in a local church, Juan Carlos Ortiz has suggested that there should be only about six different sermons a year, giving time for the truth to be thoroughly digested and applied before going on to something new. (IBITC)

*What could be done to help us work out and live out the truths
that we hear preached?*

*Father, we pray that individuals may hear what you are saying
to them and that the church as a whole may also hear what you
are saying to us as a body or family. And what you say, may
we always do.*

March 8   Aids to prayer

**We do not know what we ought to pray, but the Spirit himself
intercedes for us with groans that words cannot express.**
                                                    Romans 8:26

Most people find Bible reading helpful before prayer, because
it is much easier to speak to God once he has spoken to you.
Has he taught you, encouraged you, rebuked you, warned
you, humbled you, strengthened you through his word? Well
then, turn that into prayer. 'Pray in' those thoughts until they
take root, not only in your mind but in your heart and life.
Then use those same thoughts as the basis of your prayers for
others. You may find it helpful to make a list of persons and
needs that you want to remember in prayer. As you cannot
pray for everything every day, work out a simple prayer diary,
and pray for different people and needs each day of the week.
    Here a balance is very important. It is possible to develop
such a fixed system of prayer lists that prayer becomes
mechanical and an increasing drudgery, until perhaps you give
up altogether. It has all become quite meaningless to you in
terms of real communication with the living God. But if you
have no system at all, wishing to be spontaneous and Spirit-
led, this can so easily become carelessness and laziness. The
balance is a delicate one and lies somewhere in between. All of
us need some discipline before we can discover the immense
power of prayer. At the same time, within this discipline, we
need to discover a freedom to pray as the Spirit leads us.
(LANL)

Am I balancing freedom and discipline in my prayer life?

Lord, thank you that I have this amazing privilege of being able to talk to you, the Almighty God.

March 9   Authority in the church

I will give you the keys of the kingdom of heaven; whatever you bind on earth will be bound in heaven, and whatever you loose on earth will be loosed in heaven.   Matthew 16:19

The keys of the kingdom are symbols of spiritual authority, and Jesus gives these, not just to Peter, but to all his disciples. He gave this authority to the seventy and they returned after their first mission, thrilled at all that God had done through them. In Jesus' name they had been able to bind Satan and all his evil work and to loose those who had been bound by him in one way or another. As Christians, we have the same authority —but do we believe it or exercise it?

There was a Christian working in an area where spiritism and black magic were rife. The police were also working in the same place because drug addiction was prevalent there. One police officer after another was affected by being in those evil surroundings. One was ill, another had a breakdown, one or two committed suicide, and others were invalided out for various reasons.

'Why is it that you come to no harm,' a police inspector asked the Christian, 'when we police are coming to grief one after another?' The Christian replied, 'It is because I believe and trust in the name of Jesus Christ and in his blood, and many of you don't.' And in the name and power of Jesus, that man was able not only to be kept safe, but also to deliver many who had been bound by Satan.

But before anyone can engage in work like this — he must have Christ's spiritual authority in his life and be experiencing a very deep prayer-life. (YTL)

Lord, am I using the spiritual authority which you give me as one of your disciples?

Is there enough teaching on this topic in our church, through sermons, Bible studies, etc?

March 10   Submission to leaders

Obey your leaders and submit to their authority. They keep watch over you as men who must give an account. Obey them so that their work will be a joy, not a burden, for that would be of no advantage to you.   Hebrews 13:17

We are *to submit to those over us in the Lord.* Neither the verse above nor 1 Thessalonians chapter 5 verses 12 and 13 suggest that we are to obey these people provided we agree with their decisions. That is not the point at issue. The leaders of a church will not always be right. There may often be a need to talk and pray things through, until the will of the Lord is more clearly seen for that church. But that is no excuse for rebellion, inward or outward, silent or vocal.

Until we learn to submit to those who are over us, the Lord cannot and will not bless our work and worship. Although the time came for Jesus, as Son of God, Prophet, Priest and King, to make some stinging remarks to the Jewish leaders concerning their hypocrisy and unbelief, for many years he humbly submitted himself to the worship and leadership of his day. It was his regular custom to go to the synagogue at Nazareth on the Sabbath day, and to travel to the Temple at Jerusalem for the great festivals. This is a point worth remembering when we become impatient with the church where we worship, or with the leadership of that church. (IBITC)

How supported and encouraged are our church leaders in their God-given roles?

Father, is there any matter over which I need to submit to those whom you have placed in spiritual authority over me?

81

Make every effort to live in peace with all men and to be holy; without holiness no-one will see the Lord. See to it that no-one misses the peace of God and that no bitter root grows up to cause trouble and defile many.   **Hebrews 12:14,15**

Any gardener knows that garden weeds cause damage and need constant pulling up! But the Bible warns us against an even more damaging weed — the weed of resentment with its bitter root. It can cause trouble and defile many. Bitter people can miss the grace of God and be excluded from seeing the Lord. What terrible consequences from letting this weed grow among us!

Many doctors would say that the poisonous emotions of bitterness and resentment can cause physical pain and suffering, too.

The weedkiller for this vicious root is forgiveness — gallons and gallons of it! 'Get rid of all bitterness, rage and anger, brawling and slander, along with every form of malice. Be kind and compassionate to one another, forgiving each other, just as in Christ God forgave you' (Ephesians 4:31,32).

Jesus spoke even more strongly about this matter. 'If you do not forgive men their sins, your Father will not forgive your sins' (Matthew 6:15). (PL)

Lord, make our church fellowship aware of the 'weeds' growing among us.

Am I bitter towards anyone? What must I do?

Bear with each other and forgive whatever grievances you may have against one another. Forgive as the Lord forgave you.   **Colossians 3:13**

Forgiveness is painful. It's easier to get angry, critical or bitter, or to keep someone at arm's length than it is to sort out a wrong relationship. But just as you have to squeeze an orange to extract its juice, or crush a flower to release its fragrance, so it is through the pressures and hurts in our relationships that the love of Jesus can be shown — provided we learn to forgive.

Simon Peter wanted to know how often he was to forgive someone. He said, 'Lord, if my brother keeps sinning against me, how many times do I forgive him? Seven times?' I think he was expecting Jesus to say, 'Well done, Simon, you're right again!' The rabbis used to say one should forgive three times, and Peter must have thought, 'If I double that and add one for good measure, I'm sure to be correct!' So he was probably completely stunned when Jesus said, 'No, not seven times, but seventy times seven.' Of course, Jesus didn't mean that literally, so the Christian who is reported to have said, 'You wait till you do it the four hundred and ninety-first time,' had missed the point! What Jesus meant was that forgiveness was to be limitless.

When we feel we can't forgive, we need to dwell on what God has forgiven us in Christ, and to depend on the Holy Spirit.

Here's a practical suggestion. Make a list of the people you feel unable to forgive and then burn that list saying out loud, 'I forgive these people because God has forgiven me a million times more than I will ever have to forgive them.' (CFP)

Lord, every time I think of . . . I feel angry and hurt inside. I want to release . . . from the prison of my resentment and unforgiveness.

Try the practical suggestion.

March 13   By faith Abel

By faith Abel offered God a better sacrifice than Cain did. By faith he was commended as a righteous man, when God spoke

well of his offerings. And by faith he still speaks, even though he is dead.
Hebrews 11:4

At first sight, Abel is a curious choice for this portrait gallery of great heroes of faith. He is mentioned in only three Old Testament verses and is the victim of the first murder. His name means 'vanity' or 'mere breath'. We might say he's a bit of a 'nobody' — but God delights to make nobodies into somebodies in his sight (1 Corinthians 1:26-29).

There are three important things to notice about Abel. First, by faith he *worshipped*: he 'offered God a . . . sacrifice'. And worship is the most important thing we can do in God's sight; it's more important than work, witness or anything else. We *must* learn to worship now because heaven is filled with worship (Revelation, chapter 4 and 5). This is what we should come together to do — to offer a sacrifice of worship. People sometimes say, 'I went to such and such a church but I didn't get anything out of it.' The question is, 'What did you put into it?' First, we worship, then we receive; that's the spiritual order.

Secondly, by faith Abel *was accepted by God*: 'God spoke well of his offerings.' The story of Cain and Abel's sacrifices (Genesis 4:3-5) seems unfair at first sight, but it's almost certain that God had previously shown Cain and Abel what offering would be acceptable to him; certainly the other heroes of faith (Hebrews 11) were chosen because by faith they obeyed God's word to them. So it must have been that Abel by faith obeyed and Cain gave the sacrifice he deemed adequate and good enough.

Thirdly, by faith Abel *still speaks*. Whatever is done by faith in obedience to God's word, has the stamp of eternity on it. (YTL)

Meditate on your faith and your 'works' in the light of 1 Corinthians 3:10-14.

If my faith isn't growing, am I feeding it?

Don't talk defeat!

David thought to himself, 'One of these days I shall be destroyed by the hand of Saul.'   **1 Samuel 27:1**

When David was feeling depressed, he made some mistakes which I believe we can learn from. First, he talked defeat. One writer said, 'You said you did not have faith, and that moment, doubt rose like a giant and bound you. Perhaps you never realised that to a great extent you are ruled and shaped by your words. You talk failure and failure holds you in bondage. You talk fear and fear increases its grip on you. The answer? We must fill our hearts with "Thus says the Lord." Then, we must confess that word until it becomes part of our nature. Hold on to the promises of God.'

If we are feeling as David was, we must be positive in our words. Take a promise of God. Say it out loud and go on and on saying it until the truth grips our heart and mind. David should have done this. He had been given a wonderful promise: 'Even though someone is pursuing you to take your life, the life of my master (i.e. David) will be bound securely in the bundle of the living by the Lord your God. But the lives of your enemies he will hurl away as from the pocket of a sling' (1 Samuel 25:29). But instead of holding on to this, David talked negatively.

Words are one way in which we can take up the shield of faith against the enemy who wants to bring us and keep us low. (YTL)

Am I being negative in my words?

Father, I take hold of this promise of yours . . . for this situation today.

God's man in a crisis

When he [Ahab] saw Elijah, he said to him, 'Is that you, you troubler of Israel?' 'I have not made trouble for Israel,' Elijah

replied. 'But you and your father's family have. You have abandoned the Lord's commands and have followed the Baals.'

1 Kings 18:17,18

In Ahab's eyes, Elijah was an awkward fundamentalist prophet always talking about sin and judgment and the need to repent! He disturbed the status quo — the compromise of God and Baal. If we, like Elijah, stand up for God's word and his commands in an atmosphere of apathy or compromise, sooner or later we too will be called troublemakers or fun-spoilers.

Whatever Ahab's opinion, Elijah was God's man in this crisis. He told Ahab to bring all the prophets of Baal to the top of Mount Carmel. The scene must have been spectacular — hundreds of false prophets on one side, Elijah all alone on the other, and the people looking on.

Elijah challenged the prophets of Baal to prepare a sacrifice and call on their god to send fire down to burn it up. So the prophets called and shouted from morning to evening but there was no response. Then Elijah rebuilt the neglected altar of God and prayed that God would be known that day as God, the only true God.

It's interesting to notice that when Elijah preached, although his words were powerful and relevant, there was silence from the people. But when the fire of God fell, they all 'fell prostrate and cried, "The Lord, he is God! The Lord — he is God!"' (1 Kings 18:39). And I believe that nothing less than God's power will dislodge the apathy of people around us, and that God will not come down in power until Christians have as their one burning ambition that he will be honoured and glorified. (YTL)

If there is a crisis situation in our lives, ought we to be looking for God's man for it?

'Let it be known today that you are God' through what I say or do.

A divided heart

No-one can serve two masters. Either he will hate the one and love the other, or he will be devoted to the one and despise the other. You cannot serve both God and Money.   Matthew 6:24
No-one who puts his hand to the plough and looks back is fit for service in the kingdom of God.   Luke 9:62

Most of us would like to arrive at a happy compromise. Of course we want to seek first the kingdom of God; but earthly treasures continue to attract, tug away at the heart, cause anxiety, and lessen our faith. We may not want to be extravagantly wealthy provided we have clear financial security. However, in wanting the best of both worlds we lose the transforming power of the kingdom of God. Again we must stress that Jesus is not forbidding personal property; but when we in any way start 'craving' for these things we may well wander away from the faith and pierce our hearts with many pangs (1 Timothy 6:10).

John White says: 'We must be suspicious of any faith about personal justification that is not substantiated by faith in God's power over material things in our everyday life. Faith about pie in the sky when I die cannot be demonstrated. Faith that God can supply my need today *can* be demonstrated.'

So the question is, when it comes to the financial crunch, who or what do we really believe? Do we have faith — true faith — in Jesus? It is by faith that we are justified, and it is by faith that we shall see the power of God in our ministry. It is God's rebuke to us affluent Christians, as we hedge ourselves around with earthly treasures and securities, that God's power is today more obviously demonstrated amongst those who have little or nothing of this world's goods. But they are rich in faith. (D)

Jesus, priceless treasure — from the best bliss that earth imparts, I turn unfilled to you again.

What or who has the power to draw me? What would Jesus say about those people or influences?

Christ in you, the hope of glory.   Colossians 1:27
Praise be to the God and Father of our Lord Jesus Christ, who
has blessed us in the heavenly realms with every spiritual blessing in Christ.
                                                            Ephesians 1:3

So often we feel we need more love or power or faith or
wisdom — and we don't quite know where to get them. But *we
already have these things in Christ!* If we have received Christ
into our lives, we have wisdom and faith and power and life
and love (Ephesians 1:17-19; 2:1; 3:14-19). What we need to do
therefore is to draw on or claim these things.

Waiting at an airport for my luggage to arrive, I sometimes
notice the unclaimed baggage and think, 'Surely the owners
will come and claim their property!' But they don't always.
And many of us are like that with God's riches in Christ — we
leave them as unclaimed baggage.

Some of these riches — the gift of the Holy Spirit, grace,
peace, justification, adoption, election — are ours the moment
we receive Christ, but we may not appreciate or experience
them till later. It takes time for God's truths to cut down to
deeper layers of our lives, just as a knife cuts through to the
different layers of an onion.

We already have all we need in order to be changed
ourselves and to turn the world upside down with the revolution of love which Jesus started with a handful of disciples
nearly two thousand years ago. But we need to experience
what we have and let the truths permeate our whole being (1
Thessalonians 5:23,24), not just for our own benefit but for
God's glory (Ephesians 1:6). (AR)

*Study the Bible to discover what you actually have when you
receive Christ, and meditate on these truths.*

*Lord, help me to claim and draw on the riches of your ... for
... (a particular situation).*

For where your treasure is, there your heart will be also.
Matthew 6:21

A woman once went round her house, pausing in every room to say something like this: 'Lord, this furniture is yours, the curtains and carpets are yours.' She opened her wardrobe and said, 'These clothes are yours.' She went into the kitchen and said, 'All is yours,' and into the garage and said, 'The car is yours.' In the end, she had told the Lord that everything was his. Once she'd done that, she felt quite free to give, to lend, to share, or do whatever the Lord told her to do with her possessions.

The early church had the same feeling about their things. 'No one claimed that any of his possessions was his own' (Acts 4:32).

We need to learn today more about worship in the sharing of possessions. The church has all the money it needs, but it's in the pockets, bank balances, possessions and property of its members. The question isn't how to get more money for the work of the kingdom of God but how to release more money from the church, the people of God.

Generous giving and sharing of possessions is a vital part of our total giving to God. A friend of mine asked, 'Can your neighbours and the people with whom you work tell that you are a Christian by the way you relate to your possessions?' A man's attitude to his possessions is the evidence and measure of his commitment to Christ.

Worship means worth-ship. Do we give God his worth by our giving and sharing of money and possessions? (AR)

How do I regard my possessions?

Lord, these things . . . are yours to use for your glory.

The heavens declare the glory of God; the skies proclaim the
work of his hands. Day after day they pour forth speech; night
after night they display knowledge. There is no speech or
language where their voice is not heard. Their voice goes out
into all the earth, their words to the ends of the world.

                                                    Psalm 19:1-4

In the Bible, the 'word of God' is seen as greater than 'Bible
words', however important those words are as an objective
statement of divine truth. For example, it is by the word of
God that the heavens and the earth were created (Psalm 33:6;
John 1:1-3); in Jesus Christ 'the Word became flesh and lived
for a while among us . . . full of grace and truth' (John 1:14);
and it is through Jesus that God has spoken to us (Hebrews
1:2). Moreover God has spoken 'at many times and in various
ways' (Hebrews 1:1), not just through the scriptures. For
example, David in Psalm 19 vividly describes creation as the
silent eloquence of God's word.

     God's silent word, coming to us visually instead of audibly,
is something we need increasingly to remember in an age
dominated by television, glossy magazines and popular daily
newspapers. The creative arts can also have a part to play in
proclaiming the word which once became flesh. Drama,
dance, mime, painting, photography, architecture, tapestry:
all of these can tell the glory of God and proclaim his handiwork. At times a silent, or non-verbal presentation of God's
truth can speak more loudly than words.

     Paul makes it clear that God has already revealed himself,
even to those without the special revelation of his written
word, both in creation (Romans 1:20) and in conscience
(Romans 2:14,15). (IBIE)

*Study some aspect of God's creativity — a flower, a butterfly,
or anything else.*

*Father, help me to think about whatever is lovely, admirable
or excellent (see Philippians 4:8).*

**Then Miriam, the prophetess, Aaron's sister, took a tambour-
ine in her hand, and all the women followed her, with
tambourines and dancing. Miriam sang to them: 'Sing to the
Lord, for he is highly exalted. The horse and its rider he has
hurled into the sea.'**   **Exodus 15:20,21**

Dancing was sometimes prophetic in its associations. . . Dance
was one way by which God spoke to his people, and that is still
true today. . . It can often 'say' things very powerfully in
certain situations.

Dancing usually involved a group of women, but not
always so (2 Samuel 6:16-23). The main Hebrew word for a
pilgrim festival is *hag*, and some commentators suggest that
this term arose because of the dance of the pilgrims. Thus in
Psalm 42, for example, the psalmist remembers how once he
'used to go with the multitude leading the procession (dance?)
to the house of God, with shouts of joy and thanksgiving
among the festive throng' — the festal procession dance, *hogeg*
(Psalm 42:4).

Dancing was often the climax in worship. After Moses and
the people sang a song to the Lord, Miriam and all the women
picked up the same song and brought it to a climax in the
dance.

Dancing was one recognised form of proclaiming God's
good news and therefore should be rightly linked with
evangelism. (IBIE)

*Help me not to despise another's gift or another's expression of
love and worship to the Lord, as Michal did (2 Samuel 6:16).*

*Is there any gift or aspect of our personalities which may not be
used for God or by God? What makes a thing taboo or
unacceptable to God?*

You will be my witnesses.   Acts 1:8

Not every Christian is an evangelist, but each of us is called to be a witness. In a court of law, every person who has first-hand experience of what is being investigated can be called in as a witness, but not everyone can be a barrister — the man who persuades others of the truth of the matter. In the same way, everyone with first-hand experience of Christ can and should be a witness to him, though he may never be an evangelist, or a spiritual barrister, with his particular persuasive and other gifts.

As witnesses, we may have opportunities to share what God is doing in our lives and even to lead a person to Jesus. Therefore it's very important to work out in advance what we will say to someone who wants to know how to become a Christian.

Thousands of times over the past years I have used roughly the same method — with variations, of course. Using the Bible, I lead the person I am talking to through four basic steps.

First, he must admit his need (Romans 3:23; 6:23). He may not be aware of any need, or he may have a whole variety of needs, but it is the need to be right with God, through the forgiveness of sins, that I focus on.

Secondly, he must believe that Jesus on the cross has dealt with his sins once and for all (Isaiah 53:6).

Thirdly, he must count the cost of discipleship (Mark 8:34). If he wants Jesus in his life, then Jesus must be 'number one'.

Fourthly, Jesus needs to be invited in — he won't barge in (Revelation 3:20). (CFP)

Lord, as I grow closer to you, let my witnessing become more natural, spontaneous and genuine.

Spend time soon, perhaps today, working out the words and verses you would use in leading someone through to faith in Jesus.

When the Spirit speaks

When they [Paul and his companions] came to the border of Mysia, they tried to enter Bithynia, but the Spirit of Jesus would not allow them to.   Acts 16:7

At one evangelistic house meeting, I felt constrained to change my prepared talk at the very last moment. Consequently, I fumbled over what I was trying to say and felt that the result was very unpolished and not at all worthy of the rather sophisticated gathering at that house. Even so, I did something I rarely do in the context of a drawing room meeting: I closed the talk with a prayer of commitment for those wanting to invite Christ into their lives.

Afterwards, there was an embarrassing silence, during which I shuffled from one foot to another, feeling sure that I had blundered socially.

At last people stood up and started moving about and talking. After a moment, a mature, self-assured woman approached me and started to speak. She was angry and rude. Feeling more uncomfortable than ever, I tried to answer her gently.

Suddenly she blurted out, 'But I'm such a sinner that I'm sure God couldn't possibly love me.' Then I knew that, beneath the façade, she was longing to know God's forgiveness and peace. A few months later, we were on our knees in another room, as she opened her heart to the love of Jesus. Several others found Christ at that same gathering. The Holy Spirit had seen through to the hunger of those people and had directed my stumbling words to their hearts. (IBIE)

If the Holy Spirit wanted to speak to me, would I be quiet, relaxed and receptive enough to hear him?

Speak, Lord, for your servant is listening.

Different ways of working

There are different kinds of working, but the same God works all of them in all men.   1 Corinthians 12:6

Christ works in many different ways through his Body, the church. The church has been called the resurrected form of Jesus on earth today. We see him at work in so many ways through us. When there is real love and joy in our fellowship, and when people are healed in our services, God is at work. When gifts of money come in for the Lord's work, and when people are moved by our generous hospitality, God is at work. Juan Carlos Ortiz said that when people come into their church, 'they become part of a caring family, moving in the Holy Spirit'. This is clear evidence that God is at work in that church.

God doesn't just want to work through a few of his people; he wants to work through each one of them; his gifts are not optional extras for the spiritually élite, but for everyone.

We should not limit God's ways of working. It's nonsense to say that certain gifts such as tongues, prophecy and healing died out with the apostles and are not for the church today. True, we are told that prophecies and tongues will cease, and knowledge will pass away; but it's clear that this will happen only 'when perfection comes' (1 Corinthians 13:8,9). Then, of course, there'll be no need for healing, faith or evangelism. After all, whom would one evangelise in heaven? But for the moment, all these gifts and many others are needed, as God continues to work in different ways through his church. (YTL)

Can I see God's different ways of working through our church?

Father, help me to see more clearly where you are at work.

March 24   Church expansion

Many who heard the message believed.   Acts 4:4

How does the church expand? One way is through the witness of its members in the power of the Holy Spirit. 'Evangelism,' writes Michael Green, 'is talking about Jesus by people who've been with Jesus and who are filled with the Spirit of Jesus.' We can talk about evangelism and organise films, discussion groups, drama and anything else, but none of these is any 'substitute for the daily unspectacular witness of the rank and file Christian' (David Winter).

The church also expands through the witness of a loving, united, active church (Acts 2:42-47). When people see this kind of church, they want to know more about it (see Zechariah 8:23).

In the New Testament, the church sometimes expanded through signs and wonders (Acts 3). Those who saw the crippled man healed were 'filled with wonder and amazement' and were ready to hear the preached message. In almost every chapter of Acts, the preaching of the word and signs and wonders happened together. This combination still makes a very powerful impact today.

United prayer was the basis of all the apostles' work (Acts 4:23-31). After prayer, 'they were all filled with the Holy Spirit and spoke the word of God boldly,' and believers were added to the church.

Persecution was another means of church expansion (Acts 8). The Christians had been having a glorious time in Jerusalem, but when the persecution arose they were scattered through Judea and Samaria — exactly where they should have been if they had obeyed Jesus' commission!

Regular preaching and teaching were also very important ways of spreading the Christian message and gaining converts (Acts 11:25,26; Acts 19:8). We need to pray for those engaged in this ministry. A visiting preacher was greeted with the words, 'I hope you'll give us a good sermon today,' and his reply was, 'It'll be as good as you have prayed for.'

Also, church expansion can take place very effectively through small groups which grow, split and grow again (Acts 13:2; 1 Corinthians 16:19). (YTL)

Is our church expanding? If not, have we something to learn?

Father, help me to talk about Jesus through the Spirit of Jesus with complete naturalness and spontaneity.

After desire has conceived, it gives birth to sin; and sin, when it is full-grown, gives birth to death.   James 1:15

Read 1 Samuel, chapter 11 and you will see this verse illustrated. According to Hebrew tradition, Bathsheba was one of the three most beautiful women in the world. King David could not help seeing her and his reaction was perfectly natural. But then, instead of turning away, or turning to the Lord, he lusted after her and took steps to find out who she was. John Hercus writes: 'I don't know how David found out who she (Bathsheba) was. He may have come straight up to one of his palace henchmen and blurted out, "Who's that gorgeous little bit of fluff in the house over there with the two big fig trees in the garden?" It might have been like that, but I don't think it was.' Like John Hercus, I believe David went about matters furtively. And certainly when he found out that Bathsheba was married to Uriah, one of his select band of outstanding soldiers, he resorted to intrigue, lies and deception to get what he wanted. He committed adultery with Bathsheba, tried to trick Uriah into covering up his sin, and, failing that, arranged for his death in battle. 'But the thing David had done displeased the Lord' (2 Samuel 11:27), and David paid a heavy price for his lust — the death of his illegitimate child, and the agony of a condemning conscience, among other things.

God's laws are maker's instructions, given to us for a very good purpose. If we break them, we are not only guilty, but we will suffer the consequences.

If you have fallen as David did — it is not the end of everything. For those who truly repent there is complete forgiveness for the present and the possibility of victory in the future, as long as you are aware of your vulnerability and keep obeying and depending on God. This will involve fighting 'the good fight of the faith' (1 Timothy 6:12) fleeing 'the evil desires of youth' (2 Timothy 2:22) and presenting your body as a living sacrifice to God daily (Romans 12:1). (YTL)

What is the difference between a God-given desire for someone and lust?

Lord, through the Holy Spirit's control of my life, may I never see as beautiful anything which you hate, or see as impure anything that you have made clean.

March 26   Guilty conscience?

By setting forth the truth plainly we commend ourselves to every man's conscience in the sight of God.   2 Corinthians 4:2

Over the past years I have had the privilege and joy of seeing a number of terrorists and long-term prisoners come to a living faith in Christ. In their letters to me they have almost all used exactly the same words in describing their experience: 'For the first time I *feel free.*' No one can escape the relentless pain of a guilty conscience. Most of us try to hide sin by the cover-up of activity.

Our conscience, however, is that God-given faculty within us that is constantly vulnerable to the Holy Spirit's action. Suddenly and unexpectedly we may feel guilty over something we have done, or not done, in the past.

'Nothing is more characteristic of the human sense of guilt than its indelibility, its power of asserting itself with unabated poignancy in spite of all lapse of time and all changes in the self and its environment... The past is not dead; it can never, in this life, be buried and done with' (A. E. Taylor).

That is why the apostle Paul refused to tamper with God's word... He knew well, from his own humbling experience, how the Spirit of God could make the word of God like a two-edged sword piercing through all the barriers and defences in order to expose a guilty conscience. It is only through the awakened conscience that we shall be aware of any spiritual or moral need of God; and it is only when the Holy Spirit convinces us of this need that we shall begin to call on God for mercy and forgiveness. (D)

Lord, may the Holy Spirit renew my conscience.

Is there such a thing as an over-sensitive conscience?

If we walk in the light, as he is in the light, we have fellowship with one another, and the blood of Jesus, his Son, purifies us from every sin.   **1 John 1:7**

One of Billy Graham's associates was once on a plane with a very irritable, critical woman, who complained about everything. As he listened to her, he discerned that her real problem was some sin for which she had found no forgiveness. She felt self-condemned about this sin, but because she couldn't accept her *self*-criticism, she criticised others instead.

So this man handed her an open New Testament and asked her to read aloud for him 1 John chapter 1 verse 7. While he looked out of the window, she read, 'The blood of Jesus, his Son, cleanses us from all sin.'

'I think you're wrong,' her companion interrupted her. 'It says *some sin*!'

'Oh, no!' answered the woman. 'It says *all sin*!'

'Surely not,' said the man. 'It must be *some sin.*'

'No,' the woman insisted. 'It says here quite clearly *all sin.*'

They went on arguing like this for a little while and then suddenly the woman cried out, 'I see it! It is *all* sin!' In that moment she realised that the sin for which she was condemning herself was included in the 'all sin' from which the blood of Jesus could cleanse her. (YTL)

Lord, I hand my guilt about . . . to you, and receive by faith your complete forgiveness and cleansing.

Find and learn a promise about God's forgiveness so that you can quote it if ever you are tempted in this matter again.

'I will restore you to health and heal your wounds,' declares
the Lord.   Jeremiah 30:17

God's plan is that we should have a loving relationship with
himself, the love and care of a spiritual family, and the love
and care of a human family (Colossians 3:18-21). In this
imperfect world, people are deprived of one or all of these
provisions planned for us by God.

When small children are not given the secure protective
human love that they need, they grow up damaged physically,
emotionally or both. When they reach adulthood, they are far
from whole. Often they wear masks to hide their true feelings.
One might wear the mask of self-confidence, another that of
the constant joker and a third a 'praise-the-Lord' mask. Others
might hide behind 'shy' or 'apathetic' or 'busy' masks.

God has a plan of healing for all such. Part of that healing
takes place when we come to know God through Jesus Christ
and receive the Holy Spirit into our lives (Ephesians 3:16-19).
We can then share openly with the Lord and with others who
we are, what we're like and how we feel. He knows it all, but
we need to tell him. The healing continues as we live and
worship with our brothers and sisters in Christ (Colossians
3:12-14). Within the security of a loving Christian family, it
ought to be possible for us to share and show our true selves,
probably through small groups. Certainly we'll be hurt and
we'll need to forgive — because other Christians are far from
perfect. But through them God can and does bring inner
healing. (AR)

*Lord, make me real and help me to grow towards wholeness by
making the most of all you have provided for me.*

*Be ready in the coming days to share something of your true
self with another, or to listen to someone who wants to be real
and open with you.*

There is now no condemnation for those who are in Christ Jesus.
Romans 8:1

When I was on holiday with my family once, a bee began buzzing round my daughter who was then aged nine. I put my arm round her to protect her and got stung. So I said, 'Fiona, you're safe now. I've taken the sting and there's nothing for you to be afraid of.' When we make Jesus our Saviour and Lord, it is as though he puts his arm round us and says, 'You're safe now. I've taken the sting out of death. There's no condemnation for you to be afraid of.'

If Jesus is alive in your experience, when death comes, as it certainly will unless the Lord returns first, you need have no fear at all.

When the famous preacher William Haslam was conducting a service one day, he received a message which said, 'Father is dying and does so want to see you. Will you come?' At once the preacher left but when he arrived he was told, 'It's too late. Your father's dead.' But William Haslam went over to the bed and spoke about the lovingkindness of the Lord. His father smiled at the name of Jesus and said, 'Not dead, just beginning to live.' They were his last words.

F. B. Meyer wrote these words which were later delivered to a friend: 'I've raced you to heaven. I'm just off. See you there. Love, F. B. Meyer.' A moment later he died, or rather, was just beginning to live.

The father of a girl who had just died of leukaemia wrote these words to me: 'Although so very weak and becoming more and more delirious, she died, I know, full of faith and literally, but for the last few moments, held her right hand pointing up to Jesus as she could not speak. . . We never forget that she is now with him and we would not want to disturb her happiness even if we could.'

No one but Jesus can give people such solid hope in the face of death and judgment. (AR)

Lord, I pray for . . . who is afraid to die. Take away her fear and give her hope and peace.

Is there anything I dread? Have I shared it honestly with Jesus?

The time came when the beggar died and the angels carried him to Abraham's side. The rich man also died and was buried.
Luke 16:22

I believe Christ settled the issue once and for all as to whether there would be a second chance after death, in telling the story of the rich man and Lazarus (Luke 16:19-31). The one who loved the Lord found himself in heaven; the one who had neglected him found himself in hell. There he suddenly realised the awful consequences of his neglect and cried out for mercy, but the answer was, 'It's too late, because between you and heaven there's a huge chasm.' Then the rich man pleaded that someone would go and warn his five brothers before it was too late for them too. The answer came: 'They have the Scriptures, let them read those.' The rich man replied, 'If someone were to rise from the dead, they would listen to him!' Jesus' reply, through this story, is chilling but true: 'If they don't repent because of the Scriptures, they won't repent even if someone were to rise from the dead.'

Why should there be a second chance for those who have refused numerous chances during their life-time? God said to his people through Jeremiah, 'From the time your forefathers left Egypt until now, day after day, again and again I sent you my servants the prophets. But they did not listen to me or pay attention' (Jeremiah 7:25,26). He could say the same sort of thing about this country where all of us have access to Bibles, Christian books and services. And because of this, when some people die, God says to them with infinite sadness and finality, 'You didn't want me, now you can't have me — it was your choice.' George Macdonald said that the essence of hell for any individual is this: 'I am on my own.' (YTL)

Why is it that there's no second chance after death? Would I be able to explain this to someone asking about it, or even to show from the Bible that this is a fact?

Lord, I pray that you will prevent the devil from blinding the eyes and blocking the ears of . . . today. May he (she) hear your message clearly.

March 31   Do it now!

Today, if you will hear his voice, do not harden your hearts.
                                                   Psalm 95:8

There's a legend which is worth telling because it contains an important truth.

The devil held a passing out parade at the evil spiritual academy one year. During the course of the day he questioned three of his evil spirits. To the first he said, 'When you get out into the world what are you going to say to people?'

'Oh,' the evil spirit replied, 'I shall tell them that there is no God.'

'That's no use,' said the devil. 'Creation tells people that there is a God. Not many people will believe you.'

Then he said to the second evil spirit, 'And what are *you* going to tell people?'

'I shall say that there is not going to be a judgment,' was the reply.

'That's not much use,' answered the devil. 'Conscience tells them about judgment. Not many will believe you.'

Turning to the third evil spirit he asked, 'What about you?'

'I shall tell people that there is a God and a judgment to come,' answered the third evil spirit, 'but I shall add that there's no hurry.'

'Excellent!' said the devil. 'Many will believe that!'

I believe that the devil does try to persuade people that there's no hurry about turning to God or putting things right in the world, whereas the truth is that time is running out fast, and the right time to respond to God's voice is always now — as soon as we hear it. (AR)

Lord, perhaps time is running out for someone I know. Let me be available to that person for you — ready to speak or act in truth and love now.

What am I putting off that needs attention now?

APRIL
Christian Basics

April 1   Who's searching for whom?

Before they call I will answer; while they are still speaking, I will hear.   Isaiah 65:24
Suppose one of you has a hundred sheep and loses one of them. Does he not leave the ninety-nine in the open country and go after the lost sheep until he finds it?   Luke 15:4
I am the good shepherd.   John 10:11
You did not choose me, but I chose you to go and bear fruit.   John 15:16

At University I studied philosophy and soon discovered the truth that a metaphysician is a blind man in a dark room looking for a black cat that isn't there. Many people feel as hopeless as that about their search for God.

A social worker visited a sick boy in the back streets of Lagos and found some books on the table beside his bed. They were -- a Bible, the Book of Common Prayer, the Koran, a copy of the Watchtower, a book by Karl Marx and another with the title: 'How to stop worrying!'

Man's long search for God can be a very confusing business. But Christianity is not about man groping blindly for God, but about God seeking for individuals, because he loves them and wants them to know and love him.

Malcolm Muggeridge said: 'I've never wanted a God or

feared a God or felt under any necessity to invent one. Fortunately, I've been driven to the conclusion that God wants me.' (AR)

Thank you with all my heart for wanting me and looking until you found me.

Make up a song or prayer, expressing your joy that God actually wanted you to know him, and use it in the coming days.

Bible Study: What does salvation (past, present and future tense) mean in the Bible? Is my concept wide enough?
Starters: Matthew 1:21; Romans 10:13; 13:11; 1 Corinthians 1:18; Ephesians 2:8, 9; Philippians 2:12.

April 2   **Why the cross?**

For the message of the cross is foolishness to those who are perishing, but to us who are being saved it is the power of God. . . Jews demand miraculous signs and Greeks look for wisdom, but we preach Christ crucified: a stumbling block to Jews and foolishness to Gentiles, but to those whom God has called, both Jews and Greeks, Christ the power of God and the wisdom of God.   **1 Corinthians 1:18, 22-24**

A reporter once said to me, 'Of what possible significance is the death of a Jew in Palestine two thousand years ago?' And when we preach about Jesus dying to save us, some people are offended and others call it nonsense. But God chose this way to save people for two main reasons.

Sin really matters to God. It is a breaking of his laws and it incurs a penalty. Jesus paid that penalty because no-one else could. 'There was no other good enough to pay the price of sin.'

Pride is at the heart of all sin. When I sin, I put myself and my wishes at the centre of my world. Before we can be forgiven, God has to humble us by showing us that we can never earn his forgiveness. However respectable or clever we may be, we have to come before God as sinners, confessing our wrongs and accepting, thankfully, what God has done for us through his death on the cross for us and in our stead. (K)

O God, thank you for making it possible for me to come to you; keep me humbly trusting and obeying you always.

Work out how you would answer that reporter, basing your answer on the Bible.

April 3   Conversion or brainwashing?

He fell to the ground and heard a voice say to him, 'Saul, Saul, why do you persecute me?' 'Who are you, Lord?' Saul asked. 'I am Jesus, whom you are persecuting,' he replied. 'Now get up and go into the city, and you will be told what you must do.'
Acts 9:4-6

A well known psychiatrist wrote this about Saul's conversion: 'A state of transmarginal inhibition seems to have followed his acute state of nervous excitement. Total collapse, hallucinations and an increased state of suggestibility appear to have supervened. Other inhibitory, hysterical manifestations are also reported.' Read Acts chapter 9 and judge for yourself. Personally, I believe we have all the ingredients of a true conversion in this story.

First, there is the humble recognition of the true nature of sin. Jesus asked Saul, 'Why do you persecute *me*?' whereas the chapter opens with Saul 'breathing out murderous threats against *the Lord's disciples*' (verse 1). All sin is rebellion against Jesus and unless a person comes to see this, he will not experience true conversion.

Secondly, there is humble submission to the lordship of Christ. Before any true conversion we must be humbled and ready to obey: reporting for duty rather than giving God instructions. This matter of obedience is vitally important (Luke 6:46; Matthew 7:21), though it's not a slavish obedience, but one that springs from love. I'm convinced that what finally broke proud, intellectual, religious, independent Saul was the love of Jesus. I'm told that communists are not converted by arguments but by seeing the love of Jesus in Christians. (YTL)

In our preaching and personal evangelism, are we including these two important ingredients in conversion?

Lord, I am reporting for duty. Show me how to pray and what to do today.

April 4   Peace with God

Since we have been justified through faith, we have peace with God through our Lord Jesus Christ ... For if, when we were God's enemies, we were reconciled to him through the death of his Son, how much more, having been reconciled, shall we be saved through his life!   **Romans 5:1, 10**

It's possible to have a great sense of peace while sitting in a quiet church, or watching a sunset, or listening to music. But such an experience may have nothing whatever to do with the peace of God. And the peace *of* God is only possible for those who have peace *with* God.

In the natural course of events, we do not have peace with God. On the contrary, we are estranged and alienated from God because of our sins. The Bible even says we are, by nature, enemies of God, because we go our own way and not his.

The problem of our broken relationship with God is so serious that it could only be solved through Christ's death on the cross. The old hymn expresses it well:

> Peace, perfect peace, in this dark world of sin?
> The blood of Jesus whispers peace within.

Because Jesus' blood cleanses us from all sin, we can have peace with God and then the peace of God.

I once visited a prison and met a man who had been consumed with bitterness, resentment and hatred against the prison officers, the police, society — everyone. He was always causing trouble. Several times he had tried to commit suicide. On one of these occasions, he really believed he was dying and in that moment he cried out to Jesus for help and forgiveness. The result was that there in the prison hospital he found peace with God and began to experience the peace of God.

I found it hard to believe that he had once been one of the worst prisoners in that jail, because he was so full of peace and love and gentleness. (YTL)

Meditate on the cross — the price of our peace.

Is there anything I need to do in order to have peace with God over something? Have I done it?

April 5   What is your verdict?

He (Jesus) asked his disciples... 'Who do you say I am?' Simon Peter answered, 'You are the Christ, the Son of the living God.'   **Matthew 16:13,15,16**

Jesus didn't spend his time stating that he was the Son of God — but the disciples came to believe that he was — because of all they saw and heard of him.

They noticed the quality and authority of Jesus' teaching. 'The crowds were amazed at his teaching because he taught as one who had authority and not as their teachers of the law' (Matthew 7:28,29). And if the crowds were amazed, so were the disciples.

They also noticed his mighty healing power as he 'went throughout Galilee ... healing every disease and sickness among the people' (Matthew 4:23). Lepers were healed, demons cast out, the lame walked, the blind could see, the deaf could hear and the dead were raised to life. The crowds were astounded, and so were the disciples.

Then there were the claims Jesus made for himself. Sometimes he made these claims directly, at other times he allowed others to draw their own conclusions from what they saw and heard. This happened when he healed the paralytic (Matthew 9; Mark 12). Jesus said to the sick boy, 'Take heart, son; your sins are forgiven!' The critics — the religious leaders — cried out, 'This fellow is blaspheming! Who can forgive sins but God alone?' They were quite right. Only God can forgive sins, so either Jesus was God or he was blaspheming. There wasn't then and there never has been since, any other possibility. (K)

Lord Jesus, Son of God, we praise you for all that you are and for the way you have shown yourself to us on this earth.

Continue to make Jesus Lord of every area in your life.

April 6   An invitation Jesus always accepts

Here I am! I stand at the door and knock. If anyone hears my voice and opens the door, I will go in and eat with him, and he with me.
                                                      Revelation 3:20

It's all too easy to assume that Jesus is with you, when in fact he is not, as Mary and Joseph did (Luke 2:44), or to have no assurance that he is with you, when in fact he *is*, as was Mary Magdalene's experience (John 20:15). So how can you be sure that Jesus is with you?

If I'm given a cheque for five pounds, can I be sure I really have that money? Yes, because of the promise implicit in the cheque. Provided I act as though it were true, by taking it to my bank manager, I will then have a further promise that it *is* true, when I read my bank statement.

If I say, 'That's a beautiful cheque,' and leave it on my table, keep it in my wallet, use it only to illustrate a sermon, or even put it on the wall like a text, it will never become five pounds to me, however much I believe in it. The promise on the cheque is one which has to be proved in experience.

Almost every transaction, and certainly every relationship, depends first and foremost upon trusting a promise and acting upon it. Can I be sure that I'm married? Yes, first of all, because I've promised my life to another person, and she's promised her life to me.

Can I be sure that Jesus is with me? Yes, first of all, because of his promise (Revelation 3:20), and when I not only believe that promise but act upon it, assuming it is true, and ask him to come into my life, then I have further promises (Matthew 28:20, Hebrews 13:5, and many many others). (YTL)

Am I sure that Jesus is with me now? If not, I know what to do.

Remember a promise of Jesus next time you are tempted to doubt Christ's presence.

April 7   Seal, deposit and guarantee

And you also were included in Christ when you heard the word of truth, the gospel of your salvation. Having believed, you were marked in him with a seal, the promised Holy Spirit, who is a deposit guaranteeing our inheritance until the redemption of those who are God's possession to the praise of his glory.   Ephesians 1:13,14

In these verses Paul mentions two things we have done and must do often, and one thing that God has done for us.

We heard the word of truth. We did this when we first heard God speaking to us and responded to him. But if our relationship is to grow we must constantly, daily, listen for God's word.

We believed in Jesus, not just in our heads, but with the commitment of our whole lives to him as Lord. Again, we must constantly, daily, treat him as absolute king of our lives.

What God does for us is to seal us with his Holy Spirit — his personal stamp of ownership. In Song of Songs the lover says to the beloved, 'Place me like a seal over your heart, like a seal over your arm' (Song of Songs 8:6) — the seal being a sign of love and belonging. God's seal marks us as God's beloved, belonging completely to him.

The Holy Spirit is also 'a deposit guaranteeing our inheritance'. Once the 'deposit' of the Holy Spirit has been put down on our lives, our future inheritance is made absolutely certain — guaranteed until we actually acquire it. It's 'an inheritance that can never perish, spoil or fade — kept in heaven for you' (1 Peter 1:4). At times I can hardly wait for it! (YTL)

Am I enjoying every foretaste of heaven?

Father, thank you for the Holy Spirit, who stamps me as yours and guarantees that one day I shall be with you in glory for ever.

April 8   The priceless pearl

The kingdom of heaven is like a merchant looking for fine pearls. When he found one of great value, he went away and sold everything he had and bought it.   Matthew 13:45,46

A pearl symbolises beauty and worth. The merchant had many pearls but he was looking for one finer than the rest. In life there are many pearls — friendships, health, family life, art and music — but the kingdom of heaven, the rule of Jesus, outshines them all.

In the previous parable (Matthew 13:44), the man happens on the treasure. In the same way, some people find Jesus and enter the kingdom suddenly and unexpectedly. They may go to a camp because they want to play sport, and come away with Jesus. But here the merchant probably spent months or even years looking for the one pearl he really wanted, just as some people take a very long time to find or accept Christ and his kingdom.

In both parables, there was a price to pay. In one sense we can say that Jesus has paid the full price, through his death on the cross, so that we might receive salvation and life as a free gift. But in another sense, it's clear that in order to take this gift, we have to drop everything and hold out empty hands.

Is that a difficult thing to do? I talked to a man who thought it was impossible, but, in contrast, the man who found the treasure went out *in joy* and sold all that he had; and Paul said, 'I consider *everything* a loss compared to the surpassing greatness of knowing Christ Jesus my Lord, for whose sake I have lost *all things*. I consider them rubbish, that I may gain Christ' (Philippians 3:8). (YTL)

Am I really valuing Jesus as highly as I should be?

Father, open my eyes afresh by the Holy Spirit to see Jesus.

April 9   Turn your eyes upon Jesus

What do you think about the Christ?   Matthew 22:42

This is the crucial question, as William Haslam discovered on October 19th, 1851, when he went into his pulpit and started to preach on it. Suddenly he realised for the first time who Jesus really was and 'felt a wonderful light and joy coming into my soul'. A moment later, a man in the congregation leapt up and shouted, 'The parson's converted! The parson's converted! Hallelujah!' Then the whole congregation and the preacher joined in an outburst of praise.

Today people are hungry for Jesus, even when they are disillusioned about Christians. Something like eighteen million people watched the film 'Jesus of Nazareth' on television. This must show that outside the Christian church, there is still an enormous interest in its founder.

When people turn their eyes on Jesus, they are amazed and enthralled. Someone wrote of him: 'Born in poverty, lived only thirty-three years, spent most of his life in obscurity, never wrote a book, never held any position in public life, was crucified with two thieves, and yet two thousand years later more than 950 million people follow him.'

Dostoevsky wrote: 'I believe there is no one lovelier, deeper, more sympathetic and more perfect than Jesus,' and Tennyson: 'His character was more wonderful than the greatest miracle.' (AR)

What do I think about the Christ?

Set aside time to read about and meditate on Jesus.

April 10   His death my life

Jesus took bread, gave thanks and broke it, and gave it to his disciples saying, 'Take it; this is my body!' Then he took the cup, gave thanks and offered it to them, and they all drank from it. 'This is my blood of the covenant, which is poured out for many,' he said to them.   Mark 14:22-24

If you were moving away and wanted to give a close friend something by which to remember you with love and joy, what would it be? A photograph of yourself, or a treasured possession? When Jesus was about to leave his disciples, he had no treasured possessions to leave them, because he was poor for our sakes. But he might have chosen to leave a drawing showing a happy time, such as fishing in Lake Galilee, or a moving moment, such as any of the healing or other miracles, or a wonderful event, such as the entry into Jerusalem. Instead he chose something very different.

At his last meal with his disciples Jesus chose to be remembered by his followers for all generations by bread and wine. In other words, he wanted them above all to remember not his teaching or miracles, but his death. Memorials usually have details of a person's life, rather than anything about his death. But Jesus' death was not only the most famous death of all time, but the greatest event in history.

In the Garden alone that night, Jesus prayed in agony that God would remove the cup — not so much the cup of suffering, as the cup of the world's sin, guilt and punishment — from him, adding each time, 'Thy will be done.'

It's impossible for us to understand the full horror of what Jesus endured for us, but let's take time to meditate on the cross and to thank him, from the depths of our hearts, for the life that we enjoy because of that unspeakable death. (YTL)

Jesus, by your Spirit, help me to take in afresh something of the cost and the purpose of your death.

Meditate on the cross.

April 11   A time for reflection

A man ought to examine himself before he eats of the bread and drinks of the cup.   1 Corinthians 11:28

As we come to Holy Communion, we need to use our spiritual eyes to look in four different directions.

We need to look *back* ('Do this in remembrance of me' — Luke 22:19) to the finished work of Christ on the cross and be assured of our complete forgiveness.

We need to look *in*. 'The hand of him who is going to betray me is with mine on the table' (Luke 22:21). Paul urges us to examine ourselves (1 Corinthians 11:27-32). If our lives are not right with God and with others, it would be better for us not to take part in the service. These things need to be sorted out first.

We need to look *round*. 'Take this and divide it among you' (Luke 22:17). The communion service speaks vividly and dramatically of our oneness in Christ, regardless of denomination or tradition.

We need to look *forward*. 'I will not eat it again until it finds fulfilment in the kingdom of God' (Luke 22:16). All the blessings here and now are only a foretaste of what we shall receive in heaven when we see Jesus face to face. (AR)

Lord, show me what I am not seeing that I ought to be seeing.

How often do I remember Jesus' death and what does it mean to me? Would it mean more if I took time to prepare myself for this service?

April 12   Man of feeling

When Jesus saw her weeping. . . he was deeply moved in spirit and troubled.   **John 11:33**

Many people's image of Jesus is of someone calm, unruffled and incapable of strong feelings. Nothing could be further from the New Testament picture of Jesus. He experienced *joy* at the centurion's faith (Matthew 8:10), and told his disciples that if his joy was in them their joy would be full (John 15:11). Once his joy caused him to burst out into a prayer of praise (Luke 10:21). Perhaps if some of our Christian leaders had seen him behaving like that they would immediately have crossed him off their list of suitable speakers!

Jesus also felt deep *pain*. How it must have hurt him when thousands deserted him after he had taught them some hard truths (John 6:60), and even more when the disciples who had protested that they would never leave him — all deserted him too. At the grave of Lazarus, he was profoundly distressed, and in the Garden of Gethsemane and on the cross his agony was beyond our comprehension (Luke 22:39-46; Hebrews 5:7; Matthew 27:46).

At times, Jesus was moved with *indignation* or to outright *anger* as he was when he rebuked demons or when he saw the ravages caused by his great adversary (John 11:33,38), or when he drove out all who were buying and selling in the temple (Matthew 21:12).

On at least seven separate occasions we read that Jesus was moved with *compassion* — meaning that he felt very, very deeply for those who were in need, including the sick, a hungry crowd, a sorrowing friend, a city that rejected him, his mother at the cross, and all lost, helpless people.

115

Often Jesus was moved with *love* — as when he talked to the Samaritan woman, or the rich young ruler, or in his dealings with Mary, Martha and Lazarus, his disciples, Mary Magdalene, and others.

Jesus was a man of strong feelings, but these feelings were always under complete control. He understands our feelings and is able to forgive what is wrong and bring our emotions into obedience to God's will. (YTL)

Have I ever got anywhere near weeping for a needy neighbour or nation?

Jesus, I'm so glad you were a man of strong feelings. You understand how hard I find it to control my feelings. Help me.

April 13   **At the cross**

For you know that it was not with perishable things such as silver or gold that you were redeemed. . . but with the precious blood of Christ, a lamb without blemish or defect. He was chosen before the creation of the world.   1 Peter 1:18–20

'If you want to understand the Christian message,' said Martin Luther, 'you must start with the wounds of Christ.' Christ's death is central to the Christian message. It was planned by God before the foundation of the world. It was prophesied many times in the Old Testament. Christ talked of it constantly. Paul boasted of the cross — an extraordinary thing for a Jew to do, since crucifixion was offensive to the Jewish people. And at our communion service we celebrate the death of Jesus.

Because of his death on the cross, to take our punishment, God can treat me just-as-if-I'd never sinned — that's what justification means. And when I do sin and confess it, he can forgive me every time.

The cross is where we find peace of mind, healing of relationships, forgiveness for ourselves, and the strength to forgive others. It is God's power over all the forces of evil.

An old Christian said, 'All problems find their solution at Calvary.' I believe, from my own experience, that he was absolutely right. (CFP)

Is there any problem which I need to take to the cross? How can I do this?

Lord Jesus, by your Holy Spirit show me more and more clearly what your death on the cross can mean in my life.

April 14   A paradox to ponder

He became obedient to death — even death on a cross!

                                        Philippians 2:8

If, when we were God's enemies, we were reconciled to him through the death of his Son, how much more, having been reconciled, shall we be saved through his life!   Romans 5:10

The cross unquestionably is the badge of the Christian faith. That in itself is remarkable, since it was the cruellest form of execution known in the ancient world until it was eventually banned in the fifth century AD. What other society has as its symbol a horrifying instrument of torture and death — especially when the marks of that society are meant to be love and peace? Somebody once expressed the curious paradox about the cross in this way:

The cross is a picture of violence, yet the key to peace;

a picture of suffering, yet the key to healing;

a picture of death, yet the key to life;

a picture of utter weakness, yet the key to power;

a picture of capital punishment, yet the key to mercy and forgiveness;

a picture of vicious hatred, yet the key to love;

a picture of supreme shame, yet the Christian's supreme boast.

The Christian claims that the cross really is the key to everything. (IAT)

Lord, teach me what it means to glory in the cross of Christ.

Are there any doors in my life which need to be unlocked by this 'key'?

April 15   What's wrong with getting emotional about Jesus?

The disciples were overjoyed when they saw the Lord.
                                                              John 20:20

A dean of a college was conducting an Easter service. And as he came to the end of the service, he felt that the whole thing had been formal and dead, instead of bursting with life and joy because Jesus had burst from the grave. So after saying the usual liturgical blessing, he added, in a very unliturgical way, 'Jesus is alive! Alleluia!' All the professors and dons woke up and began looking very shocked. At the end of the service, as they filed out past the smiling dean, the Master of the college stopped long enough to say, 'Mr. Dean, I dislike all this emotion! Have you forgotten that this is an Anglican service?'

His attitude was very like that of the religious leaders on Palm Sunday. Horrified that the people were shouting praises to God, they said to Jesus, 'Stop your disciples! Stop all that noise!' But Jesus replied, 'If these people kept silent, the very stones would cry out!'

During a communion service at Canterbury Cathedral, the Holy Spirit moved in a remarkable way. Christian leaders from all over the world were present at this service and I was among their number. We were caught up in worship and praise. We sang and danced to the Lord, and some shared words of prophecy. It was a very moving experience, and our emotions were quite naturally involved in our worship and praise! (AR)

Lord, thank you for my feelings. I want them to be, with the rest of my personality, controlled by the Holy Spirit and used to worship and witness to Jesus.

Am I afraid of my emotions? If so why?

April 16   Life after death — now!

Christ died for our sins according to the Scriptures . . . he was buried . . . he was raised on the third day according to the Scriptures.   **1 Corinthians 15:3,4**
He died for all, that those who live should no longer live for themselves, but for him who died for them and was raised again.   **2 Corinthians 5:15**

'The resurrection of Jesus is either the supreme fact in history or else a gigantic hoax,' wrote Professor Norman Anderson in *The Evidence for the Resurrection*. Ponder all that follows from this supreme fact.

We know that there is life after death.

We know that God accepted Christ's sacrifice of himself as our sin-bearer.

We who belong to Christ no longer need fear death.

For us life is now filled with meaning and purpose.

Wonderful! Praise God!

But there could be no resurrection without crucifixion, either for Jesus or for us. Our self-life must be crucified if we are to know full, resurrection life. Throughout our lives God will allow many testings and trials to come our way. Do we defend ourselves, excuse ourselves, criticise others, put ourselves before others, nourish self-pity, resentment or jealousy? If so, 'self' needs further crucifixion in order that we may experience the full joy and freedom of Jesus' risen life in us.

Are we willing for the price of resurrection? (PL)

Lord, show me where I am being mild, mealy-mouthed or mousey through inferiority-feelings, rather than meek and humble like Jesus.

Start seeing life's irritants and difficulties as opportunities to shed more of your sinful, selfish human nature, through God's grace and help.

April 17   **The impact of the resurrection**

Why do you look for the living among the dead? He is not here; he has risen!   **Luke 24:5,6**

Once when I was playing rugby and had the ball, I was scared out of my wits to see a group of fierce muscled men bearing down on me. Then a voice to my left said, 'With you,' and with intense relief I passed the ball! The risen Christ comes to the sad, the depressed, the frightened, weary and confused and says, 'With you.'

Mary Magdalene was deeply sad because she thought she'd lost for ever the person whom she loved so deeply and who had transformed her life. She stood outside the grave weeping (John 20:10-18) but the Lord came to her, called her by name, and showed her that he was alive and would be with her always. She was filled with joy.

The two disciples on the road to Emmaus were very confused (Luke 24:13-23). The risen Christ came and explained the Scriptures to them and they saw everything clearly again (Luke 24:13-35).

The other disciples may well have felt frightened, weary or depressed. Their whole world seemed to have fallen apart. But then Jesus came and 'stood among them and said to them, "Peace be with you."' At first they were 'startled and frightened', but when they realised Jesus really was with them, they were filled with 'joy and amazement' (Luke 24: 36-43).

The risen Christ still comes to us, however we may be feeling, and says, 'I am with you always.' (YTL)

Jesus, you are with me here, now. Hallelujah!

Risen Lord, thankfully I hand over to you . . . (some person or situation).

**Even though I walk through the valley of the shadow of death,
I will fear no evil, for you are with me; your rod and staff, they
comfort me.**   **Psalm 23:4**

'It's not that I'm afraid to die,' said Woody Allen. 'It's just that I
don't want to be there when it happens!'

It's only through facing death, that we begin to find life. I
was told by some consultants who treated cancer patients that
some people only start living when they know they have
cancer. Often it's only when people have to come to terms with
death, that they see the value of life, or at least ask serious
questions about it.

The silence surrounding death has been broken by the resurrection of Jesus, called the 'best attested fact in history'.
Because Jesus rose from the dead, we know two things which
make all the difference between life and death.

We know that there is a glorious life *after* death. Someone
said, 'One day you will see in the papers that I am dead. When
you see it, don't believe it. I'll be more alive than ever.' When
any Christian dies physically, we can be sure that he is, from
the moment of death onwards, more alive and whole than ever
before.

We know too that there's a great life *before* death. Those
who will die well, can live well. Could you summarise in one
sentence what it is that makes life great for the Christian?

Sadhu Sundar Singh was once asked by a professor of
comparative religions, 'What have you found in Christianity
that you did not find in your old religion?' The Indian Christian
replied, 'I found the dear Lord Jesus.'

'Oh, quite, but what principle or doctrine or ethic or understanding did you find?' pursued the professor.

'I found the dear Lord Jesus,' answered Sadhu Sundar Singh.
(CFP)

*Meditate on your own death in the light of God's promises and
the fact of Jesus' resurrection.*

Father, I am not afraid to walk into your loving presence. Meanwhile, please keep me strong and healthy until my work for you in this life is done.

April 19   **Can I be sure that Jesus is with me?**

Surely I will be with you always.   Matthew 28:20
Never will I leave you; never will I forsake you.   Hebrews 13:5

We can be sure that Jesus is with us, if we've invited him into our lives, because he promises to accept such an invitation, and to stay with those who believe in him, love him and obey him. Also if Jesus is with me, there should be a new kind of joy, and a new attitude to worldly ambitions and pleasures: I no longer have the same love for them because of a new love for my heavenly Father and for Jesus Christ. There should be, too, a new peace in my heart and conscience, a new reality in prayer, a new understanding of the Bible, a new power over temptation. These things won't flower fully overnight and there may be times when temporarily this new joy, peace and love seem to be lost. But just as natural fruit grows and develops slowly but surely, so spiritual fruit in a person's life blossoms slowly but surely, if Jesus is really present. There will be results from acting on Jesus' promise. His promises will be proved in our experience.

John Newton said, 'I'm not what I ought to be, I'm not what I would like to be, I'm not what I hope to be, but I'm not what I was, and by the grace of God I am what I am.' Every Christian ought to be able to echo these words.

Are you sure, quite sure, that Jesus is with you? When I ask people that question, looking them straight in the eye, quite often the answer is, 'Well, I *think* so, I *hope* so!' But Jesus promises to come into our lives and never, never leave us or forsake us. So if we say, 'I *think* he's with me,' or, 'I *hope* he's with me,' we're insulting his faithfulness and his word, in a way. We can be wonderfully sure that Jesus is with us. (YTL)

Jesus, I go into this day, trusting and believing that you are with me all the time.

Be aware of Jesus' presence throughout the day and in the evening think about what difference this has made.

April 20 **The way of the cross**

Those who belong to Christ Jesus have crucified the sinful nature with its passions and desires. **Galatians 5:24**

What does the way of the cross mean for us today when the majority of Christians will probably not be faced with crucifixion or any other form of martyrdom? A young man once asked an older Christian, 'What does it mean to be crucified with Christ?' The older man thought for a moment and then replied: 'To be crucified with Christ means three things. First, the man who is crucified is facing in only one direction; he is *not looking back*. Second, the man who is crucified has said good-bye to the world: he is *not going back*. Third, the man who is crucified has no further plans of his own. He is totally *in God's hands*. Whatever the situation, he says, "Yes, Lord!"'

That is a fair description of what it means to go the way of the cross. (D)

Lord, you understand how I shrink from following the way of the cross. You are the only one who can lead me along this path and help me to face anything I may meet. I trust you to do this.

Has following Jesus cost me anything at all so far?

April 21 **The pressure of love**

Christ's love compels us. **2 Corinthians 5:14**

'Christ's love compels us, wrote Paul. The same word is used when the multitudes are described as surrounding and 'pressing against' Jesus (Luke 8:45). Jesus spoke the same word when warning Jerusalem that her enemies would '*hem*' her in 'on every side' (Luke 19:43), and, most strikingly, when he said, 'I have a baptism to undergo, and how *distressed* I am until it is completed' (Luke 12:50). Here Jesus felt a powerful, motivating force urging him towards the cross. He *had* to go that way; he had to finish the work. Paul knew something of this compulsion, too. The love of Christ pressed gently but firmly upon him; he felt surrounded and hemmed in by this love, as it constrained him in one clear direction. No matter what apathy or opposition he faced, no matter how tiring or painful the work might be, 'the love of Christ leaves us no choice' (*New English Bible* translation).

How was Paul so gripped by the love of Christ? As if drawn by a magnet, he comes back to the cross: 'We are convinced that one died for all, and therefore all died. And he died for all, that those who live should no longer live for themselves but for him who died for them and was raised again' (2 Corinthians 5:14,15). For Paul the cross was infinitely more than a theological statement about the atonement: Christ had died for him; Christ had suffered in his place. Paul knew, then, that he was no longer his own; he could not live any more for himself. He was bought with a price and so he must live this glorious new life for the sake of the Son of God, who had loved him and given himself for him. (IBIE)

Is my life mainly pressurised by love or by other things?

Lord, the example of Jesus and Paul put me to shame. May they also inspire me to want more of the love which compels us to action.

April 22   One-to-one evangelism

A large crowd came to him [Jesus] and he began to teach them. As he walked along, he saw Levi son of Alphaeus sitting at the

tax collector's booth. 'Follow me,' Jesus told him, and Levi got up and followed him. Mark 2:13,14

Many people owe their conversion, or at least their final decision to commit their lives to Jesus, to an individual speaking personally to them. Jesus both preached to crowds and singled out individuals—calling them to himself. Someone has said that preaching to a crowd is rather like throwing a bucket of water over rows of narrow-necked vessels. Some water might get into some of the vessels. Personal evangelism is like filling to the brim one vessel after another.

In the gospels we have nineteen records of Jesus dealing with individuals. Clearly he felt time spent in this way was time well spent.

What are the qualifications for personal evangelism?

First, the person engaged in this work must know Christ personally. It's no good having the patter like a door-to-door salesman; what comes across to people is the reality of Jesus in our lives and even in our very presence. An extrovert personality is *not* a necessity; indeed some of the shyest people make the best personal evangelists. What *is* a necessity — is that Christ is real to us day by day.

Secondly, we need to be guided by the Holy Spirit, and to obey him every time he does guide us. Philip was obviously used to unquestioning obedience, therefore the Holy Spirit could trust him to respond to the seemingly extraordinary guidance that he should leave a successful mission and go to a desert road. When we are obedient in small matters, God is able to trust us in bigger, more unusual situations. (YTL)

For meditation: We do not bear witness to Christ because we have no witness to bear.

Lord, I am ready to obey as soon as your Spirit guides me in this matter . . .

When a Samaritan woman came to draw water, Jesus said to her, 'Will you give me a drink?'   John 4:7

Much of the recorded ministry of Jesus is personal conversation with individuals, and you can pray that God will help you to develop this ministry as you mature spiritually. Read some of the incidents in the Gospels and Acts, and see what you can learn. For example, see how Jesus dealt with the Samaritan woman (John 4).

First, he *established contact*. It wasn't easy: he was a Jew, she was a Samaritan; he was a man, she was a woman. On both scores a conversation in public was definitely not done! Love will always find a way somehow, however, and Jesus asked her gently for a favour: 'Give me a drink.'

Next he *aroused her curiosity* by telling her that he could give her living water which could quench her thirst. We can do the same by talking of our own experience, by lending a book, or simply by saying, 'Come and see.'

Jesus then *touched a sore spot* by asking her to call her husband. As she had lived with six men this was a decidedly delicate issue. But Jesus knew she must sort out her wrong relationships with men before she could find a right relationship with God.

Next he *avoided a red herring*. Embarrassed by his reference to her casual sex-life, she raised a theological diversion: Where should people worship — in Samaria or in Jerusalem? Jesus dealt briefly with her question, but brought her back to a spiritual issue: 'True worshippers will worship the Father in spirit and truth.'

Finally, he *brought her to a decision*. Although she tried familiar delaying tactics, Jesus made her face up to her response to him there and then. (LANL)

How can I arouse curiosity about Jesus in people I meet?

Jesus, teach me how to talk to others.

We have different gifts, according to the grace given us. If a man's gift is prophesying, let him use it in proportion to his faith. If it is serving, let him serve; if it is teaching, let him teach; if it is encouraging, let him encourage; if it is contributing to the needs of others, let him give generously; if it is leadership, let him govern diligently; if it is showing mercy, let him do it cheerfully. **Romans 12:6-8**

Every church and every church member should be enjoying spiritual gifts. There is no sharp distinction between natural and spiritual gifts in 1 Corinthians chapter 12. They all come from and can be used for God and for good through the power of the Holy Spirit. Of course spiritual gifts can be misused. But the answer to misuse is not disuse but right use.

Ponder these truths about spiritual gifts.

They are different ways of serving Christ and his body, the Church. They are different ways in which God works in and through his church: 'living movements of Christ's body' as someone has said. God has a gift for every member of his church. He will not give it to you, or show you what it is, unless you ask him to and want the gift. If you do not use your gift, you are making God sad and robbing others of the blessing he wants to give them through you. Gifts are always and only for using to glorify Christ and build up his church.

If you are willing to use the gift God has given you, however humble it is, you may find that God has other gifts and other ministries in store for you. (CFP)

Lord, show me the natural gift you have given me which you want me to use for you, or make me desire and seek you for the spiritual gift which you are wanting me to have for your glory and the good of others.

There is nothing I have which is not a gift from God. Do I thank him enough for all that he has given?

Now to each one the manifestation of the Spirit is given for the common good.
                                                    1 Corinthians 12:7

It is *to each* that the Spirit is manifest. Every single person in Christ has a vital part to play in the body of Christ. The rest of 1 Corinthians chapter 12 spells this out. Every person has a God-given role within the fellowship where God has put him. We need to discover what this role is, probably with the help of mature Christians. As time goes on, our role may change, but there will always be one for us. Trouble comes only when we are ambitious for a role to which God has not assigned us.

'*The manifestation of the Spirit*' refers to the fact that the Spirit makes clear and visible the invisible God. I can't hear God easily, but his voice becomes clearer to me when his word is expounded. I can't see God very easily, but when I see Christians loving each other, then I see God more clearly. So through the words, life and work of the body of Christ, God can be seen and heard more clearly.

'*For the common good*' means for the bringing together, the healing, the restoring, the renewing and strengthening of the body of Christ.

Two things, above all, can endanger the common good in the matter of gifts: pride and jealousy. We can grow proud of our gift and start using it in our own strength and for our own purposes, in which case God will quickly remove it or its usefulness from the fellowship. Or we can be jealous of someone else's gift, and cover it up by fault-finding and criticism. Both attitudes are wrong and foolish, since all gifts are from God, and are simply entrusted to people for the good of others. (YTL)

Lord, I pray for. . . who have spectacular spiritual gifts, that you will keep them from pride and I pray for. . . who have more 'ordinary' gifts that you will keep them from jealousy.

Is it very evident that we are using our gifts for the common good?

Anyone who speaks in a tongue does not speak to men but to God. Indeed, no-one understands him; he utters mysteries with his spirit.   **1 Corinthians 14:2**

Tongues are neither gibberish nor ecstatic utterances. As with all the gifts of the Holy Spirit, in contrast to the gifts of an evil spirit, the recipient is in complete control of what he is doing and saying. Someone speaking in tongues can stop and start, speak loudly or silently at will. He is never taken over, or in a frenzy, as some mediums are.

Tongues have a private and public use. In *private* tongues are a God-given way of communicating with him — a language of love, praise and worship. Sometimes when we are trying to worship God, the ordinary words we use seem totally inadequate — a stumbling block rather than an aid — and we long to adore God with greater freedom. Tongues give many people this greater freedom — a new dimension in their communication with God.

Similarly, in *intercession*, we might sometimes want to pray for someone but not know what or how to pray. Tongues can help in this situation very much. We can intercede with the Spirit, by praying in tongues.

Tongues are also a means of *personal edification*. Richard Wurmbrand writes that he couldn't have endured the horrors of prison life without the release and refreshment he received through praying in tongues. When tense and tired, I too have found relief and been refreshed through this gift. It would seem that Paul had a similar experience (1 Corinthians 14:18).

Tongues are a useful *spiritual weapon* in difficult situations, when you may become very aware of spiritual warfare. (YTL)

Father, give me any gift you want to, in order that I may worship you and intercede for others better.

What should I do when I run out of words or wisdom?

Now, brothers, if I come to you and speak in tongues, what good will I be to you unless I bring you some revelation or knowledge or prophecy or word of instruction... For this reason the man who speaks in a tongue should pray that he may interpret what he says.   1 Corinthians 14:6,13

In *public* use, tongues *must be interpreted* (verse 27). Someone may ask, 'Why speak in tongues at all if they have to be interpreted anyway? Why doesn't God speak straight into English?' I believe that we find it harder to listen to God than to talk to him, and the public use of tongues is God's way of saying, 'You've done enough talking. Stop and listen to me.'

Some Bible teachers say that since tongues consist of praise and prayer, the interpretation should be praise and prayer and not a word from the Lord. But communication that's deep must be two-way, so tongues are sometimes man to God and sometimes God to man. If we were better able to hear God's voice, there would be little need for tongues or interpretations in public.

Secondly, tongues *can be a sign for unbelievers* (verse 22). People have been brought to Christ through hearing tongues in meetings.

There are various objections to tongues. Some say that tongues were given to help the disciples preach the gospel in other languages. There is no evidence of this in the New Testament. On the day of Pentecost, Peter preached in Aramaic and everyone understood it. Some say Paul discouraged the use of tongues, but he didn't: he discouraged their misuse.

Others say tongues are too emotional, but sometimes they're not emotional at all; in any case, how can emotion be totally absent when we are worshipping and adoring the Lord with all our hearts?

True, tongues are found in other religions, but they are the devil's counterfeits of the real thing.

We do well not to speak slightingly of any gift of God,

including the gift of tongues, because all God's gifts are good and beautiful. (YTL)

Father, help me not to be scornful or afraid of any of your gifts.

Are there any signs for unbelievers in any of our church services?

April 28   **Spiritual fruit**

The fruit of the Spirit is love, joy, peace, patience, kindness, goodness, faithfulness, gentleness and self-control.
                                                          Galatians 5:22,23

In one sense, every good thing in our lives, all our feelings of joy or promptings to be kind, come from the Holy Spirit. Without the Holy Spirit's activity in the world, there wouldn't be any positive good in any of us. But being influenced by the Spirit in a general way is not the same as being filled by and changed by the Spirit.

When the Holy Spirit is actively living in us, then we will be kind, even when it *doesn't* come naturally, and joyful, even when the going is tough. When we are able to offer God praise and worship in situations which wouldn't naturally produce these reactions, then we can be assured that the Spirit is filling us and producing his supernatural fruit in our lives.

As Christians, we can be moody — too easily controlled by our natural feelings. But when the Holy Spirit helps us to act spiritually, rather than react physically or emotionally, then others will be able to see the reality of Jesus through us. (K)

Lord, please so control my life that the fruit of your Spirit may be more and more clearly seen.

Take time today to stop and think, as you go about your work: 'What really controls my life most of the time?'

**The Lord appeared to Abraham near the great trees of Mamre
while he was still sitting at the entrance to his tent in the heat of
the day.**   **Genesis 18:1**

God appeared and spoke to Abraham when he was sitting
quietly — possibly thinking, meditating and resting. Perhaps
its because we don't sit still for long enough, if at all, that we
don't hear God's voice. This is how Jim Elliot, later martyred
for Christ, commented on the words, 'In quietness . . . is your
strength' (Isaiah 30:15): 'I think the devil has made it his
business to monopolise on three elements: noise, hurry and
crowds. If he can keep us hearing radios, gossip, conversations
and even sermons, he is happy, but he will not allow
quietness.'

Many people appear to be bound by these things. It seems as
though they feel insecure without them. If they were to be
quiet, they might think about the world or their own situation
and that might prove very depressing. But nothing is solved by
surrounding oneself with noise and people or by rushing busily
about. In fact these things lead to greater tension and
insecurity in the long run.

Remember Mary and Martha. One sat quietly at Jesus' feet
listening to his voice, hearing his words; the other rushed
about — anxious, troubled and distracted by many things. She
had a crowd inside her — a crowd of thoughts. For practical
people like Martha, the thought of being quiet and still and
meditative seems very hard indeed. But unless we take time to
be quiet and still before God, we will not hear his voice. (YTL)

Obey and meditate on Psalm 46:10.

Lord, I know I need to be alone with you daily. Help me in this.

April 30   Broken before God

The king was shaken. He went up to the room over the

gateway and wept. As he went, he said: 'O my son Absalom! My son, my son Absalom! If only I had died instead of you — O Absalom, my son, my son!' 2 Samuel 18:33

At this point in David's life, God is humbling him (2 Samuel 12-18). First, David's sin is exposed by Nathan and the king is convicted and begins to see himself as he really is. Then, after fasting and praying for six days and nights, David is told of the death of his baby son. After that, David's family seems to disintegrate. His son Amnon lusts after his half-sister Tamar, rapes her, and then, as so often happens, hates her. It was a terrible thing for Amnon to do, but what an example his father had set for him! Next Amnon is murdered by Tamar's brother Absalom, another of David's sons, whom David mishandles so that he emerges as a spoilt, vain young man. The moment he sees an opportunity to rebel, Absalom does so, taking half the kingdom with him. David has to flee from his own son and hide in the open country and on the hills. Next, his great friend and adviser, Ahithophel, deserts him and goes to Absalom. David suffers anguish over this (Psalm 41:9). Later, when a man called Shimei curses and stones David, the once fiery king says, 'Leave him alone; let him curse, for the Lord has told him to.'

The final breaking point comes with the news of Absalom's death. David had been a poor father, but he still loved his son: 'Be gentle with the young man Absalom for my sake,' he had told his commanders. But Absalom is killed and David is broken before God.

None of us can be really useful to God until we are broken of self and full to overflowing with Jesus. Perhaps for years God has been working to this end in your life, but now, for the first time, you realise what he has been doing and so you want to stop resisting his methods and plans! (YTL)

Father, I accept what you are doing in my life as part of your loving plan to let self decrease and Christ increase.

As I look back in faith and brokenness, can I see God's hand?

133

MAY
Committed Discipleship

May 1   **Am I a true disciple?**

Mary . . . sat at the Lord's feet listening to what he said.
                                                    Luke 10:39

Here are some questions to test our discipleship!

Am I willing to *serve*? This was a repeated lesson Jesus had to teach his status-seeking disciples, especially when he humbled them dramatically by washing their feet.

Am I willing to *listen*? When Simon Peter was full of bright ideas on the Mount of Transfiguration, God told him to 'listen' to his Son (Luke 9:36). When Martha was impatiently bustling around preparing a meal whilst Jesus was talking, she was gently rebuked for not being like Mary who was sitting quietly listening to the Master (Luke 10:41f).

Am I willing to *learn*? When Jesus spoke about his coming sufferings and death, Peter blurted out, 'God forbid, Lord; this shall never happen to you.' The stinging reply was something Peter never forgot (Matthew 16:22f).

Am I willing to *be corrected*? How well do I receive honest criticism, when others speak the truth in love (Matthew 18:15)?

How well do I *submit to those who are over me* (1 Thessalonians 5:12f; Hebrews 13:17)? Am I willing to do this even when I do not fully understand the reasons why, or even when I do not naturally enjoy what I am being asked to do?

Can I *share my life with others*, in open and honest fellowship (1 John 1)?

Am I *learning humility*? Can I rejoice with those who rejoice, and be genuinely glad when others are blessed in some way or other (Philippians 2:3f)? (D)

Is our church a place where people are encouraged to grow in discipleship?

Lord, show me where I need to change and so become a more committed disciple.

Bible study: In what ways was Jesus and in what ways should his disciples be different from others, in character, relationships, words, deeds, etc?

Starters: Matthew 5-7; Mark 8:34-38; John 13: 1-17,34; Philippians 2:1-18; 3:1-21, and see under 'committed discipleship' in index.

May 2   How committed am I?

If anyone would come after me, he must deny himself and take up his cross and follow me.   **Mark 8:34**

I once heard Brother Andrew speak of a time when he was sitting with another Christian in a bus in Vietnam. They saw a man carrying a basket and walking in front of the bus. It was during a time of intensive fighting and constant Vietcong guerrilla attacks.

'Watch out!' said the Christian. 'In the basket there might well be a bomb.'

'Why are you so afraid?' asked Brother Andrew.

'That man may be a Vietcong who will throw himself and the basket at the bus,' came the reply. 'He doesn't mind if he dies. I do!'

Brother Andrew commented on this incident: 'That sums up the ineffectiveness of so much of the church today!' How many Christians are willing to lay down their lives for Jesus Christ? Certainly many have done so. In this century alone, there have probably been more Christian martyrs than in the entire previous history of the Christian Church. However, in places where persecution is not so violent, the spirit of self-sacrifice is not always so obvious. How many are willing to lay down their worldly ambitions, their money and possessions, their privacy and privileges, their selfish desires, their comforts and securities? With the greatest urgency we need to recapture the spirit of Paul who wrote, 'I consider everything a loss compared to the surpassing greatness of knowing Christ Jesus my Lord' (Philippians 3:8); or of David Livingstone who said, 'I place no value on anything, except in its relation to the kingdom of God.' Certainly the task of evangelism is urgent in the gathering gloom and despair of today's world. (IBIE)

Lord, fill me with spiritual enthusiasm.

Has my faith involved me in hard work or any form of suffering? If not, why not?

May 3   **Lord of all**

Freely you have received, freely give.   **Matthew 10:8**
You are not your own.   **1 Corinthians 6:19**

So often we treat Christ as our servant and not as our Lord. I want him to look after *my* life, help me in *my* job, protect *my* possessions, supply *my* money, meet *my* needs, attend to *my* comforts —just like a servant! But if we are disciples of the Lord Jesus, *all these things are his.*

I found a book by Juan Carlos Ortiz very challenging. It's title is, *A Call to Discipleship* and here's a brief extract from it.

'The Lord showed us that he didn't want our houses empty — he wanted houses with us inside. He wanted houses with carpets, heating, air conditioning, and somebody who paid the light bills, telephone bills, put food on the tables and made the beds — for God. And he wanted our cars, with drivers. It meant that everything became his, even ourselves. So now, all our houses are open. When visitors come to our congregation we don't say, "Which one of you can take this brother to your house?" because all houses are given to the Lord. We tell them, "Brother, come, you're going to take these people to your house," because the house is already given to the Lord. We just thank the Lord that he lets us live in his house. We have learned to have a different perspective.' (PL)

Lord, give me this different perspective.

How possessive am I about my possessions? Is there anything God is prompting me to give to anyone now?

May 4   Counter-culture

You have heard that it was said, 'Eye for eye, and tooth for tooth.' But I tell you, Do not resist an evil person. If someone strikes you on the right cheek, turn to him the other also.
Matthew 5:38,39

In Jesus' kingdom, the kingdom of God, worldly values, aims, ambitions and standards are completely reversed. When the mother of James and John came and asked that her sons should have the top places in Jesus' kingdom, he told her and his disciples that in his kingdom the greatest would be the servant of all; and at the last supper he demonstrated this principle by taking the job of the lowest slave and washing the disciples' feet.

The sermon on the mount is full of Christian counter-culture. Jesus taught that the kingdom of God would be marked by poverty, suffering, hardship, generosity and a spirit of service. And he lived out these principles. Jesus loved people and would mix with anyone, but his life was utterly different from the lives of the people around him.

So often our lives do not differ very much from others' in

terms of money, possessions, rights, privileges, ambitions, attitudes, friends and family. And many of us do not show anything like the dedication of many members of the Communist Party for example. One young communist wrote, 'There is one thing about which I'm dead in earnest — the communist cause. It's my life, my business, my religion, my hobby, my sweetheart, my wife, my mistress, my bread and my meat.'

Are we willing to live as Jesus lived and be utterly different in what we do, say and think? (YTL)

How different am I from my non-Christian neighbours?

Father, I have not thought through the Christian difference in this area of my life. . .

May 5   **Dying to live**

I tell you the truth, unless an ear of wheat falls to the ground and dies, it remains only a single seed. But if it dies it produces many seeds.   **John 12:24**

Before there can be life, there must be death. We can see this principle at work in nature and in life — Jesus' and our own.

It is the *pattern of nature*. The world is full of visual aids on this sermon! Put a seed into a jewel case, keep it safe, and nothing will happen. Put a seed into the ground, let it rot, perish and die, and it springs up and shoots out leaves or flowers.

We see the same principle in the *passion of Christ*. He came as a suffering Saviour, his crown was of thorns, his throne was a cross and his coronation a crucifixion. The seed of his life, given over to death, bore fruit; it gave and continues to give life to millions of people. He died that our lives might be full of meaning, purpose, power and joy, now and in eternity with God.

This principle is also the *path to life* for us. The rich fool was a fool because he lived for himself. His vocabulary consisted almost entirely of four words: me, I, my, mine. He put the seed of his life into the coffin of his own selfishness and there it remained safe from God's interference, or so he thought; but the only place entirely safe from God is hell, as the rich man discovered. The one thing he had held on to in life was the very thing he had to lose one day. We have to take the seed of our life, bury it and let it die by giving it entirely to Jesus Christ to do with it as he chooses. Then and only then will it spring up into fullness of life and bring blessing to others. (YTL)

Have I really grasped this life-from-death principle?

Lord, who died that we might know life with God, help me to die daily to self and yield myself completely to you.

May 6   **The 'footwashing' jobs**

You also should wash one another's feet.   **John 13:14**

Jesus shook his status-seeking disciples by telling them that he himself had come not to be served but to serve and to give his life for others. Then, at his last meal with them, in order to teach them a lesson they would never forget, he washed their feet — a task normally done by the most menial household slave.

By nature we are selfish, so when someone performs an act of loving service like this, it speaks volumes for Christ, even though the person doing it may not say a single word.

We can perform 'footwashing' jobs in our homes, by washing up, cleaning the house, putting the children to bed, getting the tea ready, saying sorry, being ready to forgive. . . In a world characterised by selfishness, sensitivity to the needs of others, and love shown in service for others, can transform the atmosphere in our homes.

Being a 'footwasher' at work involves being punctual, honest, reliable, positive in our comments about others and refusing to fiddle the accounts or take any part in petty pilfering.

In church, we might never be teachers or evangelists, but we might have other gifts to offer — helping, giving hospitality, administering, typing, printing, plumbing, or contributing to the worship through music, art, drama or dance.

There are also many ways in which Christians can serve society and the world, and we need to explore these and make our vital contribution here. (C/LANL)

Is there a difference between being a 'footwasher' and being a 'doormat'?

Lord, make me willing to serve in the ways you want me to.

May 7   No bed of roses

Everyone who wants to live a godly life in Christ Jesus will be persecuted, while evil men and impostors will go from bad to worse, deceiving and being deceived.   2 Timothy 3:12

If anyone thinks that by becoming a Christian he is opting for a problem-free life, he's in for a rude shock. There are plenty of problems in following Jesus but at least they are problems of life.

First, there's the problem of *sin*. We do not stop being tempted to sin when we become Christians and sometimes it's very hard to say 'no' to wrong. But the Christian cannot hold on to what is sinful with one hand and on to Jesus with the other. It doesn't work. He has to keep saying 'no' to all sin.

Secondly, there's the problem of *persecution*. Sooner or later, a Christian will meet this in some form. There must be no secrecy about a person being a Christian. He has to stand up and be counted, and this will bring some suffering.

Thirdly, there's the problem of *self*. We do not lose our selfishness instantly, so it's not always easy to remain in the passenger seat, especially after years of being the driver! For the Christian, Jesus must always be in charge.

It costs a great deal to follow Jesus, but in the long run it costs infinitely more not to do so. The missionary martyr Jim Elliot wrote: 'He is no fool who gives what he cannot keep to gain what he cannot lose.' (K)

Do I make sure that someone understands the cost of following Jesus before he commits himself to this? From my own experience would I be able to assure such a person that the benefits are far greater than the cost?

Lord, forgive me for the times I've been ashamed of belonging to you and have kept silent instead of speaking out.

May 8   Don't miss God's message!

Abraham looked up and saw three men standing nearby.

Genesis 18:2

On this occasion God came to Abraham almost in disguise — just as one of three men. If Abraham hadn't been alert, he might have missed him altogether.

We need to be alert to all the possible ways in which the Lord might appear to us. It's so easy to grow spiritually blind or deaf — to read our Bibles as though they were 'just a book', to listen to a sermon and dismiss the speaker as 'just another preacher', to talk to another Christian and think, 'That's just Tom, or Jane,' or to read a Christian book as though it were 'just another story'. But if we are alert, looking and listening for the Lord, we will hear his voice through that Bible passage or sermon or fellow-Christian or book. As we read or talk or listen, there will be an inner voice saying, 'That's my message for you.'

Sometimes we come to a situation or person or book in a sleepy or critical mood, with no sense of expectancy, and we hear and see nothing from the Lord. But I am quite certain that if we come alert and expecting God to speak to us, he will do just that. He can even speak to us, as he has done to me, through a non-Christian. So be prepared. (YTL)

How much am I expecting from God each day?

Lord, keep me alert to pick up everything you say to me each day from whatever source.

May 9   How can I know what to do?

Trust in the Lord with all your heart and lean not on your own understanding; in all your ways acknowledge him, and he will make your paths straight.   Proverbs 3:5,6

The most important means of guidance is *humble prayer*. We come to God, acknowledging that we do lack wisdom and that his ways are not ours (Isaiah 55:8). In that attitude, as well as talking to God, we will be still and listen to him.

A second and very important means of guidance is *the use of our renewed minds* (Romans 12:2; Ephesians 4:23). There is a great danger in being super-spiritual and relying on dramatic experiences. There are dramatic experiences in very, very exceptional circumstances, but even when these occur, God wants us to use our minds — not our natural minds only but our constantly renewed Spirit-controlled minds.

One of the ways in which our minds can be renewed is through steeping them in God's word (Colossians 3:16). On some issues we don't need any form of guidance other than God's word, because God's will is so plain there. Paul Little once said, 'I lent a man five pounds and he's still praying about whether he ought to pay me back!' How ridiculous, when God's word is very clear about what a person should do in that situation!

In using God's word to guide us, we need to consider very carefully the context in which the words were written before applying them to ourselves in the present.

Discussion with other — preferably more mature — Christians is another useful means of guidance (see Acts 15). So are circumstances by which God can and often does open or close 'doors' to us (Acts 14:27). (CFP)

Lord, I need your wisdom in this matter . . . and I'm going to use all the means of guidance open to me to discover what I should do.

Am I really open to whatever God may say to me, or is there fear or doubt which needs to be cleared away first?

May 10   **What's the point of prayer?**

When you pray, go into your room, close the door and pray to your Father who is unseen.   **Matthew 6:6**

Some people can't see the point of prayer. They bring up three main objections to it.

The first objection is that prayer doesn't accomplish anything. The psalmist seems to have felt much the same when he cried out to God, 'How long, O Lord' (Psalm 13:1)? In another psalm the writer is even more outspoken: 'Awake, O Lord! . . . Rouse yourself' (Psalm 44:23)!

Certainly some forms of prayer don't accomplish anything — mechanical prayer, for instance, and prayer when one's heart is not right with God or with others (Matthew 6:7,14). But even assuming all is well in those ways, does prayer accomplish anything?

The answer is — it doesn't *always* change the outside world (though it often will do so), but it does always change one's inner world, transforming our reactions to events and people — and this is what really makes all the difference.

A second objection is that God knows our needs so why ask him for them (Matthew 6:8,32)? But if God automatically gave us everything, we would be like spoilt children. Besides, God's gifts are far too precious to give to any but those who really want them and will appreciate and use them well. Also, our lives are meant to be lived in total dependence upon God, so prayer is essential.

The third objection to prayer is that we cannot change God's will. But prayer isn't forcing God to do something; it's saying, 'I want your will to be done, Lord.' God graciously chooses to wait, often, for our active co-operation before he acts. (YTL)

May your will be done through me today, Lord.

Do I think of prayer as the highest possible privilege?

May 11   **Even loved ones can lead us astray!**

Abram agreed to what Sarai said.   Genesis 16:2

God had promised Abram and Sarai a son, but the years went by, they grew older and older, and nothing happened. So Sarai grew desperate, stopped trusting God and took a hand in affairs. She asked Abram to copy a pagan custom and have intercourse with a servant. Her longing for a child she could call her own overcame everything else. And Abram, knowing how depressed she was about her childlessness, agreed to do as she asked. He acted out of sympathy and affection, kindness and human love — but on this occasion his heart caused him to act against his faith and inner conviction.

Jesus knew that our loved ones might lead us astray. He said, 'A man's enemies will be the members of his own household,' and, 'Anyone who loves his father or mother. . . his son or daughter more than me is not worthy of me' (Matthew 10:36,37). He had to speak in gentle rebuke to his own mother at the wedding in Cana and in stern rebuke to Peter later on (John 2:4; Matthew 16:23).

If we are really loving Jesus more than even our loved ones, there will be times when we will be unpopular or misunderstood or criticised. But the repercussions are far worse in the long run if we choose to please them rather than the Lord.

144

Abram brought tremendous sorrow on himself, his wife, Hagar, Ishmael and on God, when he 'agreed to what Sarai said' instead of staying faithful and loyal to God. (YTL)

Lord, thank you for friends and family, but help me not to let any of them lead me into sin or persuade me to act against faith.

Would a visitor to our church services and meetings see clearly that we loved Jesus more than anything or anyone else or not?

May 12   **Handpicked by Jesus**

You did not choose me, but I chose you to go and bear fruit — fruit that will last.   **John 15:16**

In rabbinical circles, a disciple would choose his own master and voluntarily join his school. But with Jesus, the initiative lay entirely with him. Simon and Andrew, James and John, Levi, Philip and others — all were personally called by Jesus to follow him. Even when the rich young ruler ran up to Jesus and asked a leading question of this 'good teacher', Jesus replied by spelling out the costly and total demands of discipleship, and then added, 'Come, follow me.'

There may have been some who, attracted by the integrity of his person, the quality of his teaching, and the power of his miracles, wanted to attach themselves to Jesus and to his disciples, but always it was Jesus who laid down for them the strong conditions that he required. Sometimes this proved too much for them: 'This is more than we can stomach!' they once said. 'Why listen to such words?' And they left him, leaving only the twelve whom he had chosen and called to himself after a whole night spent in prayer. These were the ones in particular that God had given him.

Yet although there is a uniqueness about the twelve apostles, this fact of God's initiative and Christ's calling lies behind all those who are his disciples... When we see ourselves as disciples who have been personally chosen by Jesus, this should alter our whole attitude towards him and motivate us for the work he has given us. (D)

Lord Jesus, when I shrink from the cost of following you, remind me of how much you suffered for me.

Do I really believe I have been personally chosen by Jesus?

May 13   **What gospel?**

Jesus went through all the towns and villages, teaching in their synagogues, preaching the good news of the kingdom and healing every kind of disease and sickness.   **Matthew 9:35**

What gospel did Jesus preach and demonstrate?

It was the gospel *of the kingdom*; in other words, it was the good news that Christ reigns. Over the powers of evil, the weather, and every problem we face in this chaotic world — Christ reigns.

It was the gospel *of God* (Romans 15:16); in other words, it was the gospel which brought good news about God. Apart from the gospel, we would have no idea that God is a God of love. Other religions show him as a terrifying being who must be placated. The good news is that he loves us and wants us to be his children. It's also the gospel of God in the sense that it's good news from God. The word comes from the Anglo-Saxon *godspel* which means 'God's news'.

It was the gospel *of* or *about Jesus Christ* (Mark 1:1). There would be no good news without the life, death and resurrection of God's Son.

It was *our* or *my* gospel (Romans 2:16); in other words, it's a gospel that becomes good news to a person when he personally believes and receives it.

It was the gospel *for all men* (Mark 13:10). This, raises the problem of those who have never heard the gospel — a matter we have to leave to God, bearing in mind our responsibilities. When a student questioned Charles Spurgeon about whether those who had not heard the gospel would be saved, he replied that the question, as far as he was concerned, was whether we, who have the gospel but fail to pass it on to those who don't have it, will be saved! (YTL)

Do we preach and demonstrate the same gospel as Jesus did?

Lord, help us to see that the gospel is ours for the sake of others.

A new commandment I give you: love one another. As I have loved you, so you must love one another. All men will know that you are my disciples if you love one another.
                                                    John 13:34,35

Other religions and ideologies may imitate Christian beliefs and behaviour, but the one factor that is distinctive and unique about Christianity is *love*, the love of God made real in our hearts and relationships by the Holy Spirit. In fact this love is so different from the kinds that may be found elsewhere in the world, that the New Testament writers had to invent a new Greek word for it — one which cannot be found in any other writings of that period.

The Greeks knew all about sexual love, about natural family affection, about the special bond between husband and wife, but the word which comes 250 times in the New Testament isn't the word for any of those kinds of love: it's *agape* love, which speaks of the love of God which is supremely concerned for the highest good of the other; personal love which gives and gives and gives; a love that's willing to lay down its life for the benefit of others; a love, above all, shown by Jesus himself, especially when he died for us that we might be forgiven.

Such love can also be seen among Christians when the Holy Spirit is working in our midst. I have often talked to those from other faiths or to communists or atheists who have become Christians, and I constantly find that the one thing above all others which convinced them of the truth about Jesus and of the reality of God was the quality of love they found among Christians. Sadly the opposite is also true. Many today remain unconvinced about spiritual realities simply because they do not see this love which should always be the outstanding mark of a Christian and of the church. (C/LANL)

Is my church fellowship really showing honest, sacrificial agape *love or are we more like a club or mutual admiration society?*

Lord, make us ready and eager for your love to flood our lives.

May 15   **Commission to act**

Now that you know these things, you will be blessed if you do them.   **John 13:17**

Talking to some church leaders once, Billy Graham said, 'If God doesn't punish our society in the West, he will have to apologise to Sodom and Gomorrah.' Most people immediately think of homosexuality or some other sexual perversion when Sodom is mentioned and no doubt these things were included in their sins, but what the Bible says first is this: 'Now this was the sin of your sister Sodom: she and her daughters were arrogant, overfed and unconcerned; they did not help the poor and needy' (Ezekiel 16:49).

I find that a very disturbing indictment of the affluent West. We have many opportunities and privileges, but we have failed God's world. We *know* so much, but *do* nothing or very little; we *have* so much, but *share* nothing or very little.

Members of a church were startled when they arrived one Sunday morning to find their church doors locked. Pinned to the wood was this notice: 'You have been coming here long enough. Now go and do it.' Jesus had something similar to say to some of his so-called disciples: 'Why do you call me, "Lord, Lord," and do not do what I say' (Luke 6:46)? He spelt out the same message in the parable of the sheep and goats (Matthew 25:31-46). (AR)

Lord, if I have grown smug and uncaring, disturb and move me by your loving Spirit.

Have I learnt something new recently? How can I act on it today and in the future?

May 16   The grace of giving

Out of the most severe trial, their overflowing joy and their extreme poverty welled up in rich generosity. For I testify that they gave as much as they were able, and even beyond their ability. . . See that you also excel in this grace of giving.
2 Corinthians 8:2,3,7

Money is not an unspiritual topic. Jesus spoke more about money than he did about heaven and many other so-called spiritual subjects. Why? Because money is the commonest rival to God.

In the New Testament, we have the superb example of the Macedonian church in the matter of giving (2 Corinthians 8-9).

Their giving was a response to God's love, which so filled their lives that overflowing generosity resulted. This supernatural giving is a real sign of God's grace at work, and lack of spiritual giving is an early sign, I believe, of spiritual death.

They gave out of their poverty. What a challenge to us in the West who enjoy a very high standard of living! We need to define before God what is 'enough' and live on that, giving away the rest to 'every good work' (2 Corinthians 9:8). Under the Jewish law, the Jews were required to give a tenth of all they had and only after that did their real giving begin. We are not under the law, but how much more generous we should be now that we are under grace!

The Macedonian churches gave, as an expression of their total commitment to Christ. They gave themselves, their time, their energy, and everything else, to the Lord. (CFP)

'Thanks be to God for his indescribable gift' (2 Corinthians 9:15). May my giving be a response to that gift.

Do I really see my giving as part of my spiritual worship? If others knew how much I gave to God would they conclude that I loved him much or little? What must I do?

May 17   **Spiritual sacrifices**

At his tabernacle will I sacrifice with shouts of joy; I will sing and make music to the Lord.   **Psalm 27:6**

God's people are 'a holy priesthood offering spiritual sacrifices acceptable to God through Jesus Christ' (1 Peter 2:5). What sacrifices are we to offer?

One answer is — *the sacrifice of our praise* (Hebrews 13:15). We can praise God not only by our words, but also by our music, dance, drama and all the other aspects which could be included in our worship. In a survey in our church it was found that a third of the respondents did *not* like dance and drama, and about a third *especially* liked it! In spite of the former group, we felt that we must continue to worship God through these means. For one thing, the world is full of movement and action, and the church is starved of it. For another, movement and drama challenge the over-intellectual presentation of the Christian message. About seventy-five per cent of people are 'switched off' by words; many could respond to the gospel presented through dance and drama. Also, we need to beware of subscribing to the unbiblical idea that anything beautiful or creative is unsuitable in church. God is the great Creator, after all.

There is also *the sacrifice of our work*. God gave Adam work to do (Genesis 2:15), and Jesus worked as a carpenter for thirty years, so dignifying work for ever after. God is not just interested in our so-called religious activities; our work matters to him, too. Writing to the super-spiritual Colossians, Paul says, 'Whatever you do, work at it with all your heart, as working for the Lord, not for men' (Colossians 3:23). We need to think through our attitudes in the office, hospital ward, classroom, common room, shop floor . . .

Then there is *the sacrifice of our gifts*. 'And do not forget to do good and to share with others, for with such sacrifices God is pleased' (Hebrews 13:16). We know we are living in an age of hunger. What action have we taken about it? (YTL)

Which is my weakest area as far as these spiritual sacrifices are concerned?

Father, I want to offer you the sacrifice of . . . Help me.

May 18   **Art for God's sake**

Then the Lord said to Moses, 'See I have chosen Bezalel. . . and I have filled him with the Spirit of God, with skill, ability and knowledge in all kinds of crafts — to make artistic designs for work in gold, silver and bronze, to cut and set stones, to work in wood, and to engage in all kinds of craftsmanship.
Exodus 31:1-5

God is concerned with what we are and with the ways in which we express ourselves. The words we speak or write, the clothes we wear, the music we play, the songs we sing, the movements of our bodies, the expressions on our faces, the work done with our hands, the relationships we make with other people — all these are extensions of our personalities. And it is these personalities that, with all their variety, God wants to transform increasingly into the likeness of his Son.

Art, therefore, is intrinsically a part of the life that God has made; it is to be appreciated, enjoyed, and, for the Christian, offered back to God as part of the worship of our glorious

Creator. For the church to be afraid of art, or even worse to oppose art, is a tragic sign of a church that misunderstands its Creator, denies the humanity of its members, and has become irrelevant to the world which it has been called to redeem. (IBITC)

What do our church buildings and worship 'say' about our glorious Creator?

Thank you, Creator God, for the gifts you have given me. They are yours to use as you want.

May 19   **A gathered community**

Gather to me my consecrated ones.   **Psalm 50:5**
Many people had gathered and were praying.   **Acts 12:12**

In order to be a church we must come together (Matthew 18:20; Acts 2:1,42,46). There are still far too many four-wheeler Christians — those who come only in a pram or a taxi or a hearse to church to be hatched, matched or dispatched. In no sense do we belong to the church unless we regularly gather with God's people (Hebrews 10:25). We need each other. If I take one page, I can tear it to shreds easily. If I take a whole book, I cannot tear it at all. Others need you, even if you don't feel you need them. The church is not a vicar supported by a few volunteers; it's a gathered community of God's people who are as committed to one another as they are to Christ.

A community doesn't speak primarily of activities but of relationships. We need to build deep and loving relationships with each other seven days a week. This is a painful business for which much love, forgiveness and understanding are constantly needed.

Someone has said, 'The effectiveness of our ministry depends on the fervency of our love for one another.' An atheistic psychiatrist has said that the church has failed people because it has not yet discovered the secret of community. Whatever we call 'mine' should be shared with others.

152

Sometimes people on the fringes of church life are critical of an 'in-group' — but they shouldn't be; not if the 'in-group' represents those who have made a full response to the Lord and to his Body, while others stand on the sidelines, being critical and uncommitted. If you want to be in the 'in-group' — get more involved: give more of your love, time, prayer and of yourself! (YTL)

Do I feel that I really belong to my church? If not, why not?

Father, help me to build relationships with other Christians during the week as well as on Sundays.

And the things you have heard me say in the presence of many witnesses, entrust to reliable men who will also be qualified to teach others.   2 Timothy 2:2

The golden rule in forming groups is to start small. . . Any wise leader will concentrate his time on a small group of committed Christians — twelve probably being the maximum number for effective discipling.

One vital point is to understand exactly who is the discipler in any group. The common and natural answer is the most mature and experienced leader present. A much healthier model, however, is to see Christ as the primary Discipler, so that we all seek to encourage one another, correct one another, and build one another up in love.

When any Christian leader sees himself, or is seen by others, as the 'guru' of the group, problems are likely to follow. Dominant leadership will not help but hinder spiritual growth and development. Also every leader needs constant encouragement and even correction.

The small team I was involved with in York met at least four times a week. We usually began with a time of worship and praise. Then we shared together what God had been saying to us or doing in our lives, nearly always relating this to passages from the Scriptures that we had been reading during the previous day.

These 'sharing times' were neither pooling our problems nor just picking out nice devotional thoughts from the Bible. They were times of reality when we let down our masks, said what was going on in our thoughts or lives, and linked this with what God might be teaching us in our current situation. (D)

Lord, I long for the challenge and blessing of belonging to a small group. Guide me to people who could learn from me and from whom I could learn.

How can I develop this 'small-group' principle in my church?

May 21   **Truth experienced**

All who were sitting in the Sanhedrin looked intently at Stephen, and they saw that his face was like the face of an angel.
                                                                Acts 6:15

Three visitors came to one of our church services and afterwards one of them wrote to me like this: 'One of the most wonderful things was to look around at the faces of the congregation. They were so relaxed, so absorbed, so open and content, and of course all this created the most incredible tangible atmosphere. We all three felt it very much. I would never have thought I could go to a service lasting two and a half hours and still have been quite happy to stay longer. It seemed to solidify so many things for me. If I had had any doubts before your service, all that it gave to us and showed us would have quite decided me about the reality of Christ.'

She could see that the truth taught was experienced by the people; their faces reflected their inner peace, freedom and joy.

The Acts is full of men who experienced the truth. In his preface to the book, J. B. Phillips writes: 'These men did not make acts of faith, they believed. They did not say their

154

prayers, they really prayed. They did not hold conferences on psychosomatic medicine, they simply healed the sick. . . . The Spirit of God found what he must always be seeking—a fellowship of men and women so united in love and faith that he can work in and through them with the minimum of hindrance.'

'Truth that is not experienced is no better than error and may be fully as dangerous. The scribes who sat in Moses' seat were not the victims of error; they were the victims of their failure to experience the truth they taught' (Tozer). (YTL)

If I'm not experiencing the truth, why not?

Would I need to tell others of my faith or would they see it without my having to say a word?

May 22   **The author of life**

The letter kills but the Spirit gives life.   **2 Corinthians 3:6**

Dr Coggan once said, 'When the Holy Spirit comes on men and women, there is new life. There is often disorder too — untidy edges. But give me this every time if otherwise I have to put up with cold, lifeless orthodoxy.'

Some churches I have preached in are thoroughly orthodox but the atmosphere is almost deep-frozen! If the Holy Spirit lives in us and in our churches (1 Corinthians 3:16) there will be life and warmth there. Everything will be affected.

Without the Spirit, *worship* isn't just difficult, it's impossible (John 4:23,24), whatever we may sing, say or do. The Spirit is needed to prepare us for worship so that we come together in unity and love, by helping us to work out our grievances and resentments.

Without the Spirit, *witness* is powerless and ineffective (Acts 1:8). If we are anxious to be used by God in witnessing to others, we need to ask the Spirit daily to guide and empower us (1 Corinthians 2:4,5).

Without the Spirit, *God's word* can go dead and dry on us (1

Corinthians 2:12,14). It's a spiritual book, so we need to ask the Spirit to make it live to us.

Without the Spirit, *ministry* cannot take place (1 Corinthians 12:7,11). If you want to be used in the ministry of your church, you will need to receive from the Holy Spirit the gifts you need.

Without the Spirit, *prayer* does not reach its potential (Romans 8:26). (YTL)

Do I (we) live, work, worship, pray, walk in the Spirit?

Father, breathe new life into this area of my life. . . through the power of the Holy Spirit, for Jesus' sake.

May 23   Checks and balances in guidance

James, Peter and John, those reputed to be pillars, gave me and Barnabas the right hand of fellowship when they recognised the grace given to me. They agreed that we should go to the Gentiles, and they to the Jews.   Galatians 2:9

Even after three years' intensive thought and study of the Scriptures in the Arabian desert, Paul went and saw Peter and James to check his revelations and conclusions with theirs. Again, after fourteen years of very successful ministry, he went up to Jerusalem with Barnabas and Titus and 'set before them [the leaders] the gospel that I preach among the Gentiles . . . for fear that I was running or had run my race in vain' (Galatians 2:2). In other words, in spite of Paul's gifts, revelations, successes, knowledge of the Scriptures, and so on, he still checked out his calling to the Gentiles with the leadership of the church. This was because he was humble enough to realise that he might have got his own guidance wrong, he wanted to remain in good, open fellowship with the other leaders, and he wanted the new work to have their full approval.

If Paul realised that his own spiritual leading must be

checked by the joint leadership of the church, as well as by the Scriptures, how much more should we!

A balance is necessary however. We must not abdicate responsibility for our own decisions and leaders should never be allowed to 'play the Holy Spirit' in our lives.

A Christian leader has written: 'In the past we taught people to act as they felt led. The result, in many cases, was chaos. In an effort to help people more accurately to interpret the leading of the Spirit, we asked people to check out their guidance with a shepherd or pastor for a confirming word. The result, in many cases, was a bureaucratic system which squashed spontaneity.' Both extremes are wrong. (YTL)

Is our church life such that it would be easy and natural for us to check personal guidance with mature leaders?

Father, please help me to keep an attitude of humility which makes it possible for the Holy Spirit to tell me, through others perhaps, when I'm wrong.

May 24   **The barrier of our sin**

Search me, O God, and know my heart; . . . See if there is any offensive way in me and lead me in the way everlasting.
Psalm 139:23,24

Unconfessed sin is a barrier to spiritual growth and progress. God cannot fill our lives unless they are cleared not only of rubbish, but also of the things which, though good in themselves, are taking up space in our lives which could be better used or to which we are giving the wrong priority.

Confession of every known sin is very important. Sometimes I ask myself a series of questions. Have I been trying to give the impression that I'm a better person than I really am? Am I being honest in all my words and actions? Do I pass on to another what was told me in confidence? Am I self-conscious or self-pitying? Have I insisted on doing things about which my conscience is uneasy? Am I defeated in any part of my life? Am I jealous, angry, critical, irritable, touchy, distrustful, or impure in thought? Am I proud? Is there anyone I dislike or criticise or hold a resentment towards? If so, what am I doing about it?

We need to allow God's Spirit to search our hearts. If he convicts us of anything, we must confess that sin, repent of it and turn from it, and yield our lives fully to Jesus again. (AR)

Lord, make me willing to take time to face up to and clear up anything that is wrong in my life.

Should I take time to do what I have prayed about — now?

.

May 25   **Commitment and filling**

Be filled with the Spirit.   **Ephesians 5:18**

It sounds so easy — so why are not more of us filled with the Holy Spirit? There are several possible reasons. People may not ask for God to fill them with the Holy Spirit because they are worried about the more spectacular gifts, or because of various other fears, or because there is unconfessed and unforgiven sin in their lives, or because they are complacent.

But perhaps the greatest barrier against a person receiving the fullness of the Holy Spirit in his life, is that he is not yet fully and completely committed to Jesus Christ as Lord of every area in his life.

If I told my empty glove to pick up a Bible, nothing would happen. If I put my hand half-way into the glove, something would happen, but not much. Only when I put my hand fully into the glove, filling it all out, is that glove able, so to speak, to pick up a Bible and do a great many other things.

That glove is a picture of a life. When it is not yielded to Jesus, it's powerless and empty. When it's partly filled with Jesus, there is life, but there's limitation too. When it's fully yielded to Jesus as Lord and Master, then it's filled with power.

Remember four things. Being filled with the Spirit is not a 'once for all' experience: it can and should happen many times; you are not filled with the Holy Spirit when you *feel* that this has happened, but when you take God at his word and believe his promises; being filled with the Spirit does not answer all your problems — in fact, there will be new ones, but there will be new power too; the experience is never *only* for personal blessing — it's *always* that we might witness to Jesus and strengthen his family. (AR)

Show me, Lord, any barriers in my mind or in my life which need to come down before I can be filled with your Spirit.

Does God want me to be Spirit-filled so that I will become a crank or more Christ-like?

May 26   **Unity is strength**

All the believers were one in heart and mind.   **Acts 4:32**

God's power is essential for God's people, and not just for a few individual Christians who happen to be filled with the Spirit. One of the greatest weaknesses in the church today is individualism: 'I do my own thing my way, as I feel led.' However it is the quality, depth and unity of a Christian fellowship as a whole that is of paramount importance. Christ works through his Body. The Spirit apportions gifts to each member as he wills but they are always for the common good. It is 'the whole body, joined and held together by every supporting ligament' which 'grows and builds itself up in love' (Ephesians 4:16). Moreover, God has promised to command his blessing whenever brothers dwell together in unity (Psalm 133).

Indeed, almost every area of our Christian life can be affected by the degree of unity in the fellowship. To take only one example — prayer: Jesus promised his disciples, 'If two of you on earth agree about anything you ask for, it will be done for you by my Father in heaven (Matthew 18:19).

The Greek word 'agree' —*sumphoneo* —means 'in sympathy with' or 'in harmony with'. In other words, it is not enough that two Christians should mentally assent to the same prayer. Their lives must be in complete harmony with each other. They must be in a relationship of love and forgiveness. . . It is only when fellowship is really united and harmonious that we can ever expect any blessing at all. (OITS)

Do I even want to get closer to my fellow-Christians?

Lord, by your Spirit, make our church family one in heart and mind, for your glory.

May 27   The prophetic word

Follow the way of love and eagerly desire spiritual gifts especially the gift of prophecy. 1 Corinthians 14:1

Although the foundational gift of prophecy was given once-for-all through the apostles for the completion of the New Testament canon, even in the early church different levels of prophecy were clearly experienced. Paul envisaged this gift as a natural and healthy expression of the local church 'when you come together' (see 1 Corinthians 14). The vast majority of utterances, even in New Testament times, were not of the 'foundational' variety, but a normal part of the upbuilding of the Body of Christ in any place; this gift was clearly distinguished from that of teaching or preaching.

Whilst the written word is God's truth for all people at all times, the prophetic word is a particular word, inspired by God, given to a particular person or group of persons, at a particular moment for a particular purpose.

We should not be surprised if the prophetic utterance is in the speaker's own words and thought-forms, reflecting his or her own burdens, since God uses us as human beings, with all our human outlooks and experiences, to convey his word. Nor should we be suspicious if the prophecy is steeped in scriptural

160

phrases, since more than half the Revelation of the apostle John comes to us in that way. Nor should we dismiss prophecy if the word is simple — maybe even 'trivial' in the eyes of some. In the Old Testament we read this: 'Then Haggai, the Lord's messenger, gave this message of the Lord to the people: "I am with you," declares the Lord' (Haggai 1:13). That was all! Not another word came to God's people for a whole month. It was not the most profound or weighty word they had ever heard, but it was the word of the Lord. (D)

Lord, help our church fellowship to be prophets to one another, quietly speaking your words to and receiving your words from each other, so that everyone may benefit from this gift of yours.

Do I eagerly desire the gift of prophecy? If not, why not?

May 28   **Why prophecy?**

Everyone who prophesies speaks to men for their strengthening, encouragement and comfort.   1 Corinthians 14:3

Prophecy is of far greater value to the church than tongues. Paul tells us to 'eagerly desire spiritual gifts, especially the gift of prophecy' (1 Corinthians 14:1). Why?

Prophecy may bring fresh insight into God's truth. It may bring predictions or guidance concerning the future.

One thing is absolutely vital: prophecy is given so that the hearers will take action (Acts 11:28-30). When I realise that someone is not taking any notice of what I am saying, I soon stop talking. So, if we ignore God's word through his prophets, he will stop sending us his messages.

Prophecy may give guidance and direction to a church (Acts 13:1-3). If you receive personal guidance through prophecy, however, check this with Scripture and with mature Christians first, very carefully.

Prophecy is for strengthening, encouragement and comfort — and might include rebuke.

It can also be used in the context of evangelism. In our church a visitor, very embarrassed at our communion service, walked out halfway through. Realising she'd left her scarf behind, she returned later, hoping the service would be over. It wasn't, and as she walked up the aisle two words of prophecy were given. She was rooted to the spot, because, as she wrote to me later, 'I heard my actual thoughts in the second prophecy, something I'd never heard before. I heard God actually telling me in church with hundreds of other people, not to run as I had done so often before. I felt and experienced God's presence — something terrifying and wonderful.' There and then she gave her life to Jesus Christ. This is almost exactly what Paul says will happen (1 Corinthians 14:24,25)! (YTL)

Do we know enough about how God used prophecy in the Bible and how he uses it today?

Father, we don't want to quench your Holy Spirit. Show us where we are in danger of doing so.

May 29   **Testing the prophets**

Two or three prophets should speak, and others should weigh carefully what is said.   **1 Corinthians 14:29**

There may well be some overlap between prophecy and preaching or teaching, and real preaching should have a prophetic quality, but the two gifts are distinct. Prophecy brings a word to a particular situation. It may not be God's word for everyone, or be necessarily very dramatic or profound; but it will be God's word for *someone*.

The same criteria need to be applied to prophecy as to all spiritual gifts to test their genuineness.

Does the prophecy glorify Christ? Does it edify the Body of Christ? (Not all of them all the time, but some of them all of the time!) Is it in accordance with the Scriptures? (Here is the final authority for what we should believe.) Is it spoken in love? (It is possible to bring a stern message in love.) Is Jesus Christ Lord of that person's life? (He won't be perfect, but is he clearly under the Lord's authority?) Is that person submissive to the church leaders? (A sign of a false prophet is disobedience to leadership and a drawing away, in independence, from the main body of the church.)

Genuine prophecy is one of God's good and beautiful gifts for his people. We are told earnestly to desire (pray, seek for) these gifts, launch out in faith without being afraid of making mistakes or being corrected, and make love our first and foremost aim.

God will give us his Spirit, his love and his gifts — perhaps prophecy — if we come and ask him humbly for what we need in order to glorify Christ and edify his people. (YTL)

What is our attitude to these matters? Is it Biblical?

Father, thank you for all who enrich the life of our church and build up your people . . . (mention them by name).

May 30   Demonic con-man

The Spirit clearly says that in later times some will abandon the faith and follow deceiving spirits and things taught by demons.
1 Timothy 4:1

Satan seeks to confuse God's work with counterfeit movements, which not only deceive many, but discredit genuine movements of the Spirit of God. As the 'angel of light' he seduces deeply religious people with 'deceiving spirits and things taught by demons', bringing them into the bondage of either legalism or licence. He deludes weak Christians by those who are disguised as 'servants of righteousness' (2 Corinthians 11:15), and by 'all kinds of counterfeit miracles, signs and wonders' (2 Thessalonians 2:9). He may draw them into a false religion which has all the outward form, but none of the life and power of the Spirit of God. In the experiential mood of today, alongside genuine charismatic experiences, has mushroomed a host of occult practices and eastern mysticism. Sects that promise spiritual fulfilment and reality have grown like a wasting disease, encouraged by the spiritual barrenness of much of the orthodox church.

This has been the pattern of church history from the New Testament times onwards. The apostles and church fathers saw agnostic heresies and mystery religions as expressions of deceiving spirits... When we see the same confusing influences in both church and society today, it would be foolish to dismiss those apostolic warnings as first-century superstition. More humbly, we ought to acknowledge our own limited vision of the spiritual realm, accept the teaching of Scripture as God's word, and give due warning about the dangers of counterfeits for our churches today. (D)

May the Spirit of truth show me real from sham, true from counterfeit.

Is there any pretence in my Christian life?

May 31   **The whole armour**

Put on the full armour of God so that you can take your stand against the devil's schemes.   **Ephesians 6:11**

There is no protection for the back in the full armour God provides for the Christian (Ephesians 6:10-18)! If we turn and run, we are on our own.

We need the whole armour. One part may protect the heart but not the head; another, the head but not the heart. We need every single piece of God's armour. We cannot pick and choose what appeals to us.

However, some equipment is worn all the time in readiness, while some is used particularly in the thick of the fight. The first three pieces are the belt of truth, which is to be buckled round our waists, the breastplate of righteousness, and feet that are 'fitted with the readiness that comes from the gospel of peace'. These comprise the basic uniform of the Christian soldier. The remaining three pieces — the shield of faith, the helmet of salvation and the sword of the Spirit — are special battle gear.

Here is the picture: a soldier is sitting in his tent waiting for the battle call. He has on his belt, his breastplate and his boots. Suddenly the bugle blows. He seizes his shield, clamps on his helmet, grasps his sword, and moves out, ready for the enemy. (HW)

Father, thank you that we needn't face the foe alone or unequipped.

Think about what each piece of armour means, and how to 'acquire' it.

JUNE
Renewal

June 1   **No renewal without brokenness**

Blessed are the poor in spirit, for theirs is the kingdom of heaven. Blessed are those who mourn, for they will be comforted. Blessed are the meek, for they will inherit the earth. Blessed are those who hunger and thirst for righteousness, for they will be filled.   **Matthew 5:3-6**

During my second curacy, I became really hungry for spiritual renewal and during a period of months God spoke to me through the beatitudes, particularly the first four. I began to see that I was spiritually bankrupt and to mourn over my spiritual bankruptcy. Then God brought me to a point of meekness — to a point of brokenness before the cross of Christ, where I was willing for God to do anything he wanted with my life, so hungry and thirsty was I for something new to happen in my life and ministry.

God gave me a gift of faith to believe his promise about the Holy Spirit and I really asked him to fill me. The result was that I had a gentle but real sense of being overwhelmed with the love of God. This experience was an important leap in my spiritual life. God, and all spiritual matters, became far, far more real to me.

So when others in our church became hungry for renewal, we were able to help them to be filled with the Holy Spirit. Those who were filled found a wonderful sense of release.

They were set free for joy, praise, worship, spontaneous witness and prayer in a new way.

But the price of renewal is suffering of one sort or another, including the suffering of a broken and contrite spirit. (AR)

Spirit of the Living God, break me.

Am I really willing to pray that prayer and go on until it is answered?

Bible study: What are the marks of a person (or a church fellowship) that is brimming with spiritual life and health? What do I (we) lack? What can I (we) do about it?

Starters: Study the life and growth of Simon Peter in the gospels and the Acts, and see under 'renewal' in index.

June 2   The church doesn't own the Spirit

He who has an ear, let him hear what the Spirit says to the churches.

Revelation 2:7

The Spirit is distinct from the church. Nowhere in the New Testament is he called the Spirit of the church. No church or individual can possess or own him any more than he can own the air he breathes. It should be the other way round. As someone has said, 'If you think of him as an influence, you'll be anxious to have more of it, but if you think of him as a person, you will desire that he may have more of you.'

Just as he is not tied to the church, so no church has the monopoly of him. In recent years many Christians have been wonderfully blessed by the Holy Spirit, but they need to be careful not to judge others as unspiritual. Pentecostal and so-called 'charismatic' churches need revival and renewal just as much as others; indeed, they may be in greater need, if they fall into the error of relying on past blessing and experiences, and so fail to realise how dry and dead they are.

In the first and second centuries a group of people called the Montanists experienced great blessings through the Holy Spirit, but things went wrong when they claimed to embody the Spirit, wrote off other Christians as carnal and refused to have their teachings tested by Scripture. Consequently the church and the Montanists wrote one another off and both were the losers. This should be a lesson for us today when some claim that they have the Spirit and write off those who don't have the same experience, and others write off spiritual renewal altogether because of the attitudes, errors or excesses they see in some individuals or churches claiming this experience. None of us owns the Spirit and we all need to be constantly renewed by him. (YTL)

Does our church resemble either the Montanists or the orthodox church in an unhelpful or wrong way?

Lord of the church, let our church hear what the Spirit is saying to us today.

June 3   Willing to be God's fool

When they arrived, they prayed for them that they might receive the Holy Spirit, because the Holy Spirit had not yet come upon any of them; they had simply been baptised into the name of the Lord Jesus.   **Acts 8:15,16**

The story of the Samaritan Christians (Acts 8:4-25) is worth reading and thinking about. It would seem that they were true believers (verses 5,8,16), but they had not been filled with the Holy Spirit.

I feel this is relevant today. I am constantly meeting ministers and others who are aware of barrenness and in-effectiveness in their ministries and lives — in contrast to the New Testament pattern where the disciples, though few in number, turned their world upside down.

There are three important things to say about the filling of the Holy Spirit.

First, it's not the same as conversion. Ideally perhaps it should happen at the same time, but in practice it often doesn't happen till later.

Secondly, normally, there is clear, unmistakable evidence of the experience, such as new spiritual freedom and gifts (see Acts 2,10 and 19).

Thirdly, the purpose of it all is to glorify Christ. If he is not glorified, then any spiritual experiences are like noisy gongs or clanging cymbals!

If we want to receive the Holy Spirit in this special way, we may have to drop our prejudices. John Sherrill said there were two things he did not want to do — raise his hands and shout, 'Praise the Lord!' But these were the very things he did when the Spirit filled him. Don't let our pride and our idea of what we are prepared to accept from God be stumbling-blocks in the way of blessing. (YTL)

Am I willing to be God's fool?

Father, show me whether I really want Jesus to be glorified or am seeking something special for myself.

June 4   **Will spiritual renewal split my church?**

All of them were filled with the Holy Spirit.   Acts 2:4

Some people are frightened of spiritual renewal because they say it splits churches. Sometimes that is true, but it is not the Holy Spirit who causes divisions; he always unites Christians. Someone has said, 'I know of no story of renewal in the body of believers which has not been accompanied by disagreement and dissension. That includes the book of Acts. Such division is not created by the Spirit of God. More often, the coming of the Spirit, and the openness which it breeds, unveils the existing barriers, differences and resentments within a fellowship.'

When the wind blows, you discover where the cracks are in your walls or window frames. So when the wind of the Holy Spirit blows, we very often discover what we *really* feel about one another, and other things which have been 'swept under the carpet'.

In my experience, the Spirit binds people together and releases in them a deeper quality of love. We are the ones who cause divisions by our refusal to yield to the Spirit and by holding on to our resentments and jealousy, bitterness and anger. These things hinder the Spirit from working, which is why Paul writes: 'Get rid of all bitterness, rage and anger, brawling and slander, along with every form of malice. Be kind and compassionate to one another, forgiving each other, just as in Christ God forgave you' (Ephesians 4:31,32). (CFP).

Is the Spirit blowing in our church? What is he uncovering in me?

Lord, I want to let go of . . . so as not to grieve your Spirit.

June 5   An uncomfortable comforter

But as for me, I am filled with power, with the Spirit of the Lord, and with justice and might, to declare to Jacob his transgression, to Israel his sin.   Micah 3:8

Perhaps you have sung these words from a well known hymn about the Holy Spirit:

> And his that gentle voice we hear,
> Soft as the breath of even,
> That checks each fault, that calms each fear,
> And speaks of heaven.

Commenting on that, Dr Coggan has written: 'Gentle? It was a gale. Soft? It blew to pieces their old and most cherished patterns of life. Checks each thought? It stimulated them to such furious thinking that they could scarcely get down on papyrus the ideas that came rushing to them. Speaks of heaven? Maybe, but first of earth with its pain and sin and ignorance. They found themselves blown into a perfect vortex of problems, to share them, to wrestle with them, to master them, in the name of the Lord. True, the wind renewed, revived and freshened, but it also blew away the cobwebs and broke down the barriers. There was pain as well as joy in the experience of Pentecost.'

The Holy Spirit does not force himself on us. He waits for our willingness, but when he comes, he decides what will happen, he gives us what he knows to be right for us, and he is in control of the situation (Isaiah 40:13). He may have to be, for our good, as Micah was to the Israelites, a most uncomfortable comforter. (YTL)

Father, make me willing to receive the truth from you through anyone you choose — however painful that truth may be.

Am I willing for a fresh filling of the Holy Spirit no matter how this might unsettle my lifestyle?

June 6   **Miracles of healing today**

I will not venture to speak of anything except what Christ has accomplished through me in leading the Gentiles to obey God by what I have said and done — by the power of signs and miracles, through the power of the Spirit. So . . . I have fully proclaimed the gospel of Christ.   **Romans 15:18,19**

One reason why some people won't accept miracles today is that they believe they break scientific laws. But what is a scientific law? It's a generalisation of what normally happens. A Christian would go further and say that a scientific law is simply the way in which God normally acts, but there's no law which says that God must act in that way always. 'Our God is in heaven; he does whatever pleases him' (Psalm 115:3).

Sometimes people ask, 'Isn't the salvation of the soul far more important than the healing of the body?' The answer is, 'Yes.' Spiritual realities are of the greatest importance, and divine healing should never become the central part of our message. When Peter and John healed the cripple in the name of Jesus, they didn't say, 'Bring all your sick and let's have a wonderful healing service.' They spoke of the name and power of Jesus and preached repentance and faith. But divine healing can be a very powerful force in evangelism: it *does* reveal the compassion and power of Jesus; and it *should* lead on to greater and more important issues.

Undoubtedly miracles of healing are taking place today in many parts of the world. A doctor wrote this to me from Nepal: 'We have seen amazing things in the last few months, starting among the missionaries. Six have been filled with the Spirit, one completely liberated from real bondage and her whole life and outlook transformed in a way that everyone can see. In the leprosarium we have seen several persons healed, two instantly, another made dramatic progress in one month that would normally have taken four years.' (YTL)

What is my attitude towards miracles and healing, and what is the attitude of my fellowship?

Father, help us to proclaim fully the gospel of Christ.

June 7   The marks of a renewed fellowship

They devoted themselves to the apostles' teaching and to the fellowship, to the breaking of bread and to prayer.   Acts 2:42

In six verses, we are given some of the marks of a living Christian fellowship (Acts 2:42-47). First they were devoted to the Scriptures, to meeting one another for sharing and worship, and to prayer. I believe 'the breaking of bread' refers not only to the Lord's Supper, but also to sharing meals in one another's homes, and it was in this context that services and worship would often have taken place. Devotion to prayer is a prelude to any great work of God. Before the revival in the Hebrides, some people met three nights a week for months and months, to pray long and sacrificially.

Awe of God is another mark of true Christian fellowship (verse 43). When the Holy Spirit works powerfully in a group and the fear of God falls on them, then and then only will the world be shaken out of its complacency.

A true fellowship also shares money and possessions to meet people's needs (verses 44,45) and is full of joy and praise (verses 46,47).

There are many renewed, vital Christian fellowships today and here are some of the characteristics which have been observed in them. They talk naturally about Jesus, visit each other, care for those outside the fellowship, pray for the sick, are involved with social caring, give time, talents and money to the ministry of the church, and long for unity between all believers. (YTL)

What does our fellowship lack and what can I do about it?

Father, make us all see that real fellowship is a necessity, not an optional extra.

June 8   If we know more, we must pray more

The Lord said, 'Shall I hide from Abraham what I am about to do? ... The outcry against Sodom and Gomorrah is so great and their sin so grievous that I will go down and see if what they have done is as bad as the outcry that has reached me. If not, I will know.'   Genesis 18:17,20,21

Why did God reveal what he was going to do? Was it so that Abraham could feel thankful that he wasn't going to be among those under God's judgment? Certainly not.

He did it partly so that Abraham would 'direct his children

and his household after him to keep the way of the Lord by doing what is right and just' (verse 19).

But he did it mainly so that Abraham would pray for Sodom and Gomorrah. God's judgment on those places was not arbitrary. If I put my hand in a fire, my hand will be burnt. If people go on breaking God's commands, they will be punished; they bring it on themselves. But God has given us the secret weapon of intercessory prayer. Time and again, Moses averted God's judgment through prayer. Samuel, Job, Isaiah, Ezekiel, Jeremiah, Paul and others did the same.

We, as nations and churches and individuals, cannot calculate what we owe to the intercessory prayers of a few people. One preacher who was used again and again to win people for Jesus, once had a vision, while he was preaching. He saw the heaven opened and light streaming down from it, not on himself, but on his blind brother praying in the front pew. It was because of that brother's unnoticed intercessions that the preacher experienced such effectiveness in his ministry.

If you know something of God's truth, you have a great responsibility to pray, as Abraham did, for those in danger of God's judgment. (YTL)

Am I turning insights into prayer?

Lord, there are many evangelists and missionaries. If there is one for whom you want me to intercede regularly and whole-heartedly, please show me who it is.

June 9   Turn criticism into prayer

Do not judge, or you too will be judged. . . Why do you look at the speck of sawdust in your brother's eye and pay no attention to the plank in your own eye?   Matthew 7:1,3

If we turned our concern for other Christians more readily into prayer, we should be far more effective as a church against all the forces of the kingdom of darkness. Instead, we so often criticise one another, or slander, attack and judge. A friend of mine said that the army of Christ must be the only army in the world where its soldiers constantly fight with one another. In this way, we are doing the devil's work for him. But when we turn criticism into prayer, we lift up the shield of faith on behalf of the one being attacked, we release the Holy Spirit's power to encourage or convict (as the need may be), and we keep the love of God flowing between us when the devil is out to divide us. (D)

Pray for someone of whom you have been feeling critical.

Is it time for me to sort out, before God, those for whom I should be praying, and plan how I can actually do this?

June 10   **A new revelation of God**

When Abram was ninety-nine years old, the Lord appeared to him.   Genesis 17:1

This wasn't the first time that God appeared to Abram, but it seems to have been the first significant time for twenty-four years. And after all those years of mostly patient waiting, Abram was given a wonderful gift — a new revelation of God: 'I am God Almighty.' I believe that what God was conveying to Abram through those words was something like this: 'Abram, do you remember that promise I gave you all those years ago? By now I expect you feel that it's not going to happen, but I'm going to reveal something about my character and nature that you may not have realised up till now. I am going to tell you what sort of God I really am. Abram, listen carefully. I am God Almighty. I am God all powerful. I am the sort of God for whom nothing is impossible or too hard. What's more, Abram, that promise I gave you all those years ago will never, never be broken.' God goes on to say, 'I will confirm my covenant between me and you and greatly increase your numbers' (verse 2). And Abram, awed by this new revelation of God, simply fell down and worshipped (verse 3).

Here is a typical example of the graciousness of God. And if you hold on, as Abram did, through a time of testing when you perhaps don't understand what God is doing or why, you will not be disappointed. He will reveal himself, as he did to Abram, giving you a new insight into some aspect of his ways or his character. You may suddenly realise that Christ is alive, or that the power of the Spirit is available, or that God knows and cares and will work out a particular problem, or simply that he is — as Abram realised — God Almighty. (YTL)

Lord, as I read your word, give me a new insight into some truth about you which I or someone else will need to hold on to in the days ahead.

How does the Lord appear to his people today?

June 11   God is no spoilsport

At the beginning of creation God made them male and female. For this reason a man will leave his father and mother and be united to his wife, and the two will become one flesh. So they are no longer two, but one. Therefore what God has joined together, let man not separate.   Mark 10:6-9
You shall not commit adultery.   Exodus 20:14
It is God's will that you should be holy; that you should avoid sexual immorality; that each of you should learn to control his own body in a way that is holy and honourable.

1 Thessalonians 4:3,4

It is precisely because sex is so beautiful that God, the Maker of sex, has given us the Maker's instructions. And centuries of history have proved that his instructions are absolutely right.

The Harvard sociologist, in his book *The American Sex Revolution* describes the Russian attitude of the '20s: 'The revolution leaders deliberately attempted to destroy marriage and the family. The legal distinction between marriage and casual sexual intercourse was abolished. Bigamy and polygamy were permissible under the new provisions. Abortion was facilitated in the state institutions. Pre-marital relationships were praised; extramarital relationships were considered normal. . . Within a few years millions of lives, especially of young girls', were wrecked. The hatred and conflicts . . . rapidly mounted and so did psychoneuroses. Work in the national factories slackened. The government was forced to reverse its policy.' Indeed, Russia has returned to very strict standards of sexual morality.

When God says, 'Save sex for marriage,' he is not trying to frustrate us. He wants us to know the greatest possible joy. (ISOG)

If I am married — am I meeting my partner's needs or simply expecting my partner to meet my needs? If I'm single — do I believe that God can meet my every need?

Lord, thank you that you do not give us laws to frustrate us but to make us truly free.

June 12   **Why a body?**

There is one Body.   **Ephesians 4:4**

Why does Paul use the analogy of a body for the Christian church? First, it is because the body is one — a unity — and so should the Christian church be — 'one body' with 'one Spirit. . . one Lord, one faith, one baptism; one God and Father of all' (Ephesians 4:4,5,6).

Then, in a healthy body, every part has to function harmoniously, and the same should be true of a Christian fellowship. Everyone should have a ministry and God will give the right gifts when his people are willing to serve Christ and one another. When something goes wrong with one part of the body, the rest of the body is affected and action needs to be

177

taken to put things right. When tensions occur within the church family, these need to be dealt with quickly, so that harmony can be restored. To do this we need to learn to speak the truth in love (Ephesians 4:15).

Just as a human body starts off very tiny and grows to maturity, so the Christian church needs to grow up into Christ in every way (Ephesians 4:15). He is the head, or should be. We need to be sure that he really is Lord in our worship, our finance, our organisation and ministry.

And the life-blood of the Body is love (Ephesians 3:17-19; 4:2,15) (YTL)

What sort of a Body are we in our church fellowship — healthy, spastic, semi-paralysed. . .?

Father, this unity cannot be man-made; please bring it about through your Holy Spirit and may we be satisfied with nothing less than one supernatural Body.

June 13 Love hurts

Jesus said, 'Father, forgive them, for they do not know what they are doing.' Luke 23:34

C. S. Lewis wrote, 'To love at all is to be vulnerable. Love anything and your heart will certainly be wrung and possibly broken.' He goes on to say that if you keep your heart intact, it will become 'unbreakable, impenetrable, irredeemable'.

If we open our hearts to one another, we make ourselves vulnerable. It's sometimes with people that we really care about, that the deep bitternesses and resentments occur. Why? Because the more I commit myself to a person, the greater the pain I shall feel when he lets me down or hurts or rejects or avoids me. Also, it is only when I am close to another that I see the 'speck' in his eye and then learn the painful truth that the speck in his eye is simply a reflection of the log that is in mine. All too quickly, I notice the faults in others which are in myself.

To forgive and be forgiven in these situations is extremely painful. But think of what it cost Jesus to forgive. For him, it meant crucifixion for the sins of people he loved deeply.

Crucifixion, certainly of our pride, is necessary in our lives if we are to know Jesus' love in our experience and in our relationships. I haven't yet met a Christian anywhere in the world with a deep mature love who hasn't gone through considerable suffering in the area of relationships. So, the pressures and pains in our relationships can, if we learn to forgive and be forgiven, produce this rare and fragrant love. (AR)

Lord, help me not to shrink from the pain of opening my heart to my brothers and sisters in Christ.

Is there anything I'm resenting in others which I haven't honestly faced up to in myself?

June 14   **No battle of the sexes**

In the Lord . . . woman is not independent of man, nor is man independent of woman.   1 Corinthians 11:11

From the account of creation onwards, the Bible makes it clear that men and women have complementary roles. They are different, not only biologically (virtually the only difference that many in modern society are prepared to admit), but emotionally and temperamentally. However in no sense can either sex claim to be better than the other. They are simply different. Although it is true that man is the head of the woman, there is no thought of superiority and inferiority in this headship. Paul explains that 'the head of every man is Christ . . . and the head of Christ is God' (1 Corinthians 11:13). Just as the persons of the Godhead are equal but distinct, so with man and woman. 'You are all one in Christ Jesus' (Galatians 3:28). We should therefore learn to work together and share together, bringing to each other the mutually complementary gifts that will help to edify the whole Body of Christ.

There are many invaluable spiritual gifts and ministries that God undoubtedly gives to women, making them indispensable to the healthy working of the Body of Christ. The church that restricts women to cleaning and cooking greatly impoverishes its own spiritual life, and will often lack the warmth and love that women especially can contribute. (IBITC)

Do women and men complement each other in the life of our church?

Father, thank you that you created male and female and for giving me . . . (name your partner or close friends).

June 15   Husbands and wives

Wives, submit to your husbands as to the Lord. Ephesians 5:22

Although Paul makes it clear that marriage is a partnership that should be marked by a deep and sacrificial love, the ultimate responsibility and final authority in decision-making should rest with the man. This authority is given to him not for dominating his wife, nor for restricting her from exercising her gifts within the family; rather, just the reverse.

Paul goes on to say, 'Husbands love your wives just as Christ loved the church and gave himself up for her' (Ephesians 5:25). This headship, therefore, is for protection and support. The man gives his wife authority to act within the family (caring for the children, handling the household money, etc.) while taking the ultimate responsibility away from her shoulders and on to his. She is in this way set free to get on with her work, knowing that she has the support of her husband since he has given her authority so to act.

It means also that she can turn to someone for counsel and advice, and in practice the two of them will discuss most affairs of the house and family together. Most of the decisions will be (or should be) joint decisions; but when uncertainties or differences of opinion exist, the man should have the final say, whether or not he seems to be right in his decision. If both were to exercise equal authority in the home, inevitably tensions would arise; and this, of course, is one reason for many breakdowns in marriage. (IBITC)

If a couple were having difficulties, would they know who to turn to for help in our church?

Father, I pray for ... (a couple having a problem at the moment).

June 16   Extended families

God sets the lonely in families.   Psalm 68:6

This concept of the small nuclear family — mum, dad and two kids — is comparatively modern, stemming largely from the days of the industrial revolution when families were scattered in the pursuit of jobs. The extended family was the norm in Bible days; it remained the norm for many centuries afterwards and still is the case today in certain parts of the world. It is true that the members of these households were largely blood relations but some of the tensions of the small, modern family were considerably eased.

When some of these small family units can be expanded so that a genuine Christian community of brothers and sisters in Christ can be formed, albeit around a nuclear unit, the possibility of new, deep and caring relationships on a wider basis becomes a vital part of the good news of the gospel.

Apart from community, what real support can be given to the numerous single and divorced members of many churches ... to the widow or widower ... to those who have suffered from mental illness ... or been emotionally crippled? If it is God's plan to set the lonely in families, what practical measures can the local church take to see that this actually happens — perhaps starting within its own ranks? And it is by no means only the elderly who are lonely today. Christian ministers and clergy, not to mention their wives, can suffer acutely in this way. (IBITC)

Lord, may those of us in warm, close families remember to include and welcome those on their own.

Is our church basically geared to couples? How could we 'open out' to include others?

June 17   God's word — total communication

The word of God is living and active. Sharper than any double-edged sword, it penetrates even to dividing soul and spirit, joints and marrow; it judges the thoughts and attitudes of the heart.

Hebrews 4:12

God's word is seen in the Bible as something living and active. It achieves something, just as rain and snow does (Isaiah 55:10,11). Jesus likens it to a seed, and a seed is very powerful, having the principle of life and growth within it (Luke 8:11). It works in the believer (1 Thessalonians 2:13). It lives and endures (1 Peter 1:23). It penetrates and judges.

The Bible is part of the word of God, and a very important part at that, but it's not synonymous with it. In the opening chapter of the Bible, God's word created all that exists, and we can't say that of the Bible. Creation is also part of God's word (Psalm 19:1-4) in this wider sense — meaning God's total communication of himself to man.

We read that the word of God spread or increased (Acts 6:7; 12:24; 13:49; 19:20), referring to the church, not the Scriptures. Why did the writer use the phrase 'the word of God' instead of 'the church of God'? I believe he wanted to point out that just as Christ was the word of God made flesh, so, in some sense, is the church.

So the word of God includes the Bible but it includes other

things as well, because God is alive, and just like any other living author, he communicates in many other ways as well as through his writings. This is not to deny that the Scriptures are our final authority against which *everything else* has to be tested. Jesus rebuked those who were relying on their own reasoning and traditions and brought them back to God's written word (Matthew 15:1-9; 22:23-29). But we cannot limit God to the Bible and even the Bible doesn't truly become God's effective word to us without the Holy Spirit (2 Corinthians 3:6). (YTL)

Father, thank you that you are constantly speaking in so many ways to us.

What is the difference between God's word and God's words?

June 18   The same word

And we have the word of the prophets made more certain, and you will do well to pay attention to it, as to a light shining in a dark place, until the day dawns and the morning star rises in your hearts.   **2 Peter 1:19**

A very dangerous thing is happening in some places today. Some preachers are driving a wedge between the two Greek words: *logos* and *rhema*. They both mean 'word' but these people are saying that *logos* refers to the general objective truths of Scripture and *rhema* to what God is saying to us now — that is, to the prophetic word. They therefore stress that *rhema* is more important for our needs.

Some go on to say that our unity depends on our response to *rhema*, because if God is saying something to people now, they must respond and, if necessary, separate themselves from Christians who do not so respond. But in every good Bible dictionary or lexicon you will find that this is an entirely false distinction, and that the two words are virtually synonymous.

There is great danger in trying to build a theology round a

word. Also, the prophetic word which some are saying is more important than the written word, must always be checked by the written word and by the leaders of the church. Even more importantly, our unity is not based on our response to God's word, but on our relationship with Jesus Christ. If you are in Christ and I am in Christ, we *are* united, whether we like it or not, and whether we respond to the same prophetic word in the same way or not! If we separate ourselves from other Christians on this account, we are *not* being led by the Spirit or the written word of God. We must take heed not to be led astray or to lead others astray in this matter. (YTL)

Father, I pray that Christian leaders who have helped so many by their effective preaching and teaching may not go astray through some erroneous private interpretation of your word.

Am I studying God's word to find what is acceptable to me, or in order to face the truth and let it shape my thoughts?

June 19   **By faith Rahab**

By faith the prostitute Rahab, because she welcomed the spies, was not killed with those who were disobedient.
                                              Hebrews 11:31

What an amazing person to find in this gallery of faith (Hebrews 11)! Rahab was a pagan prostitute, possibly even a priestess involved in various fertility rites. Her life was one sordid mess. Why is she put alongside Noah, Abraham and other spiritual giants? She knew very little about God, but the point was that she responded to that little.

Faith depends on God's revelation. Rahab knew that God had given the Israelites the land, she had heard what had happened at the Red Sea and to the two Amorite kings, and she believed that the Lord was 'God in heaven above and on earth below' (Joshua 2:8-11). That was all she knew, but she believed it and responded to it in her innermost being, and that's the beginning of faith. God reveals himself to us and he looks for a personal response from us like that.

Faith *acts* on God's revelation. Faith without action is dead according to James, and he asks, 'Was not Rahab the prostitute considered righteous for what she did when she gave lodging to the spies and sent them off in a different direction' (James 2:14-26)?

Faith has very far-reaching *results*. Not only were Rahab and all her family saved (Joshua 6:17,22-24), but also Rahab was one of Jesus' human ancestors! When we obey God and take a step of faith, the consequences are incalculable.

One point needs to be made: Rahab was not saved by either her faith or her works. She was saved by *grace* (God's wonderful, undeserved love), which was received by faith and shown by works. It's the same for every one of us too. (YTL)

Lord, help me to learn from Rahab, who responded to and acted so eagerly on the little she knew of you.

Since God has shown me so much grace, do I need to show someone else some grace in any matter today?

June 20   **Lonely and afraid**

I sought the Lord and he answered me, he delivered me from all my fears.   **Psalm 34:4**

In this gloomy, depressing and often violent world, we may often feel lonely and afraid, particularly if we are in pain, or are depressed, or if we've recently been bereaved or had pressing personal problems which we cannot easily share with others.

I heard of a woman who choked on a piece of cardboard and died, but no one knew about it until she was found *three months later*. It's chilling to think how utterly alone and afraid she must have been — and yet there were people who knew her, and her family lived not far away. There are too many stories like this one. No wonder so many pop songs are about loneliness and fear! Such feelings abound in a society in which people, by and large, do not care for one another. It isn't just old people who have these feelings. In a student survey, eighty-six per cent of students put loneliness as their number one problem, and a well-known psychologist has said that fear is the great threat to mental health in our generation.

God wants to lift us out of fear and loneliness into faith. Read thoughtfully the story of Jesus and the official's son (John 4:43-53) and note the three steps of faith taken by the man whose son was sick. First, he believed in the *power* of Jesus, secondly he believed in the *promise* of Jesus and thirdly he believed in the *person* of Jesus. This is the faith that brings us into a relationship which will, as it grows and deepens, cast out fear and loneliness. (AR)

Lord, I need a closer relationship with you. Help me to make this a priority. Cast out fear and loneliness by your presence.

Is there someone I could befriend?

June 21   Enemy agents

But woe to the earth and the sea, because the devil has gone down to you! He is filled with fury because he knows that his time is short.   **Revelation 12:12**

A discerning author has written these words: 'Much of the church's warfare today is fought by blindfolded soldiers who cannot see the forces ranged against them, who are buffeted by invisible opponents and respond by striking one another.'

The devil is the ruler of this world, influencing governments, prominent leaders, revolutionary armies and terrorist organisations. His hand can be seen in unjust and ungodly political and social structures. He's also the prince of the power of the air, controlling the media and much else that influences our minds and lives.

Here are some of the goals of the so-called revolution by stealth which communists are engaged in all over the world:

The breakdown of cultural standards or morality by promoting pornography and obscenity in books, magazines, motion pictures, radio and television.

The elimination of all laws governing obscenity by calling them censorship and a violation of free speech and a free press.

The control of free positions on radio, television and motion pictures.

The discrediting of the family as an institution.

The presentation of homosexuality, degeneracy and promiscuity as normal, natural and healthy.

The degradation of all forms of artistic expression.

The elimination of prayer or any form of religious expression from schools.

These are just a few of the strategies inspired by the enemy of Christ. We need to be aware of them all and to apply all the principles of spiritual warfare to our own lives. (AR)

Lord, help me to know the enemy in whatever form he shows himself in my life and experience today.

Do I need to be more aware of Christ's victory on the cross over the spiritual enemy?

June 22   Where there's death, there's hope

Greater love has no-one than this, that one lay down his life for his friends.   John 15:13

Jesus was willing to lay down his life for us, both in service and in death, for two main reasons. First, he knew that it was only through the untold agony of the cross that there could be forgiveness for men, and it was for this cause that he had come into the world.

Second, 'for the joy set before him [he] endured the cross' (Hebrews 12:2). He knew that the best was yet to be.

187

Paul, along with the other disciples, accepted the pain of following Jesus for the same two reasons. First, although his sufferings could never atone for sin, he saw that 'I fill up in my flesh what is still lacking in regard to Christ's afflictions, for the sake of his Body, which is the church' (Colossians 1:24). His sufferings were necessary for the sake of others, that through his weakness Christ's power might touch and transform many lives.

Second, he knew that 'our present sufferings are not worth comparing with the glory that will be revealed in us' (Romans 8:18). He was abounding in hope.

In contrast, when we are not willing for the cost of discipleship, and for the price of spiritual renewal, it reveals that we are holding on to our lives, clinging to our temporal privileges and insecure in the love of God. We are afraid that if we let go, God may leave us with nothing but himself! (D)

How can I encourage someone who is going through a time of difficulty?

Pray that God will give that person the assurance of the good or glory that is going to result from his present suffering.

June 23   Discouragements in evangelism

We are hard-pressed on every side, but not crushed.
                                                    2 Corinthians 4:8

Few things will be more crushing or depressing than the passive indifference we encounter when we seek to bring people the most glorious truth on earth. I am never more vulnerable to attacks of depression than just after preaching or speaking to those who desperately need Christ but who remain totally unconcerned. . . However, Paul, profoundly conscious of the astonishing privilege of being called to be a minister for Christ, said this: 'Since through God's mercy we have this ministry, we do not lose heart' (2 Corinthians 4:1). We go on preaching Jesus Christ as Lord.

Paul also knew the crushing burden of physical and mental tiredness in evangelistic work. Even after a simple evangelistic service, the effort of preaching Christ and seeking to convince men about him, has frequently left me drained and exhausted. I can think of few activities that are more demanding. Yet how many of us have known anything approaching Paul's suffering for the gospel: beaten, stoned, shipwrecked, in constant physical danger, on frequent journeys, toil, hardships, sleepless nights, hunger and thirst, in cold and exposure (2 Corinthians 11:24-28)? If anyone might be tempted to give up through tiredness, pain or suffering, certainly Paul might have done. Yet triumphantly he asserts: 'We do not lose heart. Though outwardly we are wasting away, yet inwardly we are being renewed day by day. For our light and momentary troubles [!] are achieving for us an eternal glory that far outweighs them all' (2 Corinthians 4:16,17). (IBIE)

Lord, I pray for discouraged evangelists, especially. . .

Is my church hard-pressed, crushed or simply not engaged in evangelism?

June 24   **Judgment and evangelism**

Just as man is destined to die once, and after that to face judgment, so Christ was sacrificed once to take away the sins of many people; and he will appear a second time, not to bear sin, but to bring salvation to those who are waiting for him.
                                                      Hebrews 9:27,28

The judgment is to be for Christians and non-Christians. 'We must *all* appear before the judgment seat of Christ, that each one may receive what is due to him for the things done while in the body, whether good or bad' (2 Corinthians 5:10). Weymouth's translation is: 'We all have to appear *without disguise* before the tribunal of Christ.' I like that. We're so good at hiding behind our masks — the sanctified look, the keen expression, the charismatic countenance — while inwardly seething and rebellious perhaps! When we appear before Christ we shall be seen without disguises and as we really are.

Non-Christians will also be seen as they really are — without hope, without God, without Christ, and destined for outer darkness.

We must not forget this judgment to come. A Christian leader in Scotland has said that the failure to preach judgment in that country has cut the nerve cord of evangelism for years. If there's no judgment and everyone's going to be all right in the end, why bother to evangelise? Instead of calling the prodigal home, we might just as well make him comfortable in the pigsty. But Jesus taught that future judgment was a reality and so we must take it seriously and be urgent about it — 'Since, then, we know what it is to fear the Lord, we try to persuade men' — and consistent in our lives — 'What we are is plain to God, and I hope it is also plain to your conscience' (2 Corinthians 5:11). (YTL)

Have I thought through the implications of future judgment?

Father, show me my inconsistencies.

June 25   The Lord — my peace

He makes me lie down in green pastures, he leads me beside quiet waters, he restores my soul. He guides me in paths of righteousness for his name's sake.   Psalm 23:2,3

A true, deep peace of mind, heart and conscience is desperately rare today. Every year over thirty million working days are lost because of depression and nervous illness alone. And the National Health Service bill for tranquillisers and pep pills runs at £130 million a year.

These verses breathe a glorious atmosphere of peace. *Lying down* suggests contentment and rest. *Green pastures* speak of the tender, sweet grasses which are always rich, fresh and satisfying. There's nothing stagnant about the *quiet waters* mentioned here; they're refreshing and peaceful. *Restoring* makes one think of something broken being mended. Today we see all around us broken hearts, homes, marriages, lives and health.

Only Jesus can make these magnificent promises come true for us. The New Testament is full of references to the peace he offers. The gospel is called 'the gospel of peace' (Ephesians 6:15). Six times God is called 'the God of peace' (e.g. Philippians 4:9). 'The fruit of the Spirit is . . . peace' (Galatians 5:22). The most common greeting in the New Testament letters is 'grace and peace' (e.g. Colossians 1:2). Jesus promised peace to his disciples (John 14:27; 16:33), and Paul prayed that the Christians in Rome and Colossae would be filled with peace (Romans 14:17; Colossians 3:15). (YTL)

Teach me, Lord, to be content whatever the circumstances (Philippians 4:11).

Do I really have inner peace all the time? How should this show in what I do or don't do today?

June 26   **The impact of worship**

Exalt the Lord our God and worship at his footstool; he is holy.   **Psalm 99:5**

Clearly it would be wrong to *use* worship as a *tool* for evangelism. True worship must always be first and foremost Godward in its direction, even though the expression of worship, certainly in terms of serving and giving, may bring much blessing to other people. But when we are taken up with worship, and when we are unashamed of the fact that we are in love with God and in love with one another, that can be very powerful indeed.

The world today is starved of love, suffocated with words, bereft of joy, and lacking in peace. Therefore 'a praising community preaches to answer questions raised by its praise'. So often, today, evangelism is crippled by the prevailing apathy. Comparatively few people are asking serious questions about God, partly because there is little or nothing which they see or hear to awaken them to any sense of his reality. But when Christians are found to be really worshipping God, loving him, serving him, excited with him, and when their worship makes them into a caring community of love, then questions will certainly be asked, leading to excellent opportunities for sharing the good news of Christ. (IBIE)

Does our worship strike awe into the hearts of unbelievers (1 Corinthians 14:25)?

Father, I pray for next Sunday's worship. . .

June 27   **God's three feasts**

The kingdom of heaven is like a king who prepared a wedding banquet for his son.   **Matthew 22:1**

The first feast that God prepares for us is the gospel feast. The menu is superlative — the peace 'which transcends all understanding' (Philippians 4:7), 'inexpressible and glorious joy' (1 Peter 1:8), 'love that surpasses knowledge' (Ephesians 3:19), total forgiveness (1 John 1:9), life 'to the full' (John 10:10), and 'glorious freedom' (Romans 8:21), among other good things. Ever since the death and resurrection of Jesus, this gospel feast has been ready and God has been saying, 'Come.' But many will not come. What a feast for those who do!

The second feast God spreads for us is the communion feast (Matthew 26:26-29) — a picture of the gospel feast, since we come with empty hands, confessing our sins, to feed on Jesus in our hearts by faith with thanksgiving. The feast is free for us who come, but we need to remember that Jesus paid his life, he gave everything, to make that feast ready and available to us. We also need to remember the Body of Christ — not the bread which is a symbol of it, but ourselves who make up the Body of Christ. Our relationship as we come to this feast must be right with Christ and with every member of his Body, because we are to love him and one another as he loved us.

The third feast is the heavenly feast, a consummation of the gospel feast and the communion feast (Revelation 19:6-9). Those who are invited to that feast will be those who have already responded on earth to his invitation to the gospel feast. All three feasts are feasts of love but in this final one we will really enter into that perfect love of which we have only had foretastes here on earth. (YTL)

Do we Christians look and behave as though we're having a feast?

Thank you, Lord Jesus, for the feasts you have prepared for us here on earth and one day in heaven. Help me to invite others to come.

June 28   Think cosmic

He made known to us the mystery of his will according to his good pleasure, which he purposed in Christ, to be put into effect when the times will have reached their fulfilment — to bring all things in heaven and on earth together under one head, even Christ.   Ephesians 1:9,10

God's master plan is to unite all things in Christ through the cross. It begins with the individual being united to God through Jesus Christ, but it doesn't end there; individuals must then be united with the Body of Christ. As someone has said: 'Christianity which does not begin with the individual does not

begin. But Christianity which ends with the individual, ends.'
Some Christians have over-emphasised individual salvation,
but God wants the whole creation to be redeemed, restored
and made whole. And this healing of creation comes *from* the
individual *through* the church, the Body of Christ, and *out*
into the whole of life.

At the moment we have a divided church and therefore
creation is not being healed as it could and should be. There are
over nine thousand Christian denominations in the world
today! And I have come to realise that Christian unity is vitally
important: Jesus commanded it, prayed for it, died for it and
sent his Spirit for it.

I've no doubt at all that Jesus weeps over the church which is
not one and does not love as he loved it. Bishop Festo
Kivengere said, 'By our many denominations and divisions in
the church we tell the world how much we hate one another.'

We need to repent of our disobedience and our attitudes to
one another, come to the foot of the cross, and open our hearts
to the Spirit of truth and love and to one another, so that we
may become God's peacemakers in the world. (AR)

*Lord, show me and the other members of our church fellow-
ship what things cause you to weep as you look at the way we
live and worship.*

*Do I really accept that Christians should be one? Does the
world see the Christians in our town as one in any sense?*

June 29   Seeing God on his throne

**Whenever the living creatures give glory, honour and thanks
to him who sits on the throne and who lives for ever and ever,
the twenty-four elders fall down before him who sits on the
throne and worship him who lives for ever and ever.**

                                        Revelation 4:9,10

I was once at a conference where we were receiving much deep
spiritual teaching, but after a while I said to the leader, 'We

haven't once worshipped God. Don't you think we ought to?' He replied, 'Oh, yes. We'll have half an hour of hymn singing before the next session.' My heart sank, because worship is far, far more than that.

I'm told that when Handel was asked how he came to write the Messiah, he said, 'I saw the heavens opened and God upon his great white throne.' No wonder he wrote such a paean of worship! Unless we see God on his throne, we will not be able to worship as we should.

The book of Revelation is full of God on his throne and of worship (e.g. chapter 4). Some commentators think that jasper stands for God's utter purity, carnelian for his avenging wrath, an emerald for his gracious mercy and a rainbow as the sign of his covenant love (verse 3). The elders probably represent the whole church. They stand before the throne and see flashes of lightning and blazing lamps, which speak of God's power and his Spirit (verse 5). When the living creatures, who probably represent all nature, give glory to God, the elders fall down and worship; in other words they submit all their nature totally to this awesome, dazzlingly-enthroned, utterly holy God.

We mock God's worth and glory when we sing half-heartedly and mumble the responses. Nothing less than all our nature bowed and submitted to this same God will do. To our worship of him, we must give 'everything we've got'. (YTL)

Am I putting everything I have into my worship?

Father, with the eye of faith, I need to see you on your throne.

June 30   **What'll be missing from heaven?**

Never again will they hunger; never again will they thirst. The sun will not beat upon them, nor any scorching heat.
                                                      Revelation 7:16

There'll be no fear in heaven! 'He who sits on the throne will

195

spread his tent over them' (verse 15). When our children used to have nightmares, they would sometimes run into our bedroom and snuggle down beside us, and as we sheltered them, as it were, they would soon lose their fear and fall asleep. That's a picture of heaven where all our fears will vanish in God's protecting presence.

There'll be no hunger or thirst. That's a picture of complete satisfaction which none of us can ever know fully on earth. But when we see Jesus face to face, we will be completely satisfied — there will be no inner cravings or emptiness.

There will be no suffering: 'The sun will not beat upon them, nor any scorching heat.' There will be no more depressions, neuroses, anxieties, pressures, tensions, tiredness or old age.

There will be no loneliness: 'The Lamb at the centre of the throne will be their shepherd; he will lead them to springs of living water' (verse 17).

There will be no tears: 'God will wipe away every tear from their eyes' (verse 17). Every cause of sadness will disappear in God's presence. We will be comforted beyond measure.

In the absence of these things, we will be free to love and worship perfectly and to enter into the unimaginable joys that 'God has prepared for those who love him' (1 Corinthians 2:9). (YTL)

Father, may your Holy Spirit give me a clearer and truer vision of heaven so that I will see this life and this world in truer, clearer perspective too.

If someone were to tell me, 'You'll be in heaven tomorrow,' how would I react?

JULY
The Church Worldwide

July 1   Does this bride look radiant?

I saw the Holy City, the new Jerusalem, coming down out of heaven from God, prepared as a bride beautifully dressed for her husband.   **Revelation 21:2**

The Bible daringly indicates that our love for the Lord should be one of great intimacy. The essence of the life that God has planned for us is that we should *know* God and his Son Jesus Christ – and the word that John chooses is the one that is often used for a man knowing his wife in the most intimate sexual relationship within marriage. We are called to delight ourselves in the Lord (Psalm 37:4) and told that 'as the bridegroom rejoices over his bride, so will your God rejoice over you' (Isaiah 62:5).

Fervent love, proved by unswerving faithfulness, should be the attitude of the church towards her heavenly bridegroom; and, in return, the promise is that God will continuously pour his love into our hearts by the Holy Spirit. Have we learned to love Christ so deeply that he can expect our faithfulness, no matter what the personal cost may be?

Any bride preparing for her wedding day has to see to many demanding details. Yet they should not be a burden to her, but rather expressions of her love for the bridegroom. As Christians we have a glorious wedding day to look forward to. It is literally out of this world. (IBITC)

197

When did I last tell God that I loved him?

Lord, I love you.

Bible Study: What can be learnt through studying the names/titles given to the church or the pictures used to describe her in the Bible? *Starters:* Matthew 16:18; 1 Corinthians 1:2;12:27; 2 Corinthians 10:3; Ephesians 6:11,12; 2 Timothy 2:3,4; 1 Peter 2:4,9; Revelation 19:7, and see under 'the church worldwide' and 'church fellowships' in index.

July 2   A building still under construction

You are . . . God's building.   **1 Corinthians 3:9**

A *building* is no longer the temple or house of God; it is God's people who are now so called. A building is not to be a 'holy place'; rather God's *people* are called to be a holy people. But God's building is still under construction.

It may be helpful to remember that most buildings under construction look a terrible mess, at least to our untrained eye, until the last stage is reached.

The same is true with our church. The dust and dirt, chaos and confusion, may make it hard to believe that this could really be the temple of God. Yet, if we have faith and patience, the architect and builder is hard at work, and knows very well what he is doing. On this earth we can never claim to have arrived. The apostle Paul was well aware of this in his own life (Philippians 3:12-14).

As a church we can never afford to stand still. We can never be complacent. Nor should we ever lose heart. Always our vision should be on the promise of our future inheritance, when we shall have 'a building from God, an eternal house in heaven, not built by human hands' (2 Corinthians 5:1). (IBITC)

Meditate on the foundation of God's building (1 Corinthians 3:11).

Which is receiving more time, money and effort in our church — the material building or the people?

I will take you as my own people, and I will be your God.
Exodus 6:7

'The chief end of God in creation,' wrote Alan Stibbs, 'was to have a people of whom he could say, "I am theirs; they are mine. I will be their God and they shall be my people."' What an amazing privilege to belong to the community of the people of God!

In the Old Testament God is referred to as lord, creator, father, judge, king, helper, redeemer, rock, shield, defender — and Israel as his own, his people, his son, his vine, his servant, his vineyard, his bride and his flock.

Always it is God's *sovereignty* that is stressed. God delivered his people from Egypt, established his covenant and law, cared for them, led them through the wilderness, gave them a kingdom and sent them prophets, rescued them from exile, and, when the time was right, sent them his Son.

In contrast God's people have a history of failure, disobedience, rebellion, backsliding, sin, apostasy. Yet even in the midst of judgment, God offers *salvation* and promises of fresh love and mercy if only they will return to him (Ezekiel 36:24-26; Hosea 14:1-8).

In the New Testament there is the same picture of God's sovereignty, man's rebellion and God's salvation. The angel told Zechariah that their son would 'make ready a people prepared for the Lord' (Luke 1:17). When John grew up, he preached repentance so that the people would be ready to hear the good news which Jesus brought when he came to 'save his people from their sins' (Matthew 1:21). (YTL)

Father, help us to be much more conscious of being the people of God.

What should the people of God be like?

When Israel was a child, I loved him, and out of Egypt I called my son.   Hosea 11:1

The word used for the church, *ekklesia*, means those who have been called out or summoned together. Sometimes people speak of going to church as though this was doing God a favour, rather like tipping your cap to someone or handing over a tip. Instead, belonging to the church is a fantastic privilege, because God has called us to be part of his family, comprising people of all generations and nationalities for all time.

God's people are called *out of* sin, darkness and death (1 Peter 2:9). The clear division between Christians and non-Christians is between those who have responded to God's call and those who have not (Hosea 11:2).

God's people are called *for* a relationship with God and his Son, Jesus Christ (John 17:3). Jesus called his disciples in the first place that they might be with him (Mark 3:14).

God's people are called *to* a future inheritance (1 Peter 5:10). We have a foretaste here and now of that glory, but what it will really be like is beyond our comprehension (Romans 8:17; 1 Corinthians 2:9).

God's people are called *to be* a special people for God's own possession (Deuteronomy 7:6). He called them because he loved them and wanted them to belong to him. (YTL)

Father, thank you for the great privilege of having been called into your worldwide eternal family.

Do we as a church appreciate and enjoy our calling from God?

I have brought you glory on earth by completing the work you gave me to do.   John 17:4

In Jesus' prayer, the eight-fold purpose of the church is stated or implied (John 17:1-26).

Jesus' main purpose was to glorify God, so that must be the church's primary aim, too. We are to do this by worshipping God and offering spiritual sacrifices of praise, possessions and persons.

Secondly, we are to keep God's word. Jesus said, 'I gave them the words you gave me and they accepted them' (verse 8); the implication is that, having accepted God's word, we are to pass it on intact as the truth, the whole truth and nothing but the truth.

Then, too, the church is to be united in love: 'May they be brought to complete unity to let the world know that you sent me and have loved them even as you have loved me' (verse 23), Jesus says. If people want to see real love, they ought to be able to see it by looking at the Christian church!

Next, the church is to be filled with joy: 'I say these things while I am still in the world, so that they may have the full measure of my joy within them' (verse 13). Do people expect joy in our churches?

Fifthly, the church is to overcome Satan. Jesus prayed that his disciples would be protected from the evil one (verse 15). To be effective against Satan, we need to keep close together.

The sixth purpose of the church is to be in the world but not of it 'for they are not of the world any more than I am of the world' (verse 14). The Christian church must be in the world, but the world must not be in the church.

The church must also bring others to Christ through the gospel message (verses 20, 21).

The final, glorious purpose of the church is to be with Jesus in his glory for ever (verse 24). (YTL)

In what ways do we fall short of Jesus' ideal for his church?

'Pray in' to our church situation what Jesus prayed for his disciples.

A people alight

You are the light of the world.

Matthew 5:14

By using the illustration of light, Jesus was showing the powerful impact true Christian living can have. Yet tragically we have been foghorns more often than lights. How frequently we hear people say that Christians fail to practise what they preach! Unless we glorify God in our lives, our words are wasted. 'What the world needs to see,' said Duncan Campbell, 'is the wonder and beauty of God-possessed personalities; men and women with the life of God pulsating within, who practise the presence of God and consequently make it easy for others to believe in God.'

Paul reminded 'all in Rome who are loved by God' that they were 'called to be saints' (Romans 1:7). And a saint, in the New Testament sense, is not someone who is known for his super-piety; he is simply a true Christian who is set apart from sin for God. He has been called out of darkness into God's marvellous light. He has been called into the people of God, and his life must show something of the family likeness.

Writing to the church at Corinth, Paul uses a chain of Old Testament quotations to remind the Christians that they are to be separated from the spiritually and morally pagan society around them in order to be the temple and people of the living God (2 Corinthians 6:16-18). (IBITC)

How can we be righteous without being self-righteous?

Lord, what sort of impact should we, as Christians, be having on this area?

July 7

One for Christ's sake

May they be brought to complete unity to let the world know that you sent me and have loved them even as you have loved me.

John 17:23

The divisions within the church destroy much of the fellow-ship, love, prayer, evangelism, strength and support that Christians in a given locality ought to enjoy together. . . In many parts of the world we find tiny and struggling congregations. In the same village or small town we find a few Anglicans trying to maintain and heat a large Gothic or Victorian structure; down the road a few Methodists are doing the same in their less pretentious building; round the corner the Baptists are likewise having a battle with inflation and waning interest; and within a stone's throw a similar story holds for the United Reformed, the Roman Catholics (apart from reasonable attendance at mass), the Brethren of the Elim Church. Each little group could benefit immeasurably from the others; yet still separations persist. No wonder God is hesitant about blessing their individual efforts! No wonder the impact on the rest of the town is negligible!

Most of all, the disunity within the church is an offence to God, who, in his love, naturally longs to see his family united; it is an affront to Christ who, by his death, broke down all those walls of hostility that divide us, so as to reconcile us all to God in one Body; and it constantly grieves the Holy Spirit who has come to dwell within us to produce the fruit and gifts that are necessary for a truly united church. (IBITC)

Father, help us to hear what your Spirit is saying to us about unity today.

Do all the Christians in my town ever meet together? Should we?

July 8   A new covenant

'The time is coming,' declares the Lord, 'when I will make a new covenant with the house of Israel and with the house of Judah.'   Jeremiah 31:31

The Old Covenant failed because the people did not, could not, and did not even want to keep God's law. So God promised

203

that there would be a new covenant. It would be new in several ways including this: that God would write his law in their minds and hearts (Jeremiah 31:33) and would put a new power and spirit in them (Ezekiel 26:36) so that they would want to keep his commandments. This new spirit was the Holy Spirit and it was he who would write God's law in people's hearts and give them the power to live new lives. Jesus told Nicodemus about this when he was teaching him that he must be born again through the Spirit. Nicodemus was someone who lived a decent life by human standards. But it was a legalistic life because God's law and Spirit were not within him.

Once, Bishop Taylor Smith, when preaching on the need for the new birth, said, 'You could even be an archdeacon and not be born again.' Afterwards the archdeacon of that church wrote to him saying, 'Mine has been a hard legal service. I did not know what the matter was until you spoke about me in the service yesterday.' Later that archdeacon experienced the new birth and his life was transformed.

Others are born again through the Spirit, but then they revert to trying to keep rules. Paul wrote to such: 'Are you so foolish? After beginning with the Spirit, are you now trying to attain your goal by human effort' (Galatians 3:3)? The wonderful thing about the new covenant is that God does in us, both at conversion and afterwards, what we could never do for ourselves. (YTL)

'To do your will, O my God, is my desire; your law is within my heart' (Psalm 40:8).

What have I been struggling with that I need to hand over to God claiming his new-covenant promises?

July 9   **In trials, comfort**

Praise be to the God and Father of our Lord Jesus Christ, the Father of compassion and the God of all comfort, who comforts us in all our troubles, so that we can comfort those in

any trouble with the comfort we ourselves have received from God.   2 Corinthians 1:3,4

An oyster secretes layers and layers of a certain substance to cover an irritating object — and eventually a pearl results.

What or who is the irritating object in your life? Whatever or whoever it is, God wants to overcome it with layer upon layer of his love and forgiveness, until the jewel that he planned is created.

Put a dirty, black lump of coal under extreme heat and pressure for a long time — and you have a diamond.

What are the pressures in your life? Whether these are to do with your relationships, your work or your health, God will protect you in every conceivable situation if you stay close to him. In Psalm 91 there are twenty-five promises of God for those who cling to him in their trials.

Having experienced difficulties and God's help and comfort in them at first hand, you will be able to help and encourage others. (YTL)

Meditate on what God promises in Psalm 91 and notice any conditions involved.

Father, I name to you the thing that is bothering me at this time. I ask not only that it may not harm me, but also that you will use it to produce something beautiful in my life.

July 10   Everybody counts

From him [Christ] the whole Body, joined and held together by every supporting ligament, grows and builds itself up in love as each part does its work.   Ephesians 4:16

I believe profoundly that in any local church the ministry involves the whole congregation. I once dislocated my collar bone and I couldn't do anything properly until it was put back again. Similarly, it is only when we are rightly related to one another that the Body of Christ can work properly. A fisherman can't fish effectively if his nets are broken. So Christians cannot be effective in the world unless people are working harmoniously together.

All too often the local church is like a narrow-necked bottle, with the vicar being the cork in the bottle and the sediment at the bottom of the bottle being the pew fillers. Someone remarked that if you shook the bottle really hard, you might make the cork fly right out. That's a bit ruthless. There are other ways!

In the church I have been involved with, we have tried to learn from the New Testament principles of shared leadership. We have a system of elders, for instance, and we try to build up strong relationships with each other. I believe that the strength, harmony and love of the leadership of a church will determine the strength, harmony and love of the whole congregation. Work hard on relationships with leaders.

Then the congregation is divided into area groups for the purposes of pastoral help and counselling.

This is just one way of working out the principle of shared ministry. (AR)

Lord, help me to see the full potential of our church fellowship and give me real love for its members.

List what I do in the church fellowship, and ask about each job: 'Did I take it on because someone twisted my arm, because nobody else would do it, or because God clearly called me to do it, and the leaders recognised and confirmed this?'

July 11   Grow up

The Body of Christ may . . . become mature. Then we will no longer be infants, tossed back and forth by the waves, and blown here and there by every wind of teaching . . . Instead, speaking the truth in love . . . Ephesians 4:13,14,15.

It's a mark of our immaturity and part of the devil's tactics that we label each other and stay inside our own defensive circles, criticising anyone outside who says or does things differently, and refusing to listen to what God has to say to us through one another. We need to be mature enough not to be suspicious of each other; we need to get to know and love each other, because it is only 'with all the saints' that we can 'grasp how wide and long and high and deep is the love of Christ' (Ephesians 3:18). As we mature as Christians we will grow closer to one another.

Better teaching is vital to maturity. We need to train people to stand guard against false teachers and answer questions about the faith. Someone said, 'The average layman is as able to meet an aggressive agnostic or atheist as a boy with a toy gun to meet a tank.' Why do people get caught up in the cults? Because they are confused, and along comes someone who knows exactly what he believes and why!

And we must learn to share — particularly our weaknesses. We must be real with one another. One Swedish minister has put, near a coat hook in his hall, a sign which reads: 'Put your masks here.' Often one person is unwilling to take off his mask and share his weakness, because another person is hiding his real pain under a triumphant mask!

If you are a Christian leader — may I ask, 'Who counsels you?' I have at least two people to whom I can say anything any time. We all need such counsellors. (AR)

Lord, show me where my actions are immature and help me to mature in Christ with and through other members of the fellowship.

What opportunities, if any, are there for members of our church family to 'speak the truth in love' to one another?

July 12   How should we treat our leaders?

Now we ask you, brothers, to respect those who work hard among you, who are over you in the Lord and who admonish

207

you. Hold them in the highest regard in love because of their
work.   1 Thessalonians 5:12,13

We must hold our leaders 'in the highest regard in love' not
because we agree with them on everything, or understand all
they do, or because of their status or the fact that we
nominated them —but 'because of their work'. A leader's work
is very hard and his position makes him vulnerable to much
criticism. Worldly leaders may overcome this by developing
thick skins, but the Christian leader has to remain open and
loving and vulnerable. Leaders will make mistakes like
everyone else, but we are nevertheless to respect them and love
them because of the work they do.

We are, secondly, to imitate their faith (Hebrews 13:7). We
are not to imitate or worship their personalities — but their
faith. In the next verse we have the object of that faith — 'Jesus
Christ is the same yesterday and today and for ever.' So often
Christians lean too heavily on their leaders and this is dangerous because leaders are fallible and they come and go. What we
should do is to imitate their faith in Jesus Christ who will never
fail us and never leave us. Even if we don't like our leader, we
are to imitate his faith, as he shows us Jesus.

We are to 'obey' our leaders and 'submit to their authority'
(Hebrews 13:17). Leaders cannot lead or serve unless we receive
their leadership or service. Peter tried to dictate the service
which he would be prepared to receive from his leader, Jesus
(John 13:6-11), but we need to accept the leading or service of
our leaders whether we understand it or not. What Jesus did in
washing the disciples' feet was radical and what our leaders do
may be radical at times, for God is a God of movement and he
may want to move us, through our leaders, into fresh ways of
thought or action. (YTL)

*Has this anything to say to me in relation to my leaders or the
people I try to serve?*

Father, help me to trust, respect and love my leaders.

How long, O Lord, must I call for help, but you do not listen? Or cry out to you, 'Violence!' but you do not save?

Habakkuk 1:2

Habakkuk has three problems of faith: unanswered prayer, unabated and unchecked evil and a situation which seems to be out of control. Habakkuk had prayed earnestly but the national and international situation was as bad as ever. What was worse, God was not only allowing the cruel and violent Babylonians to go on existing, he was also going to use them for his purposes (1:5-11)! No wonder Habakkuk asks God whether he's still in control!

There are three things which help to turn the prophet's problems of faith into triumphs of faith. First, he is absolutely honest with God (1:2-4). 'Why aren't you listening? Why aren't you doing anything? I'm appalled and amazed!' he cries out.

Secondly, he reaffirms his faith in the person and nature of God (1:12-17). It all sounds a little hollow at first but he says, 'You are my God, and I know you are holy, and pure and a rock and everlasting.' Telling out what he knows to be true about God, encourages his own faith, and as he focuses on God and catches a fresh vision of his greatness, this faith grows.

Thirdly, he waits and listens for God's answers (2:1), which could be paraphrased as: 'I want you to go through these trials so that you can learn deeper lessons of faith to share with others' (2:2); 'My timing is perfect — no matter what appearances suggest' (2:3); 'My control is complete' (2:4-20).

Bring your problem of faith to God in complete honesty, fix your thoughts on God, praising him and waiting for his answers, until you have a fresh vision of his greatness and cry out in your heart, 'What a wonderful God you are!' (YTL)

Have I problem of faith which needs to be brought honestly to God?

Father, what a wonderful God you are! You have . . . (mention what God has done or is doing for the world, for you and for others).

Everyone who loves has been born of God and knows God.
1 John 4:7

The first test of the fruit of the Spirit is love (Galatians 5:22).
John has in mind both love for God and for other people, with
a particular emphasis on *other Christians*. If I really know
God, and am a member of his family by faith in Jesus Christ,
then I should have a God-given love for other Christians. If I
am in Christ, and you are in Christ, then you are my brother or
sister. We are related, so there ought to be a bond of love
between us. There is something radically wrong if we do not
love one another.

This love is not just emotional though it may well include the
emotions. Essentially it is practical. 'This is how we know what
love is: Jesus Christ laid down his life for us' (1 John 3:16). John
continues: 'And we ought to lay down our lives for our
brothers. If anyone has material possessions and sees his
brother in need but has no pity on him, how can the love of
God be in him? Dear children, let us not love with words or
tongue but with actions and in truth' (1 John 3:16-18).

How far do we love one another like that? Here is the vital
distinction between religion and spiritual reality. In the name
of religion terrible things have been done all down the
centuries. The religious leaders of Jesus' day murdered him.
Our local churches may be religious; they may also be full of
petty squabbling and resentment which grieve the Spirit of
God. But where you have a group of people who really know
God, there you will *always* find love.

Has God given you a real love for other Christians? You
may not always *like* them at first sight; you may not always
agree with them; you may not always *understand* them. But
do you *love* them? Do you see them as your brothers and
sisters in Christ? If so, that's a very good test that you know the
God of love. (YTL)

Help me, Lord, to become 'rooted and established in love'
(Ephesians 3:17).

*Take any opportunity you are given today to show love
to a Christian brother or sister.*

July 15   What is God like?

Our God is in heaven; he does whatever pleases him.
                                                Psalm 115:3

God is personal. Unlike the idols the heathen worship, he
speaks and acts and can be known personally the moment we
commit ourselves personally to him through Jesus.

God is spiritual, and must be worshipped 'in spirit and in
truth' (John 4:24). Our spirits are not just our minds or
emotions but the innermost parts of our beings and it is from
these depths, and in accordance with the truth of his word,
that we are to worship God.

God is holy: 'in him there is no darkness at all' (1 John 1:5);
and his 'eyes are too pure to look on evil' (Habakkuk 1:13).

God is just. 'Will not the Judge of all the earth do right'
(Genesis 18:25)? This is both a comfort and a warning.

God is eternal, named as the great I AM (Exodus 3:14): a title
which Jesus claimed for himself (John 8:56-59).

God is almighty. 'I know that you can do all things,' a
humbled Job tells the Lord (Job 42:2). In the physical and
spiritual realm all things are possible with God (Matthew
19:26; Luke 1:37), as long as they are consistent with his
nature. There are at least three things God cannot do because
they are *not* consistent with his character: he cannot overlook
sin, ignore the sinner, or deny himself.

God is all-present. Psalm 139 proclaims this truth to comfort
those who feel alone and afraid and to warn those who think
they can hide or run away from God.

God is all-knowing. 'Everything is uncovered and laid bare
before the eyes of him to whom we must give account'
(Hebrews 4:13).

God is all-loving. 'As a father has compassion on his
children, so the Lord has compassion on those who fear him'
(Psalm 103:13). But he can only be Father in the full sense of the

211

word to those who trust in Jesus — the One who perfectly revealed him (John 14:8,9). (YTL)

Continue to study the character of God in the Bible.

Father, I worship you because you are . . .

July 16   God's giants

Moses said to God, 'Who am I that I should go to Pharaoh and bring the Israelites out of Egypt?' And God said, 'I will be with you.'
                                                                Exodus 3:11,12

Hudson Taylor wrote: 'All God's giants have been weak men who did great things for God because they reckoned on his being with them. They counted on God's faithfulness.' The whole history of God working through his people illustrates this. Moses was a most reluctant missionary. David seemed pathetically young and inexperienced to be God's champion against Goliath. Nehemiah and friends were dubbed 'those feeble Jews' by their enemies. Jeremiah was frightened and overawed by God's call. The disciples were a motley band of ordinary folk — nervous and fearful. Even Jesus was 'despised and rejected by men'. All these, with the exception of Jesus, were men with rather obvious weaknesses, who sometimes fell into serious sin of one sort or another.

Yet God used Moses to rescue two million people from Egypt, David to slay a giant, Nehemiah to rebuild a city, Jeremiah to prophesy to a nation, the disciples to bring about the greatest revolution the world has ever known, and Jesus to procure the world's salvation.

J. B. Phillips' book title is most apt for many of us: 'Your God is too small!' Because our vision of God's greatness and faithfulness is so infinitesimally small, we see only a little of his power and glory. (PL)

Lord, I am available for you today. Please use me in the way you want to.

Have I ever realised before that my weaknesses can be a greater spiritual asset than my strengths — provided I offer them to God (2 Corinthians 12:10)?

How are the mighty fallen?

But the thing David had done displeased the Lord.
                                        2 Samuel 11:27

David was at the height of his career. He was the hero and idol of his nation, with victory after victory to his credit. It was at this moment that he crashed. The downfall of many individuals and many nations and empires has been caused by the sin that David committed — adultery — or by other forms of sexual licence and indulgence. Why did David fall in this way?

His character and temperament made him very prone to this particular sin. He was every inch a man — virile and strong — and at the same time he was sensitive and romantic — a poet and musician. All of us are vulnerable in some way, if not sexually.

His background and situation made him vulnerable too. His childhood had not been a happy one and his domestic life with Michal could not have been easy (1 Chronicles 15:29). As well as this, twenty years before, David had taken more wives and concubines from Jerusalem (2 Samuel 5:13), and this was expressly against God's law and David knew it. He never fully controlled his sexual appetite —this was a permanent weakness in his character, even after he had been forgiven and cleansed. We will find this same thing: sin indulged in 'just this once' may well leave a permanent scar and weakness.

When the other kings went off to war that spring, David stayed in Jerusalem (2 Samuel 11:1). He was lazy. Or you could say that he was in the wrong place — a very dangerous place to be for anyone. Perhaps he was lonely too, and in this state of mind, feelings — whether of fear, depression, bitterness, anxiety or passion — can easily dominate a person.

In this moment of laziness and loneliness, David saw a very

beautiful woman bathing, and his pulse quickened. So far he had only been tempted — he had not sinned. He could have brought the matter to the Lord and claimed his victory. Instead he allowed desire to grow until it gave birth to sin. (YTL)

Where am I most vulnerable? Are there any situations I should avoid?

Father, when the devil whispers, 'Just this once,' help me to see him for the liar and deceiver that he is and to claim the victory in Jesus' name.

July 18   Pride goes before a fall

He [Peter] replied, 'Lord, I am ready to go with you to prison and to death.' Jesus answered, 'I tell you, Peter, before the cock crows today, you will deny three times that you know me.'
Luke 22:33,34

Jesus' prediction came true. Peter did deny Jesus. He failed miserably. He made one mistake after another. He slept when he should have been praying in the Garden of Gethsemane (Matthew 26:40). He acted in haste without thinking (John 18:10), foolishly and uselessly cutting off someone's ear, and showing that he had completely failed to understand what was happening to Jesus and why. He followed Jesus at a distance (Luke 22:54), got separated from the other disciples and found himself in the wrong company (Matthew 26:69-75), and finally denied and disowned Jesus three times. He was like someone standing on the top of the stairs, who loses his footing and comes crashing down — bumpety-bumpety-bumpety-bump! Why did he fail? Spiritual pride was the root cause. And this had to be dealt with.

Jesus knew that Simon would be put to the test and that he would fail. And he said to him, 'I have prayed for you, Simon, that your faith may not fail' (Luke 22:32). I believe that through all that happened, Jesus was saying to Peter, "You're going to make your mark in the world as my ambassador, but I can't use you while you're proud like this. You will not know the real power of the Spirit until your pride is broken. But when you come crashing down, as you will, I can pick you up and forgive you and recommission you to go out in *my* strength and *my* love, conscious of your own inability and weaknesses, to a needy world.' (YTL)

Is the Lord saying to me:
  'These inward trials I employ,
  From self and pride to set thee free'?
                              (John Newton)

Lord, thank you that you pray for your people. Please, Lord, pray for me, as you did for Simon, that my faith may not fail.

July 19   Flaming darts

Take up the shield of faith, with which you can extinguish all the flaming arrows of the evil one.   Ephesians 6:16

A dart is noiseless and swift, especially the type that is expelled from a blow-gun by hunters in certain primitive societies. Without warning, its sudden sting pierces its target and spreads its lethal poison.

All too often, Satan has been able to do some of his most destructive work in Christians' lives while they are experiencing the glow of some spiritual success, some heightened awareness of God. Perhaps it was the inspiration of a powerful sermon, or a special insight gained in a time of rich meditation on the Scriptures, that lulled the believer into a less-than-alert attitude. Just at that point, Satan hurled a flaming dart that found its mark where he was unprotected and unsuspecting. The agony was intensified by the shock to his spirit. It may even have caused him to doubt the validity of the spiritual experience which he had just enjoyed.

Remember Paul's caution to us: 'So, if you think you are

standing firm, be careful that you don't fall' (1 Corinthians 10:12)! Satan attacks without warning, and when we least expect it.

With such demonic skills at his disposal, the enemy is not one to trifle with. It is inappropriate, to say the least, and downright foolhardy at the most, to make jokes about the devil. He is deadly serious in his war against God. (HW)

Father, I pray that you will remind me of this warning when I am on the crest of a spiritual wave and not alert.

How, in practical terms, does the 'shield of faith' 'extinguish all the flaming arrows of the evil one'?

July 20   The world and the flesh

Everything in the world — the cravings of sinful man, the lust of his eyes and the boasting of what he has and does — comes not from the Father but from the world.   1 John 2:16

Our warfare is against Satan, and two of his most powerful means of defeating us are the world and the flesh.

The *flesh*, or the self-life, is that part of us which is naturally self-centred and hostile to God (Romans 8:5-8). 'The acts of the sinful nature are obvious,' Paul writes, and he proceeds to spell them out (Galatians 5:19-21). God will frequently bring us to the point where we're so conscious of the power of our self-life, that we acknowledge that we cannot deal with it by ourselves and then recognise that it already is, or that it ought to be, on the cross. 'Those who belong to Jesus Christ have crucified the sinful nature with its passions and desires' (Galatians 5:24).

The *world* refers to everything, even that which may be good in itself, which is not directly under the control of Christ. Cain's whole life is an illustration of a worldly life — one lived away from God: 'So Cain went out from the presence of the Lord' (Genesis 4:16). Anything that is done *away from the presence of the Lord* is the world. Even Cain's worship was of the world, because it was *his* idea of sacrifice and not God's. In the same way, our religious activities may be of the world, if they are not of God and for God.

Because Cain was away from the presence of the Lord, everything he did was worldly. He built a city and his descendants became involved in agriculture or music (the arts) or manual skills (crafts) — but all these things were of the world (Genesis 4:17-22).

All these aspects of human life and achievement need to be brought under the control of Christ if they are to be of God and not of the world. As Christians, we shouldn't let the world, and its ruler, the devil, have all the best tunes, arts, crafts, cities, commerce, and other skills and achievements! (YTL)

How can I help to reclaim the world for Christ?

Father, I pray that having crucified my self-life, I may 'live in the Spirit' and 'not gratify the desires of the sinful nature' (Galatians 5:16).

July 21   Jesus believed in Satan

The field is the world, and the good seed stands for the sons of the kingdom. The weeds are the sons of the evil one, and the enemy who sows them is the devil.   Matthew 13:38,39

As soon as Jesus began his public ministry, he 'was led by the Spirit into the desert to be tempted by the devil' (Matthew 4:1). Later, when Jesus began to concentrate on his coming sufferings and death, the supreme purpose of his earthly ministry, the battle against Satan is again explicitly mentioned. When Simon Peter resisted the teaching of Jesus 'that he must go to Jerusalem and suffer many things . . . and that he must be killed', Jesus rebuked him: 'Out of my sight, Satan! You are a stumbling block to me; you do not have in mind the things of God, but the things of men' (Matthew 16:21,23). Satan constantly tries to blind our minds to the purpose of God, and tempts us to see man as the centre and standard of reference. Then again, when Jesus was facing the ordeal of the cross, he had another tremendous spiritual battle in the Garden of Gethsemane — a battle won by prayer and obedience to his Father's will.

Jesus also talked about 'the evil one' snatching away the seed of God's word (Matthew 13:19); he warned that the enemy who sowed weeds in the field was the devil (Matthew 13:39); he told the Jewish leaders: 'You belong to your father, the devil' (John 8:44); and he prayed that his disciples should be kept from the evil one (John 17:15). Much of his healing ministry involved the casting out of evil spirits and demons.

There was no doubt about the power and personality of the devil in the life, teaching and ministry of Jesus. (D)

Lord, give me a healthy fear of Satan and open my eyes to see his activity in my life and in the lives of those whom you want me to reach out to or become involved with.

What is my attitude to the devil? How does it compare with Jesus' attitude?

July 22   Violence

The earth was corrupt in God's sight and was full of violence.
Genesis 6:11
They [the wicked] clothe themselves with violence. Psalm 73:6

There is nothing new about violence. Herod, King of Judea in New Testament times, was the Stalin of his day, slaughtering his relatives, officers, rebels and even baby boys.

People may become violent for all sorts of reasons. Mao Tse -tung said, 'Political power comes out of the barrel of a gun . . . The gun must never slip from the grasp of the communist party.' Many, like him, have used violence for *political* ends.

Certain *social* conditions seem to be conducive to violence.

There is more crime in big cities and among socially deprived groups than elsewhere, for instance.

Personal factors may be involved. 'Violence is an involuntary quest for identity,' wrote Marshall McLuhan. Today, when the individual may easily feel pathetically insignificant and irrelevant, he is liable to lash out in self-defence or to attract attention.

Lack of *spiritual* certainty may also lead to feelings of frustration and despair, and so to violence. Many people are asking, 'Does God care? Is there a God who controls the chaotic world we live in?'

Sometimes people say to me, 'If I were God, I'd have made a better job of things!' But would they? How many of us would love a world filled with hatred and violence? How many of us would die in order to save people from their sins? Would we willingly suffer violent death so that some might know God's forgiveness and love? Read Isaiah chapter 53 thoughtfully. (PL)

Lord, it's so easy to react violently to violence. Help me not to do that. Help me instead to pray for those in the grip of this evil.

Meditate on 1 Peter 2:23,24, in preparation for a time when you may have to face violence in some form or other.

July 23   Protected from all evil

Surely he will save you from the fowler's snare and from the deadly pestilence.   **Psalm 91:3**

This psalm shows how great God's protection is over his people. 'The snare of the fowler' suggests a trap to entangle us and prevent us from walking along God's perfect path for our life. This trap may be a person or thing.

'The terror of night' and the 'pestilence that stalks in darkness' (verses 5,6) make me think of the fear and panic that often grip one in the middle of the night, when problems assume huge proportions.

The plague at midday (verse 6) might be having your purse stolen at the supermarket, receiving bad news or bills you can't meet, or facing change or illness.

'The lion and the cobra' (verse 13) remind us of Satan who is described in the Bible as a roaring lion or a subtle snake. He attacks with terrible ferocity or suddenness. Remember he's always hard at work, especially amongst those working for the Lord. In our anxiety, we often blame others or ourselves when the devil is the real culprit, slandering and accusing the brethren; our real battle is against him.

The psalmist mentions all these forms of evil so that he can point out that God's protection is for any and every situation. Both aspects of this protection are brought out (verse 4): its gentle, comforting quality ('He will cover you with his feathers, and under his wings you will find refuge'), and its solid strength ('His faithfulness will be your shield and rampart'). (YTL)

Lord, in Jesus' name I pray for your protection for . . . who has come under the devil's fierce attack.

Have I been blaming the wrong source for my troubles?

July 24   Why do I feel so low?

My soul is downcast within me; therefore I will remember you.
Psalm 42:5

At one time in his life, David was thoroughly low and discouraged to the point of depression. I believe there were four related factors which caused his state of mind.

He was an ultra-sensitive person. As often happens, his ultra-sensitive personality developed in early childhood as a result of emotional disturbances. David was not appreciated by his family; right from the start he was an emotional outcast.

Films which have been made of expressions on the faces of babies have shown that when a baby's mother is absent for long periods of time, the baby's face registers profound depression. We don't know whether David's mother behaved like this, but we do know that he was not appreciated when young and therefore developed this vulnerable, over-sensitive personality. As Christians we must show and voice our appreciation for one another. 'A word to the living is worth six wreaths to the dead.'

David had to cope with frustrated hopes. He was a natural leader, he'd proved his ability again and again, the people loved him and God had promised him the kingdom — but for ten years he had to be on the run, fighting for his very life. His frustration must have been very acute. Just as acute can be the frustration of a girl longing for marriage, or a childless couple longing for children.

David's struggle went on and on and on. There was no let up for him night and day, year after year. If you have a persistent illness or any other seemingly endless source of pressure or tension — you will understand just how David felt as the days, weeks, months and years passed.

Perhaps worst of all was God's apparent, continuing silence. Why didn't he do something? Didn't he care? Was that anointing for kingship one big mistake? (YTL)

Read Psalms 10, 13 and 22. Can you identify with David's feelings or gain comfort from the same sources or thoughts?

Father, when I feel low, help me to distinguish feelings from facts.

July 25   Reacting to suffering

To keep me from becoming conceited because of these surpassingly great revelations, there was given me a thorn in my flesh, a messenger of Satan to torment me. Three times I pleaded with the Lord to take it away from me. But he said to me, 'My grace is sufficient for you, for my power is made perfect in weakness.' Therefore I will boast all the more gladly about my weaknesses, so that Christ's power may rest on me. That is why, for Christ's sake, I delight in weaknesses, in insults, in hardships, in persecutions, in difficulties. For when I am weak, then I am strong.   2 Corinthians 12:7-10

It is frequently true that it is not so much our situation but the way that we react to it that counts. I once talked with two young fathers. Both had tragically lost their children aged four or five. One had died of leukemia; the other had been drowned in a swimming pool. One father had been a professing Christian but was then, through the experience, a militant atheist. The other father had been a humanist and was then, through the experience, almost a Christian. Here were two very similar tragic experiences but with totally different reactions to each situation.

These reactions are tremendously important. If I become bitter and resentful in my suffering, I still have my suffering, but on top of that I have to contend with my bitterness and resentment as well; and this may be even worse than my initial suffering. Certainly such an attitude makes things worse for other people, and I would be responsible for that.

On the other hand, if in my suffering I open my heart to the love and peace and friendship of Jesus Christ, then this will wonderfully transform the entire situation. (ISOG)

Lord, prepare me for any suffering which I shall have to face — so that I will react by softening and opening up to your will and your love, and not by hardening and closing up.

Am I reacting with bitterness to any situation?

July 26   The natural thing to do

As his custom was, Paul went into the synagogue, and on three Sabbath days he reasoned with them from the Scriptures,

explaining and proving that the Christ had to suffer and rise
from the dead. Acts 17:2,3

Guidance is usually *natural*. When Paul came to Thessalonica,
he went straight to the synagogue *'as his custom was'*, and for
three weeks he argued with them from the Scriptures about
Jesus Christ. In the absence of clear and specific guidance to the
contrary, Paul went to the obvious place where he could meet
those who believed in God. There was a considerable response
to the gospel, especially from some godly Greeks, but also
from some of the Jews. On an earlier occasion, Peter and John
were used by God to bring healing to a cripple, resulting in the
conversion of some two thousand, and all this happened when
they were 'going up to the temple at the time of prayer' (Acts
3:1), which was doubtless their daily practice. In other words,
God wants us to use our minds and common sense, because
guidance is usually thoroughly rational. In trusting the Holy
Spirit we must beware of super-spirituality which is always
looking for the unusual in God's guidance.

This isn't the *only* form of guidance, of course, and if guidance is usually natural, it is also often *corporate* and sometimes
special (Acts 15;8:26-39). (IBIE)

*Lord, I don't know what to do. The natural thing to do is . . .
Please make it very clear if this is not what I should do.*

*Would I know how to approach helping someone in need of
guidance?*

July 27   Growing faith

Now faith is being sure of what we hope for and certain of
what we do not see . . . And without faith it is impossible to
please God, because anyone who comes to him must believe
that he exists and that he rewards those who earnestly seek
him. Hebrews 11:1,6

I heard of a little girl who wrote: 'Faith is trying to believe what you know isn't true!' This is a total misconception of faith. In human relationships we exercise faith when we take someone at his word. The same is true of our relationship with God. We exercise faith in him when we believe what he says. This faith is a living thing and so it needs to be fed if it is to grow.

It needs to be fed on God's word (Romans 10:17). We need to read the Bible to discover what it is that God has said and promised.

It needs to be fed on Christian fellowship (Hebrews 3:12-14). We are in a sceptical world and we need to be encouraged in our faith by other Christians. Faith can grow infectiously as we meet with other believers.

It needs to be fed by the Spirit of God (Ephesians 3:16,17). He can make our hearts receptive to God's word and make God's word clear and relevant to us.

The language of faith is praise. The moment we humbly claim a promise of God for ourselves, having fulfilled the conditions, we need to start praising God — thus taking him at his word: 'He said he would do this, I have asked him to do it, so now I'm thanking him for doing it!' The results may be evident, sooner or later; but praise means that 'faith' comes first and then 'sight' later. (CFP)

Lord, increase my faith.

What action must I take if that prayer is to be answered?

July 28   The joy of worship

I rejoiced with those who said to me, 'Let us go to the house of the Lord.'   **Psalm 122:1**

What is clear from the Scriptures is that worship should be a delight, not a duty. The great Jewish feasts were times of exuberant joy and heartfelt celebration. Some of them contained an element of sorrow and repentance for sin; but this led to the joy of knowing God's forgiveness and mercy. They were always intended to be great and glorious festivals.

It is true that the prophets sometimes spoke disparagingly of religious feasts, but that was only when they had lost their spiritual content and had degenerated into an empty and worldly ritual. For the man whose heart was set on God, there was no greater joy than coming to worship him, especially in the presence of his people, as the psalmist made so clear: 'How lovely is your dwelling-place, O Lord Almighty! My soul yearns, even faints for the courts of the Lord; my heart and my flesh cry out for the living God' (Psalm 84:1,2). Further, when he was depressed, the psalmist remembered with longing how he once led 'the procession to the house of God with shouts of joy and thanksgiving among the festive throng' (Psalm 42:4). How many of us have experienced 'shouts of joy and thanksgiving' in our worship? (IBITC)

How does joy show in ordinary human relationships? How could it be expressed in my (our) relationship with, and worship of, God?

Father, I ask for the fruit of the Spirit described as joy to ripen in my life.

July 29   **Music in worship**

Praise him with the sounding of the trumpet, praise him with the harp and lyre, praise him with tambourine and dancing, praise him with the strings and flute, praise him with the clash of cymbals, praise him with resounding cymbals.

Psalm 150:3-5

Singing has always been a basic ingredient of praise, and although there should be some theological content in a song before it becomes a valid expression of praise, there is something to be said for what amounts to a sung meditation on the nature or character of God—especially in these days when the emphasis in the world is on speed. Therefore there can be a real place for simple and often repetitive worship choruses, provided this continues to be genuine worship and not vain repetition. After all, in Psalm 136 the words, 'His love endures for ever,' comes no less than twenty-six times! And in most of our Easter hymns we sing *Hallelujah!* over and over again. In some circles there has been an unfair and biblically unjustifiable resistance to simple and repetitive worship choruses, although certainly there are some obvious dangers which need to be watched.

When it comes to 'playing an instrument', virtually any instrument can be brought into the praise of God. Most congregations will have a variety of people who can play a variety of instruments but who are sitting passively in their pews whilst one man dominates the scene on the organ. How much better it is to use the gifts that God has already given, and to encourage maximum involvement and participation. (IBIE)

Lord, bring about a situation in which people's musical gifts can be used in the worship of our church.

Is there anything I can do to encourage people who are not yet using their musical gifts?

July 30   Surprised by joy

The kingdom of heaven is like treasure hidden in a field. When a man found it, he hid it again, and then in his joy went and sold all he had and bought that field.   Matthew 13:44

In New Testament times, people would often keep their treasures under the earth, so it wasn't at all unlikely that a man would stumble across treasure while digging in a field. Jesus said that the kingdom of heaven was like treasure for which a man would give up everything. What is the kingdom of heaven? It is the reign of the king of heaven — Jesus. This is priceless treasure, and in Jesus are countless other treasures, each one far, far outvaluing anything the world has to offer.

Think of happiness. Everyone's searching for it but, like the rainbow's end, it always seems to be in the next field. James Fox said that he'd always thought that if he could 'make it', life would be different. But he did and it wasn't! He wasn't miserable, he said, but perpetually unsatisfied, until he found the joy that only Christ can bring.

Professor Joad, who was converted from atheism to Christ, said, 'Trying to find happiness from this world is like trying to light up a dark room by lighting a succession of matches. You strike one, it flickers for a moment, and then it goes out. But when you find Jesus Christ, it's as though the whole room is suddenly flooded with light.'

Provided that Jesus is kept at the centre of our life, and this is very important, we have a priceless treasure of joy that nothing in the world can change. Richard Wurmbrand when reunited with his wife after fourteen years of brutal treatment in prison said, 'I come from the joy of Christ in prison to the joy of Christ with my family.' (YTL)

Meditate on some of the other treasures that are for those who put Christ at the very centre of their lives.

Father, I pray that this treasure of joy will increase in the life of . . .

July 31   A vision of heaven

After this I looked and there before me was a great multitude that no-one could count, from every nation, tribe, people and language, standing before the throne and in front of the Lamb.
Revelation 7:9

John had a vision of a great crowd in white robes in heaven (Revelation 7:9-17). Remember that he had this vision, and all the others in Revelation, when he was in his nineties, working in terrible conditions in a forced labour camp because of his faith.

He saw first of all *the crowds of heaven*. Perhaps John felt he was the only Christian on the isle of Patmos, just as we may feel we're the only Christian in our home, job, street, ward or group. How reassuring to have a vision of 'a great multitude that no-one could count'! They were wearing white robes (verse 9) — the robes symbolising festivity and the white, purity. The palm branches in their hands symbolised salvation.

John also saw what was at *the very centre of heaven* — and this was the throne and the Lamb. Try to visualise four concentric circles. The first is filled with the numberless crowd representing Christians worldwide throughout all time. The second is filled with all the angels (verse 11), the third with the elders symbolising all God's people, and the fourth with the four living creatures which we know from Ezekiel represent the highest order of angelic beings. In the centre of all those circles is the throne and the Lamb. The Lamb is mentioned over and over again in this Bible book. Why? Because the Lamb speaks powerfully of the death of Jesus on the cross without which there would be no heaven at all for anyone. And in heaven, the focus of all eyes and all worship will be — the Lamb. (YTL)

Does my worship of the Lamb now give me any insight into what it will be like for me in heaven? If not, what's missing?

Father, help me to meditate on all that the Lamb symbolises and represents.

AUGUST
Spiritual War

Endure hardship . . . like a good soldier of Christ Jesus.
2 Timothy 2:3

The church of the New Testament must never forget its role as
the army of God . . . 'No-one serving as a soldier gets involved
in civilian affairs — he wants to please his commanding officer'
(2 Timothy 2:4). In *every* age we are to 'fight the good fight of
the faith' (1 Timothy 6:12).

Although the battle and victory are the Lord's (2 Chronicles
20:15) we still need to be thoroughly trained and disciplined as
soldiers in the army of Christ. Thinking of the famous
Isthmian Games (second only to the Olympic Games) that
were held every three years at Corinth, Paul wrote to the
church in that city about the spiritual contest in which they
were all engaged: 'Everyone who competes in the games goes
into strict training. They do it to get a crown that will not last;
but we do it to get a crown that will last for ever. Therefore I do
not run like a man running aimlessly; I do not fight like a man
beating the air. No, I beat my body and make it my slave so
that after I have preached to others, I myself will not be dis-
qualified for the prize' (1 Corinthians 9:25-27).

The astonishingly rigorous and disciplined training schedule
of an athlete who is out to win should be a constant challenge
and rebuke to the flabbiness and laziness of many Christians.
Everything, even a good and harmless pursuit, is put to one

side if it might in any way hinder the training. The Christian, likewise, is to lay aside not only every sin, but also every weight, which might hold him back as he seeks to run the race, looking unto Jesus (Hebrews 12:1,2). (IBITC)

How can I start some kind of spiritual training or discipline?

Lord, show me where I am flabby and undisciplined.

Bible study: What does the devil tempt you to *doubt* and to *fear*? List these and find and learn words of God which you can have ready to use against him every time he suggests a fear or doubt.
Starters: Matthew 14:22-32; 28:17; John 20:24-29 (situations of doubt or fear); Romans 8:28;38,39; Hebrews 13:5,6; 1 John 1:9; Revelation 3:20 (some promises), and see under 'spiritual war' in index.

August 2   **There's a fight to be fought**

Consider him who endured such opposition from sinful men, so that you will not grow weary and lose heart. In your struggle against sin, you have not yet resisted to the point of shedding your blood.   **Hebrews 12:3,4**

Although in Christ we are now in the kingdom of God where grace reigns — and in that sense we are freed from the authority of sin and Satan over our lives — the spiritual battle is very strong and powerful until that day comes when Christ will put all his enemies under his feet. We are free in Christ, yes; but we are free to fight. . . The Christian is certainly in the realm of grace, and has died once for all to the realm of sin. Paul therefore repeatedly exhorted his readers, 'Become what you are!'

To maintain our freedom and fruitfulness in Christ will be neither quick nor easy. That is why we need the mind of Christ, who 'humbled himself and became obedient to death — even death on a cross' (Philippians 2:5-8)! We should note carefully the example of Christ's sufferings, and follow in his steps (1 Peter 2:21). We should not be 'surprised at the painful trial . . . but rejoice that you participate in the sufferings of Christ, so that you may be overjoyed when his glory is revealed' (1 Peter 4:12,13). (D)

Who or what am I 'fighting'? Is this fighting my own private battle or part of the spiritual battle?

Lord of hosts, show me where I am wasting my time fighting against things, people or situations I should accept, and lead me to where you want me to be in your battlefield.

August 3   Spiritual war

For our struggle is not against flesh and blood, but against the rulers, against the authorities, against the powers of this dark world and against the spiritual forces of evil in the heavenly realms. Therefore put on the full armour of God, so that when the day of evil comes, you may be able to stand your ground, and after you have done everything, to stand.

Ephesians 6:12-13

C. S. Lewis pinpointed two 'equal and opposite errors into which our race can fall about devils; one is to disbelieve their existence; the other is to believe and to feel an excessive and unhealthy interest in them. They themselves are equally pleased by both errors and hail the materialist and the magician with the same delight.'

We have to approach this subject with caution. But remember that Jesus was intensely aware of the spiritual battle in which he was involved. So was the apostle Paul.

Study the description of the devil and of his activities in the Bible and you will realise that we have a terrifying enemy. What are we to do?

First, we must stand together in Christ, so that we may be 'strong in the Lord and in his mighty power' (Ephesians 6:10).

Secondly, we must put on the whole armour of God (Ephesians 6:13-17): the belt of truth, which speaks of integrity; the breastplate of righteousness, which speaks of right relationships with God and with one another; the shoes of peace; the shield of faith, which speaks of protection; the helmet of salvation, which speaks of having our minds protected from doubt; and the sword of the Spirit, which is the word of God.

Thirdly, we must be totally dependent on him — praying 'in the Spirit on all occasions with all kinds of prayer and requests' (Ephesians 6:18). (CFP)

Make me aware enough of the enemy to rely on you, but not so conscious of him that I feel overwhelmed and fearful, Lord.

How can I put on the whole armour of God?

August 4   **Know your enemy**

The Lord said to Satan, 'Where have you come from?' Satan answered the Lord, 'From roaming through the earth and going to and fro in it.'   **Job 1:7**

It is vital that we should know our enemy. We must not be ignorant of Satan or of his devices.

A Scotland Yard inspector was once asked if he believed in the devil. He replied like this: 'Yes, I do, although I have never seen him. Sometimes in London there is an outbreak of petty crime and the quality of the criminals caught shows that they are not intelligent enough to have planned the crime. So we know that there is a new leader, and we open a new file — "Mr X". We then build up a picture of him and from that we seek to find him. In the same way, as I cross-examine people on how they got into the mess they are in, I find there is a "Mr X" who is twisting our lives. That "Mr X" is the devil.'

He is the mastermind behind all the evil in the world (John 12:31).

232

He is the prince of the power of the air who seeks to manipulate the philosophy, the thought-forms, the moral standards of our life, often through the influence of the media (Ephesians 2:2).

He is the god of this world, who can blind the minds of unbelievers, often by the paralysis of apathy, and who can change the patterns and structures of society so fast that many are left bewildered and depressed (2 Corinthians 4:4).

He is the angel of light, who works through false teachers and false prophets (2 Corinthians 11:14).

He is the father of lies, who will cause you, if he can, to doubt God's word, to question God's love, to deny God's control, to disbelieve God's faithfulness (John 8:44).

He is the roaring lion, who can spring sudden and fierce attacks so that we are startled by overwhelming depression that pins us down, or by overpowering feelings of lust, greed, anger, jealousy, ambition, resentment, that leave us wounded and helpless (1 Peter 5:8). (IBITC)

Lord, if I need to be made more aware of my enemy and yours, the devil, make my spiritual eyes and ears more sensitive.

Study the Bible passages relating to the devil so that you know his tactics. See the passages above and others, e.g. Revelation 12:9,10;20:2.

August 5 Use your weapons

The weapons we fight with are not the weapons of the world. On the contrary, they have divine power to demolish strongholds. 2 Corinthians 10:4

What are these weapons with divine power in them?

First, we need the weapon of the Bible: 'the sword of the Spirit, which is the word of God' (Ephesians 6:17). Jesus drove away Satan with the word of God (Luke 4:1-12).

Then there is the weapon of prayer. 'Pray in the Spirit on all

233

occasions with all kinds of prayers and requests' (Ephesians 6:18). Although we should all be prayerful and exercise increasing authority in prayer, I believe some have a special burden and ministry for it. We accomplish more by talking to God about men than by talking to men about God, so we should praise God for those with a special prayer ministry. I was in the Royal Artillery in the army and we had to barrage the enemy with fire before the infantry went in. In the spiritual battle, before a guest service or mission or some other important advance into enemy territory, I believe a barrage of prayer is needed before the spiritual infantrymen go into the new situation.

The cross of Christ is another powerful weapon. Through it Christ 'disarmed the powers and authorities' ranged against us (Colossians 2:15). The enemy army is still there but no weapon they can fashion against us can prosper if we are trusting Christ and his victory on the cross.

The weapon of praise was shown in all its effectiveness when Judah routed her enemies (2 Chronicles 20:21,22).

Fellowship is another effective and essential weapon for Christians (Ecclesiastes 4:12). The armour of God is to be put on by the whole fellowship together (Ephesians 6:10-20).

Not to be neglected is the weapon of a disciplined life (1 Corinthians 9:25-27). (YTL)

If you are discouraged in the battle, read and meditate on Romans 8:31-39. (Or share this with someone who is discouraged.)

Father, I have been neglecting this weapon . . .

August 6   He sets the prisoner free

Having disarmed the powers and authorities, he made a public spectacle of them, triumphing over them by the cross.
                                                        Colossians 2:15

On the last day of a mission, a colleague and I were called in to see a girl who was said to be demon-possessed. My immediate reaction was; 'I don't believe it.' And at first I thought she was just hysterical. But when we spoke to her of Jesus, she began to curse and blaspheme horribly, and we saw that she was in the grip of powerful satanic forces. She came at us with knives and broken glass and was extremely violent, but after four hours she was released and gave her life to Jesus and we prayed that the Holy Spirit would fill her.

During that long battle these were what had the most powerful effects: reading Isaiah chapter 53, the story of the crucifixion in the gospels, and verses of Scripture about the cross, and claiming the victory of Jesus Christ on the cross.

About eighteen months later I had a letter which said: 'Do you remember that night when you helped to release a girl from bondage? Well, I was that person. The reason for this letter is to share just a little of the wondrous works of Christ.' The letter went on to speak of her involvement with a live church and in outreach, and then ended: 'Praise the Lord, for his is the victory now and always.' I continue to hear from her and to learn of God's continuing victory in her life.

Through the cross, we have been freed from our old lives and been given new ones (Romans 5 and 6). However, it may take us a while to realise our freedom, just as someone newly escaped to West Berlin from the East may take a little time not to feel threatened every time there's a knock on the door. But when the devil accuses us and tries to lord it over us, we can claim the victory of Christ on the cross over him and send him packing. (AR)

Lord, I pray that you will make the victory of Jesus on the cross real in my experience, particularly in relation to . . .

Do I need to persist in claiming Christ's victory for myself or another?

David thought to himself, '. . . The best thing I can do is to escape to the land of the Philistines.'   1 Samuel 27:1

As well as talking defeat when he felt depressed, David gave up the battle. He was tired of waiting patiently for the Lord. There was too much effort involved. So he went off and lived in the land of the enemy. They welcomed him and he settled down comfortably. The pressure was off. He had 'peace' at last.

But this sort of peace is always a delusion. It's like a drug of which the effects wear off quite soon. It was the kind of 'peace' which forced David later on in this chapter to murder and plunder, lie and deceive; the kind which the prodigal son experienced after leaving the pressures of his father's house — until he found himself in a pigsty; the kind which some young people know when they opt out of moral and social responsibilities — until they find themselves trapped by evil. It may also be the sort of 'peace' a Christian girl tastes when she marries a non-Christian man because she can no longer wait patiently for the Lord, only to discover she has opted for a life that is — as she is painfully aware — much less than the best.

Whenever you take the easy way out and give up the spiritual battle, whenever you stop praying and reading your Bible, whenever you stop going to church or taking part in Christian fellowship — you may find temporary 'peace' but you will certainly not find the long term answer to your depression. At such times, force yourself to come into God's presence and join in with Christian fellowship. When David at last enquired of the Lord (1 Samuel 30:8) he was given an answer and a victory.

Don't rebel or run. Be still (Psalm 46:10). Stand firm (2 Chronicles 20:17). (YTL)

Nobody knows the trouble I'm in. (Not true.) Nobody knows . . . but Jesus. (That changes everything.) Glory, hallelujah!

Father, I'm ready to give up, but in obedience to your word I'm going to hold on to you and to your word, trusting that you know all about the trouble I'm in and have everything under control. (If you do not need this prayer, someone else might.)

The fool says in his heart, 'There is no God.'   Psalm 14:1

Many people fail to realise that there are different kinds of knowing. There's mathematical knowledge, based on reasoning, scientific knowledge, based on testing hypotheses, and there's personal knowledge. If you try to explain personal knowledge in either mathematical or scientific terms, the result is ludicrous — like this definition of a kiss, found in a communist textbook: 'A kiss is the approach of two pairs of lips with reciprocal transmission of microbes and carbon dioxide.'

It is through personal knowledge that God can be known, because he is a person. Personal knowing comes about through mutual commitment of persons. So knowing God comes about only when we commit ourselves to him. He cannot be known, or at least proved, by scientific or mathematical methods. Nor can he be mathematically or scientifically *disproved*.

At a house-meeting, a brilliant scientist said, 'I not only believe there is no God, I *know* there is no God.'

'Do you know the total truth about the whole universe?' I asked him.

'Of course not,' he replied.

'Do you know one per cent of the total truth?' I asked.

'Of course not,' he answered again.

'Do you know point one per cent?' I persisted.

'Not even that,' he said.

'Supposing for the sake of argument that you did,' I replied. 'Isn't it logically possible that God is both in the ninety-nine per cent plus that you *don't* know, and in the point one per cent that you *do* — but you don't recognise him?'

The man was quiet for some time afterwards. Perhaps he

237

realised that though you cannot prove God's existence, neither can you disprove it. (AR)

Father, help me not to despise 'fools' but to pray for them, and expect opportunities to share your wisdom with them.

List all the things you have personal knowledge of, regardless of whether they can be scientifically or mathematically demonstrated. Praise God for these certainties.

August 9   **Knowing and believing**

If anyone acknowledges that Jesus is the Son of God, God lives in him and he in God.   **1 John 4:15**

Do we believe that Jesus is divine — is God? John writes: 'Who is the liar? It is the man who denies that Jesus is the Christ. Such a man is the antichrist — he denies the Father and the Son' (1 John 2:22). Because the Jehovah's Witnesses, Mormons and members of the Divine Light Mission deny that Jesus is the Son of God, equal with his Father in heaven, they are false prophets — and we need to insist that this is so.

The divinity of Christ is central to Christian belief; people are divided by it into those who have the spirit of error and those who have the spirit of truth. There are no 'in-betweens' on this issue. There is only one person who can lead you to a true knowledge of the living God, and he is Jesus Christ, Son of God, Saviour of the world. 'I am the way . . . No-one comes to the Father except through me' (John 14:6), Jesus said. Peter adds: 'Salvation is found in no-one else, for there is no other name under heaven given to men by which we must be saved' (Acts 4:12). Knowing God is only possible through Jesus Christ, the Son of God. That is why it is essential to receive Christ into your life and not simply to believe in God.

Knowing God is simply not possible without believing in and receiving Jesus as God's Son. (YTL)

238

How would I answer someone who said, 'Jesus didn't go round saying, "I am God's Son"?'

Meditate on the familiar quotation: The Son of God became the Son of Man to make the sons of men the sons of God.

We know that we have come to know him if we obey his commands.   **1 John 2:3**

If we really know God and have a personal, loving relationship with him, we shall *want* to please him. Jesus said, 'I always do what pleases him [God]' (John 8:29). Paul said, 'We instructed you how to live in order to please God' (1 Thessalonians 4:1).

If a husband and wife have a truly loving relationship, they will do what they possibly can to please one another. At the wedding service, the bridegroom promises to love and cherish his bride. And — at least in some versions of the marriage service — the bride promises to love, cherish and *obey* her bridegroom. Some brides jibe at that word 'obey'; they shouldn't do so. Not only is it biblical, but also, if you love a person, you'll *want* to please him. We are to submit to one another in love.

Jesus said, 'If you love me, you will obey what I command' (John 14:15). To know God is to love God, abide in him and keep his commandments.

If in your home, place of work, private and social life, you have one supreme aim — not to be religious, but to love and obey God, that is a very good test that you know him. (YTL)

Father, show me your will in this matter . . .

'Do whatever he tells you' (John 2:5).

No longer will you be called Abram; your name will be
Abraham.
                                                        Genesis 17:5

In Bible times a name was very important: it stood for a
person's character and nature. God always revealed himself by
a name. He called himself 'the Lord who heals', 'the Lord will
provide', 'the Lord is there', 'the Lord is my shepherd' or 'the
Lord Almighty'. These names showed different aspects of his
character. Jesus did the same thing. He said, 'I AM the bread of
life,' 'I AM the light of the world,' and so on.

When men and women came into a new relationship with
God in Bible times, they were often given a new name, to
signify a new nature and relationship. Jacob meaning
'deceiver' was called Israel meaning 'prince with God'. Simon
became Peter — 'a rock'. And God sealed his covenant relationship with Abram and Sarai by giving them new names.
Abram meaning 'exalted father' was to be called Abraham
meaning 'father of a great multitude'. In other words when
Abram came into a new relationship with God two things
happened: first, God, not he, was to be exalted from now on;
secondly, he was to be a blessing to other people. And Sarai
meaning 'struggler' or 'fighter' was to be called Sarah meaning
'princess' or 'queen'.

We can apply these names to ourselves when we become
Christians and so have a new relationship with God. We can
put God first and be a blessing to others; we can stop struggling
to win God's favour and start enjoying all the riches of his
palace. (YTL)

*If I were given a new Christian name in keeping with my
character and nature what might it be?*

What is your new name for me, Father? Help me to live up to it.

I have given them your word and the world has hated them,
for they are not of the world, any more than I am of the world.
My prayer is not that you take them out of the world but that
you protect them from the evil one.   John 17:14,15

This is the vital thing, that we should be *in* the world but not *of*
the world. Just as a boat should be in the water but the water
should not be in the boat, so a Christian should be in the world
but the world should not be in the Christian. And for the sake
of those for whom Christ died and who are going to believe in
him through our word, we should sanctify ourselves, and
maintain our determination to abide in him. There is no other
place of safety and power.

Generally speaking, we will probably not want to spend a
large proportion of our time on 'worldly amusements'. We
have found something far more satisfying in the unsearchable
riches of Christ. But if we really love him, there may be times
when we can safely find ourselves in situations, or with certain
people, that might surprise some other Christians.

In that case there are two things for us to watch very carefully. First, 'be careful . . . that the exercise of your freedom
does not become a stumbling block to the weak' (1 Corinthians
8:9). Then, 'if you think you are standing firm, be careful that
you don't fall' (1 Corinthians 10:12)! An electrician may
handle a 'live' wire. If he knows what he is doing and takes
adequate precautions, he will be quite safe. So it is with the
Christian and the world. (HW)

*In the course of my daily life, do I get close enough to any non-
Christians to be able to understand and so speak and behave
relevantly towards them?*

*Lord, show me whether I'm too much 'of the world' or not
sufficiently 'in the world'.*

You . . . are controlled not by the sinful nature, but by the Spirit, if the Spirit of God lives in you. And if anyone does not have the Spirit of Christ, he does not belong to Christ.

Romans 8:9

The Holy Spirit is given many names — the Spirit of adoption, glory, grace, counsel, wisdom, knowledge, understanding, truth, and so on. But he is chiefly called the Spirit of God or the Spirit of Christ. Why?

He comes to glorify Christ (John 16:13,14). To some, the Christian life might look like a rather dull box. But what the Holy Spirit does is to open the box and reveal Jesus as the jewel inside it. When the Holy Spirit came at Pentecost, the disciples burst into spontaneous praise and worship of Jesus and Simon Peter had great clarity and authority as he preached Christ.

I received a letter which excited me very much. It said, 'The first time I came to your church I went home and told my wife, "I have seen the Lord".' Everything we say or do *should* have that aim, and everything that the Spirit does *will* have that effect.

The Holy Spirit comes also to make us like Christ (2 Corinthians 3:17,18). He takes the veil from our eyes, so that we see Christ as he really is and as we go on and on looking at him, he changes us to be like him, more and more. But almost certainly this will involve some form of pain or suffering.

Thirdly, the Holy Spirit unites us into the Body of Christ (1 Corinthians 12:13). Our disunity is a scandal and an offence to God the Father, who longs that his children should be in one family, to God the Son who died to make us one and to God the Holy Spirit who came to unite us into one Body in Christ.

So the Holy Spirit *glorifies Christ*, which may be wonderful, *makes us more like Christ*, which may be painful, and *unites us in the Body of Christ*, which may shake us up considerably. (YTL)

Are people seeing the Lord Jesus through us?

Father, if I am seeking anything for myself from the Holy

Spirit, please show me and give me a greater longing to be like Jesus.

August 14   No colourless personalities

He [Apollos] was a learned man, with a thorough knowledge of the Scriptures . . . He vigorously refuted the Jews in public debate, proving from the Scriptures that Jesus was the Christ.
Acts 18:24,28

Trusting the Holy Spirit does not mean suppressing our human personality. The desire to be 'hidden' in order that Christ may be seen, can lead to colourless Christian lives which will hardly commend the Author of life or the abundant life that he promises to bring. The biblical record is that God has always worked through human personality, created, fashioned and inspired by his Spirit. See the strong and varied personalities of the apostles or prophets. See Moses striding down Mount Sinai to smash the golden calf to bits, and yet he was known as the meekest man on the face of the earth. See Peter at Pentecost, or Paul on Mars Hill, or Philip at Samaria, or Stephen before the council.

As John Stott aptly writes: 'What Scripture lays upon us is the need for a proper combination of humility and humanity — the humility to let God be God, acknowledging that he alone can give sight to the blind and life to the dead, and the humanity to be ourselves as he has made us, not suppressing our personal individuality, but exercising our God-given gifts and offering ourselves to God as instruments of righteousness in his hand.' (IBIE)

Lord, help me to become more truly myself as you created me to be.

Do we (Christians) strike people as being more fully alive than others or not?

Peter, filled with the Holy Spirit, said to them (the Sanhedrin):
'Rulers and elders of the people . . . it is by the name of Jesus
Christ of Nazareth, whom you crucified but whom God raised
from the dead, that this man stands before you completely
healed.'
                                                              Acts 4:8,10

Little by little, God trained Simon Peter for leadership in the
church.

First, his natural strength was broken. Although naturally
strong and a born leader, he had to learn through Christ's
stinging rebuke (Matthew 16:23) and his own failure (Luke
22:54-62) not to place any confidence in himself. He must have
been shattered on both these occasions, but the person whom
God uses must learn that his strongest points are his weakest
points and that without the grace of God he can do nothing of
lasting worth.

Secondly, his faith was built up — slowly but surely.
Looking at Jesus, he was able to walk on the water — but
looking at the waves and trying to work out what was
happening intellectually caused him to start sinking. Many
Christians have swallowed today's rationalism which believes
only what it can understand. Christ wants childlike trust from
us. Peter learnt this and became full of faith and boldness.

Thirdly, Peter learnt to listen to God with a willingness to be
directed into new attitudes and actions (see Acts chapter 10).

Also, Peter was totally committed to other Christians as well
as to Christ. All who believed were together and shared all
their good things. Peter knew the importance of 'living stones'
in God's building all fitting together well (1 Peter 2:4,5).

Most important, Peter was filled with the Holy Spirit.
The difference in him before and after Pentecost is quite
astonishing. (PL)

*Meditate on how a childlike trust can result in faith and
boldness.*

Are we willing to lead if we are called?

What, after all, is Apollos? And what is Paul? Only servants, through whom you came to believe — as the Lord has assigned to each his task.   1 Corinthians 3:5

We cannot have an effective ministry in the church until we are willing to serve. The church of Corinth made the common mistake of putting their leaders on to pedestals, and because of the differences between them, the church members were obviously saying things like this: 'Apollos is my favourite preacher because he's so eloquent,' or, 'Paul's my favourite speaker because he's so deep and clever.' Have you ever heard talk like that?

Paul has no time for such comparisons. 'What is Apollos? What is Paul?' he asks, and then answers his own questions: 'Only servants.' Later he writes to the same church, 'We do not preach ourselves, but Christ Jesus as Lord, and ourselves as your servants for Jesus' sake' (2 Corinthians 4:5).

In fact in the New Testament the Greek word for *minister* was the word used for the lowest slave. This was in keeping with Jesus' teaching about ministry and service. While the disciples argued about who was the greatest, Jesus taught them again and again what true greatness was. He said, 'Whoever wants to become great among you must be your servant, and whoever wants to be first must be slave of all' (Mark 10:43,44), and, 'I am among you as one who serves' (Luke 22:27).

Our spiritual maturity and our readiness to be leaders of any kind could be measured by our willingness to serve others. Could you honestly say to those around you in a church service, 'I am here to serve you. I am your servant for Jesus' sake'? (YTL)

Next time you go into church, really look at the people there and say in your heart to them, 'I am here to serve you.'

Lord Jesus, to think that you took 'the very nature of a servant' for me! How can I ever refuse to serve others for you?

Whoever wants to become great among you must be your servant, and whoever wants to be first must be your slave — just as the Son of Man did not come to be served, but to serve, and to give his life as a ransom for many.

Matthew 20:26-28

Unfortunately, some forms of evangelism today encourage people to remain thoroughly self-centred, instead of urging them to become God-centred. In this advertising age it is all too easy to present Christ as the one who will meet all your needs. Are you anxious? Christ will bring you peace! Are you lost? Christ will give you new direction! Are you depressed? Christ will fill your life with joy! All this is true, and it is part of the good news of Christ that he longs to meet the deepest needs of each one of us. But that by itself is only one half of the story. The other half is that we must turn from self to God and to others.

Jesus repeatedly found that he had to correct his disciples as they fell into two equal and opposite temptations, which crippled the spirit of service in their lives. The first temptation was ambition... This is the spirit of the world: seeking for status instead of service. Jesus rebuked them... He later demonstrated this spirit of service in a way they never forgot, when he wrapped a towel around his waist and washed their feet.

The second temptation was self-pity. 'Lo, we have left our homes and followed you,' said Simon Peter as he began to feel the considerable cost of discipleship... We need to be honest and real about our weakness and pain, but the moment we fall into self-pity we hinder God's working in our lives.

If we are taken up with our own personal needs first and foremost, or if we are looking for position and status in the church, we shall be no use to God. We are called to serve; and a servant must go where his master sends him and do what his master commands. (D)

Lord, show me where self is hindering you from doing anything in me or through me.

Has selfish ambition any place in my life and work? Or self-pity? What can I do?

This man is my chosen instrument to carry my name before the Gentiles and their kings and before the people of Israel.

Acts 9:15

God chose and blessed Paul not for his own benefit but that he might carry the good news to others. He always chooses and blesses for a good purpose.

'You are a chosen people, a royal priesthood, a holy nation, a people belonging to God,' writes Peter, *'that you may declare the praises of him who called you out of darkness into his wonderful light.'*

'Arise, shine, for your light has come,' writes Isaiah, and adds, 'Nations will come to your light, and kings to the brightness of your dawn' (Isaiah 60:1,3).

Jesus promised his disciples that they would receive power. Why? So that they would be his witnesses to the ends of the earth (Acts 1:8).

The gift of Jesus, the gospel, the Holy Spirit — and all God's other blessings — are given to us for the sake of others. William Temple said that the church is the only society which exists for the benefit of its non-members.

How effective are we in communicating the gift of Jesus?

We must never be complacent. We have been chosen for the sake of others. But we need not be despondent in the face of such a huge task, because the Lord reigns and because the Holy Spirit has never been withdrawn. (YTL)

How am I and how is my church benefiting the non-members around?

Father, help us to fulfil the task for which you have chosen us.

You are . . . a royal priesthood.   1 Peter 2:9

Instead of being content to fill a church with new believers in Christ, it is important to see the New Testament picture of every Christian in the Body of Christ as a minister for Christ — nothing less: 'It was he who gave some to be apostles, some to be prophets, some to be evangelists, and some to be pastors and teachers, to prepare God's people for works of service' (Ephesians 4:11,12). 'In this way,' comments Juan Carlos Ortiz, 'the entire church is composed of ministers. The ministers are not a special breed of sheep coming from the seminary. They are simply believers who go on growing. Thus the purpose of the pastor is to make disciples, who make disciples, who make disciples, who make disciples.' Aiming towards this ideal will involve a radical rethink for many Christians. First there is no distinction between 'clergy' and 'laity': all priests are laymen (from *laos*, the people of God), and all laymen are priests (1 Peter 2:9). All too often the vicar or pastor is the bottleneck of the church: everything must pass through him or go out from him. With such a constriction it is not surprising that there is an acute shortage of gifts and ministries in most churches; they are simply not allowed to flow and develop. (IBIE)

How could we involve more people in our church in the action?

Father, help us to understand more of what it means to be a member of your 'royal priesthood'.

August 20   The local church an entity

For in Christ all the fulness of the Deity lives in bodily form, and you have been given fulness in Christ who is the head over every power and authority.   Colossians 2:9

Each individual *ekklesia* (local church, group of churches, or denomination), is not *the* church, but *fully represents it*. For example, each local church is not just a section of the whole church, and the whole church is not just the sum of all the local churches. Instead the *whole* gospel, the *fulness* of God, the *finished* work of Christ together with the 'immeasurable greatness' of his resurrection power, the *complete* gift of the Holy Spirit together with the full range of his gifts and ministries, and the 'very great promises' of God offering *full* salvation — all these are available in every place, wherever the church, great or small, is to be found. (See Matthew 18:20.)

Thus the local church does not merely *belong* to the universal church as some junior, smaller and greatly inferior part of the whole; the local church *is* the church and is therefore *complete* in Christ. Paul pointed this out to the Christians at Colossae who were being deceived into believing that there was something more to be had apart from Christ. Not so! God has blessed us in Christ with *every* spiritual blessing (Ephesians 1:3); there is nothing to discover for our spiritual well-being that is outside him. (IBITC)

Thank you, Father, that our church doesn't have a bit of Jesus, but all of him and therefore we have all we need.

Is our church growing into more of an entity?

August 21   **You are vital**

God has arranged the parts in the body, every one of them, just as he wanted them to be.   **1 Corinthians 12:18**

Determine to find your place within the local fellowship of Christians where you are, certainly in a local church and also, if applicable, in the Christian Union of your college, school, factory, unit, or office. You may not find it easy, initially. When Saul of Tarsus met with the living Christ, he at once attempted to get involved with the local Body of Christ. But he was given a cool and negative reception. They doubted his conversion and were suspicious of his motives. And there were other natural barriers, too. Saul was a gifted intellectual, highly educated and influential, a Jewish leader and Roman citizen: his pedigree was impeccable. Humanly speaking it could not have been easy for him to have joined a despised minority group consisting of poor, illiterate fishermen and those who once were cheats, traitors, prostitutes and thieves. Moreover Saul had hated and persecuted this Christian 'sect' with persistent and skilful ruthlessness. And now he had changed sides! Indeed it was this social, religious, and intellectual aristocrat who later wrote: 'There is neither Jew nor Greek, slave nor free, male nor female, for you are all one in Christ Jesus' (Galatians 3:28).

Therefore, even if your natural reaction to, or from, your local group of Christians is cool, and even if there are marked social, cultural, racial, and intellectual differences, realise that, with them, you *belong* to God's building and Christ's Body. You need them and they need you (I Corinthians 12:12-27). (LANL)

Have I found God's place for me in our church fellowship? If not, is there someone I could talk to about this?

Lord, help me not to be so busy or preoccupied that I miss an opportunity or a person prepared by you for me.

August 22   What is an elder?

Paul sent to Ephesus for the elders of the church. When they arrived, he said to them: '... Guard yourselves and all the flock of which the Holy Spirit has made you overseers. Be shepherds of the church of God, which he bought with his own blood.'   Acts 20:17,18,28

In the New Testament church, the spiritual leaders of the church were elders (sometimes called bishops, overseers, guardians or shepherds) and deacons. The deacons could be described as assistant elders, having similar functions apart from teaching or preaching, perhaps, but with the emphasis on pastoral and administrative responsibilities.

A very important part of an elder's responsibilities (and in the New Testament eldership was always shared — never the task of one man) was leading and speaking at meetings and services and undertaking church discipline — this latter being a much neglected function today. Another way of putting it is to say that elders were to feed and protect the flock and refute false teaching. Paul writes: 'I know that after I leave, savage wolves will come in among you and will not spare the flock' (Acts 20:29). Such people are to be silenced, Paul tells Titus (Titus 1:10-16).

Another task of the elders was to 'encourage the timid, help the weak, be patient with everyone' (1 Thessalonians 5:14) — a much needed ministry today!

Also elders were to be an example to others in love, faith and purity (1 Timothy 3:1-7), and ready to pray for the sick (James 5:14).

No one elder could do all these things, but together they could perform these ministries and so build up an increasingly harmonious, united, loving and joyful fellowship. The distinctive marks of eldership, as of any form of leadership, are submission to Christ and genuine service to others. Serving does not mean being servile or giving people what they want, but meeting their true needs. (YTL)

Is there a need for elders in our church? How would they be chosen and appointed?

Lord of the church all over the world and of our church, guide us in the matter of leadership. May spiritual leaders be seen to be at least as important as administrative ones.

August 23   **Unity through renewal**

You are all one in Christ Jesus.   **Galatians 3:28**

The way to achieve continuing Christian unity is continuing spiritual renewal. Someone has said: 'Christian unity will not be inaugurated in any particular year. It was inaugurated on the cross, is given by God and wrought by the Spirit in the hearts of his people. History teaches us that when revival comes the Spirit takes virtually no notice of denominational labels and, what is more, those who experience revival do not worry about them either.'

Cardinal Suenens stated: 'I believe that the solution of ecumenical disunity will not finally be the result of the dialogue between the church of Rome and the church of Canterbury or the church of Moscow; it will not be a dialogue between the churches as such, but a dialogue between Rome and Jesus, Canterbury and Jesus, Moscow and Jesus, so that we can become more and more united in him.'

When we open our lives to the Holy Spirit, he lifts us more consciously into the presence of Jesus, and the nearer we come to Jesus, the nearer we come to each other.

In these difficult days we need more than ever to be closely joined to one another, so that we can stand firm, and so that the world can see the reality of Jesus. (AR)

Lord, help me to care about the divisions between members of your Body — throughout the world and in my church and locality. Show me if there is anything I can do to further unity in any way.

Is everything in our church life geared to bringing us all closer to Jesus?

August 24   **No unity without humility**

Be completely humble and gentle; be patient, bearing with one another in love.   **Ephesians 4:2**

We need humility in order to put wrong relationships right. There was real tension between my wife and myself one

Friday and I went into my study and waited for her to come and apologise. I was due to preach on 1 Corinthians chapter 13, so I looked for my carefully prepared and filed notes. I couldn't find them. In one file after another I looked, but still I couldn't find them. So I said, 'All right, Lord, I've got the message. I'll go and apologise and you show me where my notes are.' But then I had another look in the first file, which I had checked several times — and there were my notes. Of course, I still had to keep my side of the bargain and say sorry to my wife.

We do need to put right our wrong relationships with God, and where someone has been hurt, with that other person too.

We also need humility in order to respect and value the gifts of others, whether these are gifts of leadership, or apostolic gifts, used for pioneering work or the encouraging of the churches, or hearing gifts, used to discern what God is saying to the churches, or growing gifts, used in evangelism and for adding more members to Christ's Body, or caring (pastoral) or knowing (teaching) gifts. All are needed. All are important.

Charles Hummell wrote: 'Suppose you are walking near a lake and suddenly hear a cry for help. As you turn towards the water, you see a child has fallen in. So you run to the spot and pull the youngster out. It's absurd to argue about which member of the body was most important for the rescue: the ear which heard the cry, the eye which saw the child, the feet which ran to the spot or the hand which pulled him out. All are necessary and if any had failed, the rescue would not have happened.'

We need humility to use our own gifts and to value those of others so that we can serve the Body of Christ and reach out more effectively into the world. (AR)

Lord, show me any area where I need humility to act in some way today.

Who in our church fellowship — as well as myself — needs the humbling work of the Holy Spirit in their lives? Pray for these people.

Confess your sins to each other and pray for each other, so that you may be healed.   James 5:16

Acknowledgement of sin in the presence of another brother is a safeguard against self-deception. It is a curious fact that it is invariably easier to confess our sins privately to a holy and sinless God than openly to an unholy and sinful brother. If that is true, 'we must ask ourselves,' writes Bonhoeffer, 'whether we have not been deceiving ourselves with our confession of sin to God, whether we have not rather been confessing our sins to ourselves and also granting ourselves absolution. And is not the reason perhaps for our countless relapses and the feebleness of our Christian obedience to be found precisely in the fact that we are living on self-forgiveness and not a real forgiveness?'

That is perhaps why James, in the context of open confession to another brother, gives the assurance that any sins committed will surely be forgiven. Once sin is brought out into the light, it can be forgiven and forgotten. Its power has been broken. It can no longer hold the believer in bondage, or tear the fellowship apart. The sinner can honestly be a sinner, and still enjoy the grace of God and the love of the brethren. This is the moment where fellowship in Christ becomes a profound reality. 'In confession the Christian gives up all and follows. Confession is discipleship. Life with Jesus Christ and his community has begun' (Bonhoeffer). (D)

Lord, show me whether I am really confessing my sins to you or to myself.

Do I need to obey James' instruction with regard to some wrong in my life?

It was he [Christ] who gave some to be apostles, some to be

prophets, some to be evangelists, and some to be pastors and
teachers.   Ephesians 4:11

It was when Christ ascended to heaven that spiritual gifts were
given to the church. It is when Christ is glorified in our
personal lives and in our relationships that the same thing
happens today. Take a closer look at some of these spiritual
gifts (Ephesians 4; 1 Corinthians 12).

Apostles: I believe these are people sent out through
the local church to establish a church or to renew the
churches.

Prophets: These have a definite, authoritative word for the
church in a particular situation. We need to ask ourselves as we
listen: 'What are you saying to me, Lord, through this
word?' as well as, 'Is this word according to the written word
of God?'

Evangelists: These are not necessarily to travel all the time,
but may — like Philip — be primarily involved in a local church,
while going out from there occasionally.

Pastors: These have responsibilities for counselling,
visiting, correcting, disciplining.

Teachers: They need to teach in small groups as well as from
the pulpit.

Other gifts include: the message of wisdom (the ability to
know what to do in a difficult situation); the message of knowledge (perhaps in a counselling situation); faith; healing or
other miracles; the ability to distinguish between spirits;
tongues and interpretation (1 Corinthians 12:7-11); serving;
encouraging; contributing to the needs of others; showing
mercy (Romans 12:6-8).

The two vital points about gifts are — they are for the
common good and must be used only in the context of love (1
Corinthians 12:7; 13:1-3). (YTL)

*Lord, I long that you will be glorified in my life and in all my
relationships.*

Do I know what gift God might have given to me?

Concerning this salvation, the prophets who spoke of the grace that was to come to you, searched intently and with the greatest care, trying to find out the time and circumstances to which the Spirit of Christ in them was pointing when he predicted the sufferings of Christ and the glories that would follow.   1 Peter 1:10,11

The Spirit is relevant. He takes old truths and makes us see how contemporary they are. He focuses our attention on something we need to know this week. Perhaps we need to return to our first love, or be humbled or encouraged. Whatever it is, the Spirit will bring something to our attention, through the Bible, other Christians, prayer and so on, and say, 'That's for you now.'

But he cannot do this unless we are really sensitive and open to him, listening and waiting and expecting him to speak. It is said that Christians are so heavenly minded that they're no earthly use, but I believe that it's the other way round. Most Christians are far too earthly minded to be any heavenly use — and that's more serious.

I read of an Indian woman in South America who was dying and some Indian Christians and two missionaries gathered to pray for her, but she relapsed, after a slight improvement, and was on the point of death. The Indian Christians prayed again, but this time they did not invite the missionaries to join them. The sick woman was completely healed and got up and made supper for them. As they talked about this, one missionary asked why they had not been invited to the second prayer meeting and the answer was, 'Because you don't really believe, and you cannot heal by God's power when you have unbelievers in the circle.'

The missionary who told this story against himself wrote later, 'I am now deeply aware that my western Spiritless culture has given me an acute hearing defect to the voice of the Holy Spirit.' It's true of many of us. We need to learn to discern what the Spirit is saying to us each day in every situation. (YTL)

What is the Spirit saying to me at this time in my life?

Father, with your help, I intend to spend far more time listening to you, learning to discern the voice of your Spirit to me.

August 28   **How does God heal today?**

When you enter a town and are welcomed, eat what is set before you. Heal the sick who are there and tell them, 'The kingdom of God is near you.'   **Luke 10:8,9**

The New Testament disciples were specifically commissioned by God to heal the sick, and it's a historical fact that for eight hundred years after the ascension of Christ, the church continued its healing ministry. Then that part of the vision was lost. But today there's a new and lively interest in healing. People often say, 'Doesn't God heal through doctors nowadays?' The answer is that he does, but not *always* and *only* in that way. In the New Testament, healings were first and foremost signs and wonders — they were signs of the presence of the living God and of the truth of the message proclaimed and they evoked wonder in the hearts of those who witnessed them.

I believe in this materialistic age that we need to see God at work in unmistakable power and that we should pray for this and expect it. I asked a young Muslim who had become a Christian whether it was the Christian message which had convinced him. He replied that it hadn't — he'd heard many religious messages. But what had convinced him was witnessing two healing miracles. A deaf woman had been healed and that had impressed him but not convinced him, because she could have pretended to be deaf. But then he'd seen a twisted leg straighten out before his very eyes and this had convinced him that the living God was at work.

In places where God's Spirit is clearly at work, people are being converted mainly through healings, deliverances or direct visions of the Lord. (YTL)

257

Am I willing to change my ideas when I see God at work in new and unexpected ways?

Father, thank you for the signs and wonders in New Testament times and today, which are helping people to see your power and believe in the name of your Son Jesus.

August 29   **Comparisons are out!**

Peter replied, 'Even if all fall away on account of you, I never will.'   **Matthew 26:33**

Peter was guilty of spiritual pride. He compared himself favourably with others: '*They* may let you down; *I* won't.' Certainly, he had been greatly blessed. He had been the first to recognise who Jesus was and Jesus had blessed him for it (Matthew 16:13-20). A week later, he and two others had seen something of the glory of God on the Mount of Transfiguration (Matthew 17:1-13). Perhaps with all these happy experiences behind him, it was natural for him to think, 'I won't fall away. I know too much. I've experienced too much.'

When God blesses you in some special way — be very careful. The church at Corinth had experienced tremendous spiritual blessings and gifts — healings, prophecies, tongues and other miracles. And yet spiritual pride led them into all sorts of excesses and evil so that Paul had to write, 'If you think you are standing firm, be careful that you don't fall' (1 Corinthians 10:12)!

In my own spiritual life, my greatest crash followed on the heels of my greatest spiritual blessing since conversion — because of spiritual pride. You may think this will never happen to you, but be careful, because it has certainly happened to many others. (YTL)

Lord, make me aware of the times I compare myself favourably or unfavourably with others.

Study 2 Corinthians 10:12-18, especially noting verse 12b, for guidelines on the whole matter of comparisons and feelings of inferiority or superiority.

August 30   **Personality cults**

No more boasting about men! All things are yours, whether Paul or Apollos or Cephas or the world or life or death or the present or the future — all are yours, and you are of Christ, and Christ is of God.   **1 Corinthians 3:21-23**

Paul rapped the foolish Corinthian Christians over the knuckles for their rivalry and party-spirit. They were boasting of the different personalities and gifts of their leaders. What a silly and unspiritual thing to do, he wrote. The very differences between Paul, Apollos and Cephas meant an enriching variety for the whole church, and therefore of every member of that church. If the Corinthians failed to see this, they had not begun to see what it meant to belong to the Body of Christ or to the temple of the Holy Spirit.

Today, the cult of personality is rife, especially within certain sections of the church. Such immature rivalry is a mark of the lack of real spirituality within the church. If we are guilty of this, we are 'acting like mere men' (1 Corinthians 3:3).

The same is true of tensions between churches in the same town or city, or between clergy and ministers. Once we have in any way grasped what it means to belong to the Body of Christ, we ought to thank God for one another, and for the great variety of gifts and ministries that God gives within his church. (IBITC)

Am I relying too much on a human leader?

Father, protect those who are in danger of being put on a pedestal.

We are therefore Christ's ambassadors, as though God were making his appeal through us — we implore you on Christ's behalf: be reconciled to God. God made him who had no sin to be sin for us, so that in him we might become the righteousness of God.
2 Corinthians 5:20, 21

The cross is the final compelling motive behind all evangelism. When Jesus died at Calvary, it was as though he took man in one hand and God in the other, bringing the two together by being made sin for us. These are devastating words! They speak of God pouring all the filth of our sin into Jesus so that, as Luther once expressed it, Jesus became the greatest liar, perjurer, thief, adulterer and murderer that mankind has ever known — not because he committed these sins but because he was actually made sin for us.

Therefore, because he was made sin for us, God made peace with us by the blood of his cross. It is not an easy thing being a peacemaker. It cost Jesus his life. It meant that he had to appropriate the filth of our sin upon himself. Thus when Jesus said, 'Blessed are the peacemakers, for they will be called sons of God' (Matthew 5:9) — he knew that calling us into this peace-making ministry as sons of God, or ambassadors for Christ, would involve us in considerable sacrifice — in some cases the ultimate sacrifice of our lives. But this is the only way in which God can make his appeal through us to the world. We may be tempted to lose heart, perhaps on numerous occasions. If so, 'consider him who endured such opposition from sinful men, so that you will not grow weary and lose heart' (Hebrews 12:3). (IBIE)

Help me, as I can bear it and little by little, to understand more of what it meant for the Lord Jesus to be made sin for us, so that my heart will overflow with love and gratitude and the desire to share this incredibly good news with others.

Is there any situation from which I am shrinking because of what it may cost me? Should I take time to think this through with God today?

SEPTEMBER
Mission

September 1   **God is a missionary**

The field is the world. . . The harvest is the end of the age.
Matthew 13:38,39

God is a missionary. His redemptive work in the world is missionary work. . . Since his harvest field is the world, it is up to the Lord of the harvest to place his workers where he wills. No Christian can serve his Lord on condition that he lives in, say, the comfortable surroundings and social environment that he has always enjoyed. He is to be available to Jesus for work in Godalming or Guatemala, Chicago or Chile. As far as personal preferences are concerned, the Lord of glory would hardly have chosen the cattle shed in Bethlehem or the carpenter's bench in Nazareth; but he went where his Father sent him, and 'though he was rich, yet for your sakes he became poor, so that you through his poverty might become rich' (2 Corinthians 8:9).

A healthy church will always be especially concerned about its missionary work both on its own doorstep and overseas. It will try not to be insular and parochial, but develop steadily a worldwide perspective of the work of God, and encourage everyone to be directly involved in some form of missionary concern. There should be a constant flow of candidates for the harvest fields abroad; and these men and women should be strongly backed by the church in terms of finance, prayer and personal links forged through letters and gifts at regular intervals. (IBITC)

*How much time, teaching and money in our church is given to
missionary work anywhere?*

*Lord, give us all enthusiasm for your missionary work through
us.*

Bible study: What should we be telling and showing the world and
how?
Starters: Matthew 20:28; 28:16-20; John 4:1-42; Acts 1:8; 2:1-47;
17:1-34; 1 Corinthians 2:1-5; 2 Corinthians 5:17-21; Philippians
2:5-11, and see under 'mission' in index.

September 2   Community evangelism

**We do not preach ourselves, but Jesus Christ as Lord, and
ourselves as your servants for Jesus' sake.   2 Corinthians 4:5**

For too long we have neglected to see the tremendous
evangelistic impact of a church that is a real, loving, warm
Christian community. Certainly the preaching of evangelism
is Christ and not the church (1 Corinthians 1:22-24) but the
purpose of evangelism and the agent of evangelism *is* the
church.

God's purpose in saving an individual is to add him to his
church, where he will demonstrate, with all the others, God's
new lifestyle and relationships. Loving other Christians is one
test of genuine spiritual life (1 John 3:14). 'Follow-up' shouldn't
be an addition to evangelism; making sure new converts are
absorbed into their local churches and involved with their new
family should be part and parcel of it.

In evangelising, God works through the church, and he can
work more effectively in those churches which are true
Christian communities. These will show a lifestyle completely
contrary to that of the people around and will astonish and
challenge the world, just as the New Testament church did, by
its generosity, its care of widows and of the weak, sick and
infirm, its concern for prisoners, slaves and the down-trodden,

its hospitality, sexual purity and hatred of injustice and cruelty, and its good citizenship.

Graham Pulkingham has written that so much evangelism is like a bodiless arm reaching out. His point was illustrated by a girl who said she was reluctant to evangelise the needy young people she worked amongst, because she knew her church members would not provide the loving after-care that these sad and mixed up youngsters would need.

Where the church really is God's new society, putting into practice, in its life and worship, Christ's teaching and standards, there you will have effective — natural, continuous and complete — evangelism. (YTL)

Are we astonishing and challenging non-Christians in any way?

Father, help us to see how much we need each other and belong to each other in Christ.

September 3   Principles of personal evangelism

The eunuch asked Philip, 'Tell me, please, who is the prophet talking about, himself, or someone else?' Then Philip began with that very passage of Scripture and told him the good news about Jesus.   **Acts 8:34,35**

Philip came to the right person, at the right time, with the right message and the right ministry (Acts 8:26-40).

The eunuch was a God-fearer (verse 27), he was a seeker (verse 28), he was honest and open (verses 30,31) and he really meant business (verse 36). He was *the right person*. We need to pray that God will guide us to the right people — those in whom the Holy Spirit is already at work.

Philip came up at just *the right moment* — when the eunuch was reading from the prophet Isaiah and wondering who was being referred to (verses 30,34). In personal evangelism, we need to know when to speak and when to be silent. I know of someone who was warming to the gospel when a well-meaning person barged in and 'witnessed' very strongly. The seeker was put right off. We must 'be prepared in season and out of season' (2 Timothy 4:2), but we must let the Holy Spirit teach us sensitivity about when to say something and when to say nothing.

Philip had *the right words* (verses 30,35). He asked a relevant question, and then answered the eunuch's counter-question, beginning from where the man was in his thinking and reading. Would we really have the right words if someone were to ask us today, 'How can I find God?'

Philip had *the right ministry*, and so will we, if we can so bring a person into touch with Jesus that he goes on his way rejoicing (verse 39). (YTL)

Who should be involved in personal evangelism?

Lord Jesus, give us a desire to talk about you to others.

September 4   Telling others

They were all filled with the Holy Spirit and spoke the word of God boldly.   Acts 4:31

Someone has said, 'Compared with evangelism, everything else that is happening in the church is like rearranging the furniture when the house is on fire.' I have a growing sense of urgency about obeying Jesus' great commission to preach the good news throughout the world.

On the day of Pentecost, it was not enough for the Spirit to fall on the disciples with great power. Peter had to stand up and preach the good news about Jesus Christ. It was not enough for the cripple to be healed. Again Peter had to stand up and proclaim salvation through Jesus (Acts 3).

Luke uses thirteen different Greek words in connection with the preaching of the gospel; preaching, heralding, testifying, proclaiming, teaching, exhorting, arguing, disputing, confounding, proving, reasoning, persuading, pleading. Clearly the early disciples used words in every possible way in order to make their message known and understood.

They used every possible opportunity, too. Paul argued in the hall of Tyrannus every day for two years. He and the other disciples used initiative and imagination in this matter. They talked to people in streets, market-places, courts, council chambers.

I have a friend, a gifted evangelist, who uses every opportunity, just as the disciples did long ago. He was once sitting near a well known runner, and he asked this man, 'Why do you spend all your life running round in circles?' That pertinent question helped the man to find Jesus as his Saviour and he later entered the ordained ministry.

Why is my friend so effective in evangelism? First, because he cares about people as people. Secondly, he does *not* care what other people think of him. All that matters to him is to be the Lord's messenger. Thirdly, he prays very hard for this gift of evangelism. Fourthly, he practises this gift wherever he goes. (AR)

Am I an evangelist? If not, am I supporting, praying for, and encouraging at least one local and one overseas evangelist?

Lord, make me bold but not brash in the way I speak to others about you.

September 5   Home-made evangelism

They broke bread in their homes and ate together with glad and sincere hearts, praising God and enjoying the favour of all the people. And the Lord added to their number daily those who were being saved.   **Acts 2:46,47**

The home is still undoubtedly one of the best of all settings for evangelism. Frequently I have seen the value of the home, with gatherings ranging from six to 150, but usually between twenty and forty. Here is the ideal framework for genuine communication, providing an opportunity for declaring the good news of Christ, together with come-back, discussion, debate, argument and spontaneous testimony from other Christians present.

It is a relaxed environment for those who might feel uncomfortable and on the defensive in a church building. It provides a setting in which people's personal difficulties and doubts can be expressed and, perhaps, resolved.

The home is a marvellous field for evangelism and Christians who catch a vision of this have an immense contribution to make for the kingdom of God today. (IBIE)

My home is your home, Lord. Use it as you will and show me clearly how I can co-operate with you in this matter.

If I am house-proud — who am I making my home spotless for and why have I chosen to spend so much of my time in this way? If I'm inclined to let things go — is my home a fit place for God to be and to use — or do I need to lavish a bit more time and care on these 'earthly' things for his sake and glory?

September 6   Anyone can and everyone should do it!

When they saw the courage of Peter and John and realised that they were unschooled, ordinary men, they were astonished, and they took note that these men had been with Jesus.

Acts 4:13

The disciples had no special qualifications; they weren't theologically or academically trained. You don't have to be a specialist to be an active witness for Jesus. The only BA you need is 'Born Again', followed by a first hand experience of Jesus.

Of course we must also know what we believe and keep thinking it through, as well. What impresses many about some of the sects is the fact that their members know exactly what they believe and have answers ready for most questions. In this way, they are a rebuke to many Christians, as well as in their zeal to spread their message. But it's possible to have a real grasp of one's faith without studying at a theological college. Speaking as a minister, I would say that the non-professional witness for Jesus is more effective than that from a man who is paid to do it. People expect their ministers to speak about Jesus, but they may not expect to hear a neighbour or workmate talking about him, and that may well impress them far more.

Theological training may not be necessary, but something else *is* essential before anyone can be an effective witness for Jesus. The disciples themselves felt completely unable to obey Jesus' commission, until they had this essential 'qualification'. They needed to be filled with the Holy Spirit. Only then were they able to witness boldly and effectively for Jesus.

Anyone who is empowered by the Holy Spirit *can* be a witness for Jesus, and everyone who knows and loves Jesus *should* be witnessing for him! (YTL)

Lord Jesus, help us not to hide behind shyness, ordinariness, or lack of education, when we have such a treasure to pass on and such power available to us.

Which is my point of weakness: speaking inadvisedly of Jesus, or staying silent when an opportunity to speak is given to me?

September 7   The good news — shown as well as spoken

Jesus went into Galilee, proclaiming the good news of God.
                                                    Mark 1:14

Jesus not only *said* that he had come for sinners, but scandalised his critics by actually eating a meal with 'tax collectors and sinners'. Constantly we find the living demonstration that he actually meant what he said. He was demonstrating good news. We cannot take the verb 'to evangelise' out of its meaning. It was never the bare proclamation of words. Always it was words set in action: not just 'signs and wonders', of course, but numerous examples of the love, care and compassion of the one who had come to bring good news. It is therefore not surprising that Luke says of his first volume: 'I wrote about all that Jesus *began to do and to teach*' (Acts 1:1). Here the *doing* comes even before the *teaching*! And the implication of Luke's words is that Jesus went on doing and teaching through his Body, the church.

This, in fact, is exactly what we find. Throughout the whole of Acts, in almost every chapter, we see a demonstration accompanying the proclamation of the gospel.

Without some concrete reality of the gospel, words become empty and meaningless. From New Testament days to the twentieth century it remains true that, unless there is a demonstration of the power of the Spirit, the proclamation of the gospel will be in vain. It will not be evangelism. (IBIE)

What has James 2:14-26 to say about this?

Father, I know I'm more inclined to talk (do) than to do (talk). Help me to get the balance right today.

September 8   **Depression for spiritual reasons**

Then a great and powerful wind tore the mountains apart and shattered the rocks before the Lord, but the Lord was not in the wind. After the wind there was an earthquake, but the Lord was not in the earthquake. After the earthquake came a fire, but the Lord was not in the fire. And after the fire came a gentle whisper.   **1 Kings 19:11,12**

Depression is not necessarily a sign of spiritual failure in the depressed person's life. Some of the greatest saints have suffered from depression. But depression can sometimes have a spiritual cause or aspect. Part of Elijah's depression was due to spiritual failure on the part of God's people: 'The Israelites have rejected your covenant, broken down your altars, and put your prophets to death with the sword' (19:10).

God's answer to this is to take Elijah back to the mountain of God, Horeb, and to speak to him, not this time through fire, or earthquake or wind, but through a gentle whisper. What he was saying, in effect, was this: 'I know you're depressed, Elijah, because there hasn't been a revival in spite of all that has happened. I know you want me to come down in a dramatic way on my people, but I'm not doing so. However, I am in control, I haven't forsaken you, I love you still, and I am working, as I often do, so secretly and silently that you hardly notice it. I have allowed this time to teach you to trust me, not only when I am working in great power, but also when nothing seems to be happening and you are in a deep, dark tunnel of depression.'

God says the same to us: 'The greatest expression of my love there has ever been on earth was in the darkness of Calvary.' If we only trust people when we can see what they are doing, then our trust isn't very deep. Real trust in God means believing in his love even when we *can't* see or understand what he's doing. (YTL)

Father, I pray for . . . who is going through a time of great pain and perplexity. Please deepen his (her) faith and trust in you, in spite of everything.

Am I waiting for fire while ignoring the gentle whisper?

September 9   The Lord — my provider

You prepare a table before me in the presence of my enemies.
Psalm 23:5

According to a Palestinian shepherd, the ground where sheep are to graze has to be cleared of all danger. In particular there are two hazards not obvious to the casual observer — poisonous grasses which are deadly if eaten, and small, venomous snakes which lurk in holes and then dart out and bite the grazing animals.

So, using his rod and staff, the shepherd digs out the deadly grasses and ferrets out and kills the poisonous snakes. Then he puts them on the rocks to shrivel up in the hot sun.

There are enemies around us, too. Just as it would be impossible for the sheep themselves to deal with the poisonous snakes and grasses, so it's impossible for us to deal with our spiritual foes; 'for our struggle is not against flesh and blood, but against the rulers, against the authorities, against the powers of this dark world and against the spiritual forces of evil in the heavenly realms' (Ephesians 6:12).

In particular, our greatest foe, Satan, is both very strong and very subtle — the great deceiver who attacks us very unexpectedly at times.

But he is also a defeated foe. Just as the sheep can graze happily in full view of the dead snakes and withered grasses lying on the rocks all around them, so we can feast on the spiritual table prepared for us in the presence of our enemies. Satan cannot harm us when we are trusting in the name and blood of Jesus, the Good Shepherd, who is stronger than the strong. (YTL)

Lord, I praise and worship you for all you provide for me. . .

Am I aware of my spiritual enemies? How can I allow Jesus to defeat them for me today?

September 10   Super-Peace

A furious squall came up, and the waves broke over the boat, so that it was nearly swamped. Jesus was in the stern, sleeping on a cushion . . . He got up, rebuked the wind and said to the waves, 'Quiet! Be still!' Then the wind died down and it was completely calm.   **Mark 4:37-39**

Two kinds of peace are illustrated in this story, and Jesus is the

270

source of both. When Jesus says to the situation all around you, 'Peace, be still,' and you find that he sets you free from the storm of sickness, or loneliness, or tragedy, or bereavement, or broken nights, or demanding children — that's one kind of peace.

Jesus displayed the other kind of peace when he lay asleep, utterly relaxed, while the storm raged all around him. This is a deeper kind of peace — the sort the world cannot give or take away.

A Christian woman was wonderfully and dramatically healed of cancer in direct answer to prayer. One week after her return home, her husband suddenly collapsed and died. Her first reaction was to cry to God, 'Lord, you can't do this to me! You've healed me of cancer, but why take my husband away just when I need him badly?'

But because she was a Christian, she was able to kneel down and pray, and as she did that, she discovered — as she expressed it — 'the most wonderful comfort I have ever experienced'.

When this woman's cancer was healed, she knew the peace of a storm stilled — or the peace that comes after the storm. But when she found comfort in her bereavement, she was entering into a deeper experience — that of peace in the middle of a storm. (YTL)

Father, you know my problem. I pray to you for peace in this situation.

Is there anyone I know who might find today's reading helpful? How can I share it with that person?

September 11   Can I claim God's protection?

He who dwells in the shelter of the Most High will rest in the shadow of the Almighty.   Psalm 91:1

It's possible to be presumptuous in claiming that God will protect us. We are reminded, in this psalm, of the devil tempting Jesus to throw himself off the temple pinnacle, because God's angels would protect him (verses 11,12). But such an action would have been rash, pointless and out of God's will, so Jesus refused to take it. In the same way, it's presumptuous for me to claim God's protection against ill health, if I'm neglecting or abusing my body, or in spiritual battles, if I'm not spending time with the Lord, or if I'm neglecting Christian fellowship, or ignoring the principles of spiritual warfare. Nor can I launch into a new work assuming that God will provide, unless God has very clearly guided me into it — such guidance to have included advice from mature Christians and not just my own feelings.

In other words, we can only claim God's protection with assurance and truth, when we are in the centre of God's will. This will involve certain actions or attitudes on our part and these are linked with three words — translated in the Revised Standard Version as *cleaves, knows* and *calls.* Cleaving means setting one's heart on someone in such a way that absolutely nothing will affect the bond of love one has with that person. Knowing God's name means knowing his nature, and this psalm is full of helpful images and descriptions of God. For instance, he is the 'Most High'. Therefore since we are in his shelter (verse 1) we can, with him, look down on our problems. But first of all, God waits for us to call. He does not rush to our rescue automatically; if he did, we would quickly take him for granted, and taking anyone for granted spells the beginning of the end of that relationship. (YTL)

Meditate on the names and nature of God mentioned in this psalm and how knowing these helps me.

Father, help me to understand more of what it means to dwell and rest in your shelter and shadow.

Even though I walk through the valley of the shadow of death,
I will fear no evil, for you are with me; your rod and staff, they
comfort me.   Psalm 23:4

The valley of the shadow of death was the name given to a very
narrow, steep-sided, steaming gorge between Jerusalem and
Jericho. For David this valley was a picture of depression. One
commentator has called it 'the gorge of gloom'.

In his valley of depression, David found two sources of
comfort. First he had the Lord's *presence*. The writer of Psalm
139 stresses that God's presence is everywhere and the New
Testament makes it very clear that once a person makes Jesus
his own shepherd, he is never alone; Jesus is with him all the
time, as the good shepherd from whose hand no one can snatch
his sheep (John 10:28).

Secondly, David knew the Lord's *protection*. The rod refers
to the short powerful club which a shepherd would use to drive
away wild animals wanting to harm the sheep. And the staff
was used both to help him bring back straying sheep and to
examine the flock as they came back into the fold for the night.
The shepherd would position his staff in such a way that the
sheep would have to lower their bodies and squeeze themselves slowly under it, giving him a chance to examine them for
injuries which might need attention.

In the same way our Good Shepherd drives away our
enemies (Romans 16:20), draws us back when we stray, and
brings us low in order to heal our wounds. Having to crouch
under the shepherd's staff is a humbling experience, but it may
be an essential one, if we are to emerge from the gloom of
depression. (YTL)

*Loving Shepherd, 'is my gloom, after all, shade of [your] hand
outstretched caressingly'? (From 'The Hound of Heaven',
Francis Thompson)*

*How can I remind myself continually that God is my
protector?*

By faith Enoch was taken from this life, so that he did not experience death; he could not be found, because God had taken him away. For before he was taken, he was commended as one who pleased God.   **Hebrews 11:5**

Reading Genesis chapter 5 is rather like walking through a cemetery and finding that all the gravestones have similar inscriptions, until suddenly one is different. All the others have the name, date of birth and death and nothing more, but this one has an epitaph too — the most wonderful epitaph in the Bible: 'Enoch walked with God' (Genesis 5:22,23).

What does walking with God mean? Two people who walk along together choose to do so, or agree to do so; they don't *have* to do so. So Enoch must have *agreed* to walk with God because God wouldn't have forced him to. He doesn't force us either, but he invites us to, and we can agree to the suggestion or not.

Walking with God, or anyone else, means walking in the same direction. It also means walking at the same pace.

By faith Enoch walked with God or, to express it in another way, he pleased God. Does my way of life, this friendship, my use of time and money, and so on, please God? If not, I am not walking with God.

By faith Enoch also spoke out for God against the evil of the society in which he lived (Jude 12-16). It was a society which left God out, an *ungodly* society, just like ours. It is time for Christians, ordinary family men and women like Enoch and his wife, to speak out against the evils in our society, if we care about our children and young people.

By faith Enoch was taken up to be with God, just as we shall be, if we're Christians and still alive, when Jesus comes again (1 Thessalonians 4:16,17). (YTL)

Do I really see life as a walk with God, and death as his invitation to stop walking and stay in his house?

Father, help me to walk with you at your pace, neither rushing ahead nor lagging behind, like an impatient or a reluctant child.

I am the Lord your God, who brought you out of Egypt, out of the land of slavery. You shall have no other gods before me.
Exodus 20:2,3

What is a god? It's an object of worship — a dominating influence in our lives. Keith Miller defines it as 'the object of your life's most intense focus'. It's where our treasure and our heart is, to use Bible terms, and it can be another person, an ambition, a lifestyle, a pastime — any thing or person that takes the central place in our lives. The things that often crowd God out of people's lives are the 'worries of this life and the deceitfulness of wealth' (Matthew 13:22) as well as 'the cravings of sinful man, the lust of his eyes and the boasting of what he has and does' (1 John 2:16). All these are false gods.

God will brook no rival. After all, he created and redeemed us: 'I am the Lord your God, who brought you out of Egypt, out of the land of slavery.' Jesus expressed it in this way: 'Do not set your heart on what you will eat or drink. . . Seek his kingdom' (Luke 12:29,31). 'Our hearts have room only for one all-embracing devotion' (Bonhoeffer).

I have a great burden that all Christians should come to God for forgiveness and for the filling of the Holy Spirit, to enable us to live out this commandment and all the others, so that there will be a greater sense of the presence of God throughout our land. (YTL)

Who or what are we really devoted to?

Father, please make me sensitive enough to realise when anything or anyone is taking up too much of my life.

275

To do your will, O my God, is my desire.   Psalm 40:8

All *power* is given to God, so we worship him by trusting him in every situation, knowing he can keep us from falling and present us faultless and filled with joy (Jude 24).

All *riches* belong to him, so we worship him by the generosity of our giving, in response to what he did: 'though he was rich, yet for your sakes he became poor, so that you through his poverty might become rich' (2 Corinthians 8:9).

All *wisdom* belongs to him, so we worship him by allowing his Spirit to guide us, following wherever he leads, even when it's confusing, painful or difficult to do so.

All *strength* belongs to him, so we worship God by sacrificial acts of service, trusting that as our days so shall our strength be (Deuteronomy 33:25).

All *honour* belongs to him, so we worship him by helping others to find Jesus, and bow the knee to him now before the judgment day when 'every tongue' will 'confess that Jesus Christ is Lord' and every knee shall bow to him (Philippians 2:10,11).

All *glory* belongs to him, so we worship God by praising and thanking him for the 'glory of the one and only [Son], who came from the Father, full of grace and truth' (John 1:14).

All *blessing* belongs to him, yet he pours out blessings for us, so we worship him by pouring ourselves out for other people, by using every gift he gives us for the benefit of others, and by sharing what we have — 'for with such sacrifices God is well pleased' (Hebrews 13:16). (YTL)

Do I believe these words from a hymn: 'My will is not my own, until I make it thine'?

Father, I do want to worship you by surrendering my will to your great and glorious purposes now and always.

Since we live by the Spirit, let us keep in step with the Spirit.
Galatians 5:25

How do we keep in step with the Spirit, making steady
progress, growing and maturing in the centre of God's will?
One way is by not gratifying 'the desires of the sinful nature'
and by crucifying 'the sinful nature with its passions and
desires' (Galatians 5:16,24). Self still dominates many of us in
different forms — selfishness, self-centredness, self-seeking,
self-pity. We think, 'If only others knew how tired I am (or how
confused I am, or what a frantic week I've had, or what bad
nights I've had, or what battles I've fought, or what compli-
cations face me) they'd be overwhelmed with sympathy for
me!'

A colleague of mine in the course of a mission threw himself
down on his bed one evening and said, 'Lord, I'm shattered.'
And the Lord answered him with one word: 'Repent.' If we are
going to keep in step with the Spirit, continuously renewed by
him, we need to repent continuously of all selfish and negative
feelings towards any person or situation. All complaining
about the weather, the boss, the family, the church leaders,
other Christians, our status or lack of it — are out. These are of
the flesh and grieve the Spirit.

One day I found my secretary on her hands and knees with a
dustpan and brush sweeping my study carpet. I asked her,
'Why don't you use the hoover?' and she replied, 'That doesn't
really get into the corners.' Our repentance needs to be more
than a general 'hoovering' of our lives. We need to attack the
'corners' of our lives with a spiritual dustpan and brush, and
sweep out deeply entrenched negative and selfish attitudes
which may have gathered dust for years. Let me warn you that
this will not be easy. (YTL)

Lord, I acknowledge that this attitude . . . has been with me for
years. I want to bring it right out into the open before you.
Cleanse me and free me from it and may your Holy Spirit blow
in and fill that newly empty space in my life.

Am I prepared to pray that prayer over every aspect of 'self' in my life over and over again until it is answered?

September 17   God — alive and active

This is what the Lord Almighty says: 'In those days ten men from all languages and nations will take firm hold of one Jew by the edge of his robe and say, "Let us go with you, because we have heard that God is with you."'   **Zechariah 8:23**

Why have godless sinners of all kinds poured into churches during times of revival? What has attracted the members of the community who normally would not be seen dead inside a church? The answer is this: they see that God is very clearly with his people — and they feel compelled, almost irresistibly, to take a look for themselves at his amazing power at work.

It was the same at Pentecost. Why did the crowds 'from every nation under heaven' come flocking round that small group of disciples? Why did Peter have the opportunity of preaching to so many with such dramatic effect? It was because God was powerfully and evidently with them, and the amazed onlookers knew it. 'We hear them declaring the wonders of God in our own tongues!' they exclaimed to each other (Acts 2).

Unless that is true of our church fellowship, all our publicity, our restored buildings, our music, dance, drama, area groups and everything else, will largely be in vain. (PL)

O living God, show me and the rest of my church family what is our greatest need at this time.

Have I ever heard a visitor to our church commenting on a powerful sense of God's presence there? Do I know that God is active in my own life?

278

I will obey your word ... I reach out my hands for your
commandments which I love, and I meditate on your decrees.
                                            Psalm 119:17,48

We must listen carefully to God's word. Jesus said we need
every word that God speaks (Matthew 4:4) — and he speaks to
us every day in different ways.

We need to read and study God's written word, so that we
can correctly handle the Scriptures, as a skilful workman
correctly handles his tools (2 Timothy 2:15), and not be
ashamed and unable to answer when people ask us about our
faith.

We need to obey God's word. In a book called *The Devil's
Dictionary* a Christian is defined as 'one who believes the New
Testament is a divinely inspired book admirably suited to the
needs of his neighbour'! We each need to see that it's admirably
suited to our needs, too.

Through it, our minds, so easily brainwashed by the world,
can be renewed to think God's thoughts. It is there to guide our
lives in every situation. We are to use it to overcome temptation as Jesus did. He used three quotations from
Deuteronomy chapters 6 and 8, which might well have been
the passages he was meditating on, during his time of fasting in
the desert. At any rate, he was able to use God's word as a
sword and drive the devil away with it. We, too, should know
this word so well that we can use it to defeat our enemy, or to
help depressed or sad people, or those wanting to find Christ.

If we listen to God's word, study and obey it, we will be able
to stand firm when the winds, floods and storms of life come
along. (YTL)

*Do I need to start learning some verses and references which
might be useful to me personally or to others in certain
situations?*

*Pray through Psalm 119, making the psalmist's responses to
God's word my own.*

There are different kinds of gifts, but the same Spirit.
1 Corinthians 12:4

There is a rich variety of gifts listed in the New Testament
(1 Corinthians 12:8-10;28-31; Ephesians 4:11; Romans 12:6-8;
1 Peter 4:10,11) and these lists are not meant to be exhaustive.
God's gifts are as rich, varied and plentiful as creation suggests.

There is no sharp distinction between natural and spiritual
gifts, either. They are all gifts of God, even though some are
more unusual than others. The word for gifts is 'charismata'
and the New Testament is full of different kinds of 'charismata'
— God's forgiveness, eternal life, fellowship, leadership,
marriage and celibacy: these are all 'gifts of God's love and
grace' which is what 'charismata' means. The important thing
is not whether a gift is natural or spiritual, but whether we see
it as God's, not ours. Something which may be a natural part
of your being can become a spiritual gift and blessing to the
whole church, if you recognise that it comes from God and use
it in complete dependence upon him; otherwise it is self-
display. As someone has said, 'When gifts are no longer an
expression of Christ's actions, they are not only useless but
harmful in their effect. They are counterfeits which offer my
neighbour nothing, but positively deceive him.' (YTL)

*Am I looking for personal fulfilment from my gift, or do I see it
entirely as God's gift which he could remove at any time if it
doesn't glorify him or benefit others?*

*Father, help us to see where pride or jealousy is hindering the
effective use of our natural and spiritual gifts in the church and
in the world.*

September 20   The healing of the cripple

Peter said, 'Silver or gold I do not have, but what I have I give
you. In the name of Jesus Christ of Nazareth, walk.' Taking

**him by the right hand, he helped him up, and instantly the
man's feet and ankles became strong.** Acts 3:6,7

Look at the timing of this miracle! We read that the man had
been crippled since birth, that he was carried to the temple gate
every day, and that he was over forty years old. Since Jesus
frequently went to the temple to preach and teach, he must
have seen this man often. Why didn't he stop and heal him?
The answer was that God had planned that this man's healing
would be a vital sign at a crucial moment in the proclamation
of the true gospel.

In all healing, the sufferer must submit totally to God's will
as to whether he will heal him, and if so how and when. I don't
believe we can ever presume to command God to heal *now*,
unless God has given us a specific gift of faith for a particular
person or occasion.

Look at the healing itself. The cripple himself wasn't full of
faith; he wasn't even asking for healing: he was asking for
money. Of course faith is necessary if healing is to take place,
but as this story shows, it may not be the faith of the sick
person. The challenge of faith should not rest on the sick
person alone, or even, in some cases, at all. If it does, and
healing does not take place, the sick person has deep
depression to cope with, as well as illness. In this case, I believe
Peter and John, who must often have seen the cripple, were
given a specific gift of faith at that moment to heal that man
that day. Otherwise their words would have been sheer
presumption.

The result of the healing was that Christ was glorified. If you
are seeking for healing, I would urge you to have nothing
whatever to do with any so-called faith-healer or healing
which does not have Christ, crucified and risen again, at its
heart and centre. Jesus himself warned us about false signs and
miracles (Matthew 24:24). (YTL)

*Father, I pray that we may be ready to receive the gift of faith
whenever you choose to glorify Christ through a very clear
sign of your love and power.*

What is the danger in wanting healing at any price?

I am jealous for you with a godly jealousy. I promised you to one husband, to Christ, so that I might present you as a pure virgin to him. But I am afraid that just as Eve was deceived by the serpent's cunning, your minds may somehow be led astray from your sincere and pure devotion to Christ.

2 Corinthians 11:2,3

Who are the spiritual adulterers within the church? It is those who are doctrinally corrupt (verse 4). . . . If the church is to be the faithful bride of Christ, its doctrinal purity is extremely important. The New Testament, however, is quite clear about the need to be faithful to apostolic teaching. This needs to be stressed in a day when there has been such a sharp reaction to cold, doctrinaire orthodoxy that almost anything goes. An article in *The Times* on the Church of England's Doctrine Commission Report made this comment: 'What the eighteen theologians hold in common is a belief in the likelihood of God, and reverence for Jesus. . . . The impression given . . . is that Anglicanism is a religion without doctrine.'

The same can be said of most other denominations. In 1961 one of the top pollsters of the United States made a survey of Protestant seminaries. Of ministers in training, fifty-six per cent rejected the virgin birth of Christ, seventy-one per cent rejected life after death, fifty-four per cent rejected the bodily resurrection of Christ, ninety-eight per cent rejected a personal return of Christ to this earth.

Although there has, more recently, been a healthy return to biblical studies and to a renewed acceptance of the authority of the Scriptures as the written word of God, there are still many within the church who question, and sometimes categorically deny, the most basic truths of the Christian faith. (IBITC)

How much doctrine do I know?

Father, I believe your every word. Your words to me are . . .

When I kept silent, my bones wasted away through my groaning all day long.   Psalm 32:3

As we read the story of David's adultery and what followed (2 Samuel 11 and 12), it might seem that for a whole year David was untroubled about the sins he had committed against Bathsheba and Uriah. But I believe his uncharacteristic behaviour and words revealed his inner turmoil due to a very guilty conscience.

Why should he send for Uriah, urge him to go home and rest, and give him a present? To try to salve his conscience and cover his sin. But it didn't work, and he must have felt worse than ever when Uriah said, 'How can I eat, drink and sleep with my wife when my commander and colleagues are living rough and fighting hard?'

I believe David felt desperately guilty as he wrote the despatch to Joab which made Uriah's death virtually certain. In normal circumstances, he would never have done such an evil thing. It's hard to believe that this was the same man who had been too honourable to harm his enemy Saul when he had had him at his mercy.

When David heard of Uriah's death, his reaction was uncharacteristic again: 'Don't worry, these things happen,' he said calmly. It is hard to believe that this was the same man who had publicly mourned when he'd heard of the death of Abner his enemy (2 Samuel 3); now the death of one of his best soldiers does not seem to upset him at all. But Psalm 32 probably gives us an insight into David's true thoughts and feelings at this time.

When we are trying to suppress a guilty conscience, our behaviour, our words, our attitudes and even our appearance will betray us. Even if we could hide the truth from ourselves and our friends, we wouldn't be able to hide it from God. (YTL)

How does a guilty conscience affect the way I behave, think or speak?

Thank you so much, Lord, that as your child I need never carry a guilty conscience round with me.

September 23   No fragrance without brokenness

While he [Jesus] was in Bethany, reclining at the table in the home of a man known as Simon the Leper, a woman came with an alabaster jar of very expensive perfume, made of pure nard. She broke the jar and poured the perfume on his head.

Mark 14:3

An alabaster jar was a sealed jar. This one might have been a fine-looking jar but the really precious thing was the ointment inside it. Until the jar was broken, no fragrance could be experienced.

The New Testament tells us that we are to have the fragrance of Christ about us, but often we have a hard outer crust which needs to be broken before this can happen. When people meet us, they're conscious, perhaps, of our gifts, abilities, ideas and opinions, instead of becoming aware of Jesus. A hard lesson which many of us have to learn is that unless our outward self is broken none of our gifts and abilities will bring anyone closer to Jesus. I believe many people who would never come to a church, would genuinely like to see and know the living Christ. But we won't be able to show him to them unless we can say with Paul, 'I have been crucified with Christ and I no longer live, but Christ lives in me' (Galatians 2:20). God is probably using difficulties in our lives to bring us to the point of brokenness. So if you're experiencing the buffeting of illness, disappointment, failure, trouble of one sort or another, it may be that God in his love wants your life to be filled with the fragrance of Jesus by his Spirit. (YTL)

'Thanks be to God, who always leads us in triumphal procession in Christ and through us spreads everywhere the fragrance of the knowledge of him' (2 Corinthians 2:14).

Can I honestly echo Paul's words (Philippians 1:21)?

Give me oil in my life

You anoint my head with oil; my cup overflows. **Psalm 23:5**

As the sheep returned to the fold at night, the shepherd would sometimes use his staff to make them lie down so that he could examine them for scratches and other injuries. If he found wounds, he would apply to them the oil often used for healing such injuries. In the same way, the Good Shepherd heals our wounds and injuries.

In the Bible, oil is a symbol of the Holy Spirit and of God's anointing — and so it conveys the idea of God's healing love and peace, which we can experience in the thick of the battle when we are feeling bruised and battered.

Jesus was about to enter into the hardest spiritual battle of his life when Mary, longing to show her love for him, brought her most precious possession, a jar of ointment and poured it over his feet, which she then wiped with her hair. We read that 'the house was filled with the fragrance of the perfume' (John 12:1-3).

When Jesus anoints our head with oil and applies his healing love and peace to us in the throes of our spiritual battles, the area around us is suddenly filled with fragrance too. (YTL)

As others look at my life, do they see a dried-up or an over-flowing personality?

Lord, give me 'the oil of gladness instead of mourning and a garment of praise instead of a spirit of despair' (Isaiah 61:3).

Amazing love

God demonstrates his own love for us in this: while we were still sinners, Christ died for us. **Romans 5:8**

The essential nature of God is love. It is *all-embracing* love, since God desires that all should be saved (1 Timothy 2:4). It is *unmerited* love, in that while we were yet sinners Christ died for us (Romans 5:8,10). It is *sacrificial* love, marked by God giving us his Son and even making him to be sin for us (John 3:16; 2 Corinthians 5:21). It is *merciful* love, since God longs to wash away our sins; he does not keep his anger for ever (Ephesians 2:4; Psalm 103:8-10). It is *conquering* love, enabling us to overcome the trials and temptations that God in his wisdom allows us to experience for growth into full maturity (Romans 8:37). It is *inseparable* love, which nothing can ever break — neither depression, disease, demonic forces, nor death itself (Romans 8:38,39). It is *chastening* love, since this too is necessary for our 'highest good' (Hebrews 12:8). It is *everlasting* love as the Scriptures remind us some 180 times. It is also *jealous* love, in that God expects the total devotion of our lives to him who has given himself unreservedly to us (Exodus 20:5). (D)

Thank you, Father, for your breathtaking love for me.

Meditate on God's kind of love and on how you can receive it more fully or believe more fully that you have received it.

September 26   No love without judgment

For God so loved the world that he gave his one and only Son, that whoever believes in him shall not perish but have eternal life.
                                                     John 3:16

A vicar once collected a visiting preacher from the station and took him to the church. As he drove along, the vicar said to the visiting preacher, 'By the way, I'd rather you didn't preach about judgment. We don't like that sort of thing in our church. What *are* you going to preach about?' The man replied, 'My text is John chapter 3 verse 16.' 'Excellent! Excellent!' said the vicar.

   Once in he pulpit, the preacher announced his text and started to read it. Just before the word 'perish' he paused and said, 'Excuse me,' to the congregation, then turned to the vicar and asked, 'Vicar, may I go on?' The vicar blushed and gave a little nod, so the speaker completed the verse.

The point is, we cannot really understand the love of God until we see it in the context of judgment. What does it mean when we say, 'God is love'? Does it mean that he sits up in heaven smiling down and saying, 'I love you'? No wonder people ignore God today if they think that's what his love means! No wonder the faith of some Christians is so flabby! They have never really understood the love of God, because they've never really seen what God has saved them from, or what Christ actually endured for them on the cross. Christ, who more than anyone else showed us the love of God, taught us more than anyone else did about his judgment. It's a judgment that comes on all who reject his love — and love always risks being rejected. Ask anyone who's ever loved! (YTL)

What does 'God is love' really mean? Could I spell it out with Bible references to anyone asking me about it?

Father, help me to love people enough to risk rejection by them.

September 27   Fire and brimstone today?

The cowardly, the unbelieving, the vile, the murderers, the sexually immoral, those who practise magic arts, the idolaters and all liars — their place will be in the fiery lake of burning sulphur. This is the second death.   **Revelation 21:8**

During a mission, I talked one evening about hell and a God of love. As I spoke, I became aware that a number of clergy and other religious leaders were growing angrier and angrier. The next day I had a phone call from a local vicar who had some very uncomplimentary things to say about my message. How apt is Malcolm Muggeridge's comment: 'When I talk about

Christ in public, the people who go for me the hardest are not bankers and shopkeepers, but clergy.'

Many clergy and others today reject, or are not preaching about, the judgment of God. They say, 'It's positively mediaeval to preach about hell and God's judgment in the enlightened twentieth century.'

I was reading through some sermons of George Whitefield and came across many statements like this: 'As the Lord lives, in whose name I speak, if you will not come to Christ to have life, you must hear him pronounce you damned to all eternity.' Such preaching would no doubt be offensive today, but thousands came to hear George Whitefield proclaiming both God's judgment and his love, and the result was revival in our nation. Today there's no preaching like this, and no revival either. It isn't that such preaching is a technique for revival; it's that judgment is a major emphasis in God's word. You'll find a warning of God's judgment on almost every page of the Bible, and many of the prophecies of judgment came dramatically true. (YTL)

What is the right motive for warning anyone about God's judgment on those who reject Jesus?

Father, thank you that 'no condemnation now I dread', since 'Jesus and all in him is mine'.

September 28   Satan silenced by the cross

When you were dead in your sins and in the uncircumcision of your sinful nature, God made you alive with Christ. He forgave us all our sins, having cancelled the written code, with its regulations, that was against us and that stood opposed to us; he took it away, nailing it to the cross. And having disarmed the powers and authorities, he made a public spectacle of them, triumphing over them by the cross.

Colossians 2:13-15

The cross saves us from the power of Satan. He accuses the saints before God night and day (Revelation 12:10). He can also cause Christians to be filled with doubts and with guilt feelings. But when Jesus died on the cross, he shouted in triumph, 'It is finished!' That word was one which was stamped across bills after they had been paid.

If a firm sends me a bill for something I've already paid, all I need to do is to produce the receipt — or the bill with 'paid' stamped across it, and the firm will have no power or authority in the matter and no right to charge me again.

In the same way, when Satan accuses me, saying, 'Look what a mess you've made of things! Now you're for it!' — I can, so to speak, point him to the cross of Jesus and say, 'That matter has been fully settled. The bill has been paid. Jesus dealt with my sins once and for all and you have no right to try to make me pay up again.'

So when Jesus died, he stamped 'paid' across our account, and deprived Satan of any rights over us. We are safe from him through the cross of Jesus. (K)

Thank you, Lord, that you have paid in full for all the wrong I have done or will do. May this fill me with a hatred of wrong and love for you.

Is there someone I know who feels self-condemned? How can I help that person through today's reading and comments?

September 29   **Together through the cross**

Those who belong to Christ Jesus have crucified the sinful nature with its passions and desires. . . Let us not become conceited, provoking and envying each other.

Galatians 5:24,26

The true basis for all fellowship is when two or more persons kneel at the foot of the cross of Jesus Christ, trusting wholly in his mercy and love. It may well be in fellowship with other

Christians that the light of Christ will shatter my self-righteousness and expose my sinful heart. At that point of reality, I see how my sins crucified Christ and how they wound his Body, the church, today. Once I really face that, nothing that I can say or do should surprise me concerning the image I have about myself. Also, as I turn towards my brother, nothing he may say or do should surprise me about him. I can no longer be critical or judgmental, since there, at the cross, I have discovered the state of my own sinful heart.

Since the cross is at the heart of all fellowship, it is only by way of the cross that fellowship is deepened and matured. This will involve the frequent and painful crucifixion of all forms of self — self-seeking, self-centredness, self-righteousness — and the willingness to remain weak and vulnerable in open fellowship with other Christians. Often we try to meet each other from positions of strength. We talk about our gifts, blessings and achievements in the name of Christ. Mutual encouragement along these lines may sometimes be necessary and helpful. But true fellowship, which binds our hearts together in love, begins when we meet at the point of weakness. When I am willing to be open to you about my own personal needs, risking your shock or rejection, and when I am willing for you to be equally open with me, loving you and accepting you with unjudging friendship, we both find ourselves at the foot of the cross, where there is level ground, at the place of God's healing and grace. (D)

Lord, help me to be real in my relationships.

Is the fellowship at my church like that of a club, rather than being truly based on the cross? What can I do about this?

September 30   Grumblers anonymous!

When they came to Marah, they could not drink its water because it was bitter. . . So the people grumbled against Moses, saying, 'What are we to drink?'   Exodus 15:23,24

**They camped at Rephidim. . . But the people were thirsty for water there, and they grumbled against Moses. Exodus 17:1,3
All the Israelites grumbled against Moses and Aaron.**

Numbers 14:2

Have you ever noticed how often God's people grumbled in the Old Testament? Exodus chapters 15, 16, and 17 have some striking examples. They grumbled immediately after God's wonderful deliverance at the Red Sea, they grumbled after God's miraculous provision of water, and they grumbled after the spies had returned from exploring the land of Canaan.

Usually their grumbling was apparently directed at their leaders, but as Moses warned them, 'You are not grumbling against us, but against the Lord' (Exodus 16:8). And none of the grumblers entered the Promised Land.

Grumbling is a sign of unbelief; it shows that we don't believe that God is in control. We may appear to direct our grumbling at other people, but ultimately we are complaining against God through a spirit of unbelief. The writer to the Hebrews has some solemn things to say on this matter (3:7-19; 4:1-3; 12:14,15).

Jesus said that if we have a complaint, we should go straight to the person concerned (Matthew 18:15). And a spirit of grumbling needs to be cast out by unconditional repentance, by accepting Jesus' forgiveness, and by asking God to fill us again with his love. We cannot be full of God's love and be grumblers at the same time! (PL)

Lord, drive out my spirit of grumbling by a fresh filling of your love.

If someone comes up to me and starts grumbling about the church or another church member, I must be prepared to speak out, change the subject or walk away — not smugly, but gently.

OCTOBER
Prayer

October 1   **Prayer works!**

He [God] will deliver us. On him we have set our hope that he will continue to deliver us, as you help us by your prayers.
2 Corinthians 1:10,11

A small boy sat on the quayside, dipping his toes into the cool, refreshing sea. Beside him sat an old weather-beaten Cornish sailor.

'What is the wind?' asked the boy suddenly. There was a long pause while the two sat watching the breeze ruffle the water.

'I don't know,' answered the old sailor at last. 'I can't tell you what the wind is. But I know how to hoist a sail.'

'How does prayer work?' some people ask, to which I, along with many others, would reply, 'I don't know. I only know that it *does*!'

Paul the apostle was confident that God would deliver him — yet he asks for prayer. Almost all his letters have an appeal for prayer support. Young, inexperienced Christians are urged to pray constantly for the mighty apostle! Even Jesus asked his disciples for their prayers. Why? Again, I don't know. But I do know that when we pray, God works. (PL)

Lord, teach me to pray deeply, effectively and often.

Is there a united prayer meeting in my church fellowship? If so, do I go? If not, why not?

Bible study: What can we learn from Bible prayers?
Starters: 1 Samuel 1:10-12; 2:1-10; Nehemiah 1:5-11; Daniel 2:20-23; Habakkuk 3; Matthew 6:9-13; 11:25-26; 26:39,42; John 17; Acts 4:24-30 and see under 'prayer' in index.

October 2   Living prayer

The Lord would speak to Moses face to face, as a man speaks with his friend.   Exodus 33:11

Although we need to set aside some time each day for specific prayer, it's good to practise the presence of God wherever we go — walking along the street, driving a car, riding a bicycle, sitting at home or in the office, working at a bench. Anywhere and everywhere we can turn our thoughts to God, thanking him for anything good that has happened, asking for his help for what we're about to do, confessing our anger or selfishness, praying for someone in need; in other words, sharing our lives with him, and talking to him as we would talk to our best and closest friend.

Look at the psalms. Every mood, emotion, thought and situation is shared by the psalmist with the Lord. Nothing is too great for God's power and nothing is too small for his love.

Some people find a structure helpful for the more specific times of prayer. One suggestion can be remembered easily because it consists of four words of which the opening letters spell the word 'acts'.

A is for adoration. It's good to begin by remembering God is with us and reflecting on his greatness and glory, his compassion, understanding and love. This leads us to worship and adore him in our hearts, perhaps using a psalm or song.

C is for confession. We tell him about anything on our consciences and, with his help, turn away from those things, trusting in his promise of forgiveness.

T is for thanksgiving. We thank him for the many good things we receive daily, and for answers to our prayers.

S is for supplication. We pray for others and ourselves.

We can use this framework when we pray alone or with others. There is special power in prayer when Christians join together. It was not for nothing that those first Christians gathered frequently to pray as a group (Acts 1:14). (C/LANL)

Meditate on the fact that Jesus is 'closer than breathing, nearer than hands and feet'.

Lord, as I go about the day's activities and work, keep me talking and listening to you.

October 3   Meet him in the morning

Very early in the morning, while it was still dark, Jesus got up, left the house and went off to a solitary place, where he prayed.   Mark 1:35

There is no doubt that the most important time of prayer for the vast majority of Christians is first thing in the morning, if possible before breakfast and the rest of the day starts. It helps us to tune in to God from the start thus enabling us both to commit the entire day in prayer to God, and to turn to him much more readily at various times throughout the day.

In any war, communications are vital. Every day begins with a careful check on these communications, so that throughout the day orders can be passed on immediately and calls for help can be instantly heard. Without this, any army would be in total disarray. Exactly the same applies within the army of Jesus Christ.

Before we think that we are one of those whose metabolism makes all this impossible, however, let me say that I have personally never found it easy to get up in the morning to pray! Virtually every day is a real battle; but because I believe it to be a battle worth winning, I have taken active and practical steps to 'beat my body and make it my slave' (1 Corinthians 9:27)! For many years I have used two alarms to wake me up, since I sometimes find that one on its own may fail to wake me. I used to have one alarm clock by my bed, then another cheap but very noisy alarm outside my door set to go off ten minutes after the first. Because the second alarm would wake the whole household (and make me thoroughly unpopular), I had some motivation to get out of bed as soon as the first alarm had sounded. This scheme never failed!

In many ways I am ashamed to have to resort to such methods when rising to pray means rising to enjoy the Great Lover; nevertheless I am grateful to those who helped me to see that this is an important daily battle to take seriously and win! (D)

Lord, show me when is the best time for me to be alone with you every day. Strengthen my will to keep that time free for you.

Are there any practical steps I can take to help myself (or another) to begin the day with God?

October 4 A pattern for intercessory prayer

Then Abraham approached him [the Lord] and said, 'Will you sweep away the righteous with the wicked? What if there are fifty righteous people in the city? Will you really sweep it away and not spare the place for the sake of the fifty righteous people in it?' Genesis 18:23,24

Read the whole intercession (18:23-33). What can we learn from this prayer?

Abraham was *confident*. He 'approached' the Lord, knowing that he was right with God by faith, just as we can know that we have an open door into God's presence if we have a personal faith in Jesus. But he was also *reverent*. 'I am nothing but dust and ashes,' he said (verse 27). He knew he had no *right* to ask for *anything* from God, unlike some people today who pray as though they have a right to ask him for *everything*.

Abraham was *fervent*. He felt strongly about this. 'Far be it from you to do such a thing,' he said (verse 25). He was also *definite*, in contrast to some of our vague prayers asking God to bless everyone everywhere; this was possible, because he knew the facts and based his prayer on them. He knew that God was both loving, holy and just. He knew that Sodom was a wicked place and deserved punishment. So he prayed a bold, definite, specific prayer.

He was *persevering*; he pleaded with God six times.

And yet Sodom was destroyed. Why? Because Abraham wasn't praying for any 'ten righteous' in Sodom: he was praying for his nephew Lot, his wife, two sons, four daughters and two sons-in-law. And he was assuming that because Lot was righteous, his family were too. But this wasn't so. Lot's sons and sons-in-law would not listen to him when he told them of God's coming judgment, so Lot left with his two unmarried daughters and his wife only, and even his wife wasn't with him for long. (YTL)

What would have happened if Abraham had asked God, 'What if only one righteous person be found there?'

Lord, for whom or what should I be persisting in prayer now and in the coming days, weeks, months or even years?

October 5   United prayer

Again, I tell you that if two of you on earth agree about anything you ask for, it will be done for you by my Father in heaven. For where two or three come together in my name, there I am with them.   **Matthew 18:19,20**

Jesus promised that he would be present in special power whenever two or three of his disciples met for prayer. The early church was always praying together, devoting itself to prayer. In this way we encourage one another, stimulate faith, identify ourselves as members of the Body of Christ, and bring spiritual gifts to build each other up in him.

Corporate prayer often needs good leadership by those who are sensitive to the Spirit. It may be helpful to start with a time of worship, consciously lifting our minds and hearts from ourselves to the Lord. Too many prayers are earthbound. We are to set our minds on things above, encouraging one another to know that the Lord is with us. We need to raise the level of corporate faith and expectancy. Short bursts of praise and prayer from as many as possible are far better than the long prayers of the 'professionals'. Such perorations might impress some like-minded saints, but they will kill most prayer meetings. Encourage sensitivity both to the Spirit and to one another. It helps when one theme at a time is 'prayed through', rather than jumping randomly from one topic to another. We have a New Testament model for such gatherings: everyone should have some contribution, each bringing different gifts to glorify Christ and to strengthen his Body (1 Corinthians 14:26). (D)

Lord, unite our church fellowship in regular, persistent, sensitive prayer.

Do I long to pray with fellow Christians? If not, what's amiss?

October 6   Victorious prayer

They raised their voices together in prayer to God. 'Sovereign Lord,' they said, 'you made the heaven and the earth and the sea, and everything in them.'   **Acts 4:24**

Read the verse in its context (Acts 4:23-31), to discover the secrets of victorious prayer.

First, the disciples prayed *together*. There is always a special sense of Christ's presence and power when believing Christians raise their voices together in prayer to God. Christians in some parts of the world know this so well that they are willing to risk imprisonment, or even death, in order to attend prayer and fellowship meetings.

Secondly, they prayed *to the Sovereign Lord*. Before they touched on their problems, they turned to God, as he had revealed himself in the Scriptures. They saw that the God of the Bible was in control over everything, starting with creation, and including the recent crucifixion of his Son Jesus — and so they were able to pray believingly.

Thirdly, they prayed *specifically* and *boldly*. Notice that they did not pray for protection, but for 'great boldness' to 'enable your servants to speak your word' (verse 29), and for God's power to be seen in signs, wonders and healings in the name of Jesus (verse 30).

We need to take united prayer far more seriously than we do. We need to focus on the one to whom we are praying, through the biblical revelation we are given of him, so that we can pray with a faith kindled by the truth of God's word. We need to be clear as to what it is we are actually asking God, the Sovereign Lord, to do for us. (YTL)

What do I (we) need to learn about victorious prayer?

Sovereign Lord, enable me, your servant to . . .

October 7   Persisting in prayer

Then Jesus told his disciples a parable to show them that they **should always pray and not give up.**   Luke 18:1
We . . . will give our attention to prayer and the ministry of the word.   Acts 6:3,4

There is possibly no area in our lives where we can be so careless and lazy as in the matter of prayer. We may neglect it altogether. We may give lip-service to it by reeling off a few familiar phrases, while our hearts and minds are elsewhere (Mark 7:6). Certainly God works in our lives by grace and, thankfully, not by what we deserve. He may therefore answer even our casual prayers; but normally he waits until our whole being is concentrated on him... The Scriptures are full of examples of men and women who gave themselves unreservedly to the Lord in prayer.

Jesus also told his disciples that 'they should always pray and not give up'. He underlined this principle in his stories of the importunate widow and the friend at midnight. God wants us to rely on him for everything — only then shall we enjoy his love — and thus in his wisdom he sometimes delays in answering our prayers, to see how much we really want something for his praise and glory alone.

The first disciples knew the absolute importance of persistence in prayer. After the ascension of Jesus into heaven, when they knew they could not witness to him in their own strength, they 'all joined together constantly in prayer' (Acts 1:14). They refused to give up or get discouraged; they determinedly stuck to it; they knew it was essential. Later, when the church in Jerusalem was growing by leaps and bounds, the apostles checked on their priorities. They appointed others to attend to the increasing pastoral and administrative demands so that they could give their attention to prayer. (D)

Show me, through your Holy Spirit's inner voice, where I should be persistent in my prayers and give me the desire to continue.

Be prepared to hear God telling you in his own way where you ought to be persisting in prayer about any matter.

October 8   Three priorities

Now the tax collectors and 'sinners' were all gathering around to hear him [Jesus]. But the Pharisees and teachers of the law muttered, 'This man welcomes sinners and eats with them.' . . . [Jesus said]: 'I tell you that . . . there is more rejoicing in heaven over one sinner who repents than over ninety-nine righteous persons who do not need to repent.'   **Luke 15:1,2,7**

Worship should always be the first priority of the Christian.

Next to worship, evangelism should be our greatest concern, for heaven is especially filled with joy when even one person turns to Christ, and Christ has commanded his people to take his message to the ends of the earth.

A third priority is caring and serving. As well as spending time deepening his relationship with his disciples, Jesus gave himself to the crooks and the prostitutes, the sick and the poor, the devil-possessed and the social rejects of his day. He saw each individual as vitally important to God.

If we profess to follow Jesus today, we must pray for the same self-sacrificing compassion. Millions will starve to death — do we care? Families need to be housed. Loneliness plagues countless people.

The church needs to become a loving welcoming community or family. This is a high priority. (PL)

Lord, show us in our church fellowship where our priorities are wrong at the moment — whether in our worship, our caring or our evangelism.

What is my contribution in these areas? Is it enough?

October 9   **The means and motive for mission**

The Spirit told Philip, 'Go to that chariot and stay near it.'
Acts 8:29

It is the Holy Spirit who empowers evangelism and initiates mission. The Acts of the Apostles are really the acts of the Holy Spirit. He told Philip to approach the chariot of the Ethiopian eunuch; he confirmed the vision that Peter had received (Acts 10:17-19), which led to the inclusion of Gentile believers; he told the church to set apart Barnabas and Saul for missionary work on a large scale (Acts 13:2). It must have been just as shocking for Peter to enter Cornelius' home and see the Spirit falling on Gentiles as it is for some Protestants today to hear of the Spirit renewing Catholic churches all over the world!

It is the Holy Spirit who fills us with the love without which all our evangelism and mission and everything else is useless (Romans 5:5; 1 Corinthians 13:1). We grieve the Spirit by our lack of love — our bitterness, rage and malice (Ephesians 4:30,31). We can even quench the Spirit or 'put out the Spirit's fire' (1 Thessalonians 5:19) in various ways. Instead of that, we are to 'be filled with the Spirit' (Ephesians 5:18) for mission and service according to God's will. (YTL)

Where do all the new ideas in our church come from?

Lord of the church and of my life, please may the Holy Spirit be the initiator of any changes or new directions.

October 10   Pointers in personal evangelism

Then Ananias went to the house and entered it. Placing his hands on Saul, he said: 'Brother Saul, the Lord — Jesus, who appeared to you on the road as you were coming here — has sent me so that you may see again and be filled with the Holy Spirit.'   **Acts 9:17**

Opportunities for talking about Jesus come in so far as we want them to. The crucial question is: 'Do I really want to speak about Jesus to others?' I remember being on holiday once and not wanting to speak to anyone about anything, but I believe the Lord challenged me near the end of the holiday and I said, 'All right, Lord, I'm willing to speak to anyone in this hotel about you if you guide me to someone.' And he did, immediately after breakfast that morning.

Most people, if not all, are hungry for God, however self-confident or uninterested they may appear to be. I discovered this with the man at the hotel. He appeared to have everything but he quickly admitted that he didn't know which way he was going in life. Many times I have found appearances to be deceptive in this matter.

Have a vision for unlikely people. Often the most unlikely

301

people are crying out for God. When Philip went to the desert road and met the caravan, he might well have wondered whether he was to speak to one of the servants or a soldier about Christ, but instead the Spirit said, 'Go and join that Rolls-Royce chariot with the V.I.P. sitting in it' (Acts 8:26-39)!

Have ready for use at any time a simple, clear explanation of how a person can become a Christian. Here are three words and three verses which might be useful as you work out your way of leading a person into faith in Christ: repent (Acts 3:19), believe (Isaiah 53:6), receive (Acts 2:38). (YTL)

Do I believe that most people, if not all, are hungry for God?

Father, give me a vision of some unlikely person in whom your Spirit is working, and show me what I can do to share Jesus with that person.

October 11   Never miss an opportunity

The next day the rulers, elders and teachers of the law met in Jerusalem. . . They had Peter and John brought before them and began to question them: 'By what power or what name did you do this?'
                                                                 Acts 4:5,7

Peter and John were in a tough situation. Their master had been crucified and they were in danger of the same fate. Here they were in front of the religious leaders who had brought about Jesus' death. They could have chosen to answer cautiously, guardedly. Instead Peter declared, 'It is by the name of Jesus Christ of Nazareth, whom you crucified but whom God raised from the dead, that this man stands before you completely healed' (Acts 4:10).

Someone has written, 'Reticence can be as harmful as unguided speech, and it is not always what Christians say, but what they *don't* say, that misrepresents the things of God.' If we say nothing about these things, people will assume that they are not important. Worse still, if we remain silent when we have an opportunity of speaking for Christ, we are virtually denying him.

Why are some people so bold and others so reticent in speaking for Jesus? The answer lies partly, but not wholly, in temperament and personality. John Stott has said, 'Nothing shuts the mouth, seals the lips, ties the tongue, like the poverty of our own spiritual experience. However shy we are, if our spiritual experience is rich, if we are filled with the love of Jesus, and if spiritual issues are very real to us, we will witness to others in word and life.'

I believe we need to pray daily for a fresh vision and experience of Jesus and his love and a fresh understanding of spiritual realities. We cannot rely on a great spiritual experience in the past. We need the Holy Spirit's presence and activity each day as we read the Bible, pray and go about our daily lives. Otherwise Satan will soon get us preoccupied with matters of secondary importance. (YTL)

Would I even recognise an evangelistic opportunity?

Lord, show us anything that is hindering us from seeing or taking opportunities to speak for you.

October 12   Dance as evangelism

The Lord announced the word, and great was the company of those who proclaimed it.   **Psalm 68:11**

In this verse the Hebrew word for 'those who proclaimed it' is the feminine form of the word 'evangelist'. . . In practice, the good news of God's victory was proclaimed in a great procession led by women, some of whom were prophetesses, who were singing and dancing. This was one God-given way in which the Spirit of God encouraged people with the sense of God's presence and power, and consequently led them out into worship. Here all the faculties of mind, soul and body were united in praise, and this was one authentic way of enjoying and sharing the experience of the living God.

I have, on numerous occasions, witnessed the same moving of the Spirit of God through united singing and dancing, springing out from the sharing of lives together in Jesus Christ. Not only has this stimulated God's people to worship and praise, but outsiders, with no professed belief at all, have often tasted, perhaps for the first time, something of the joy and presence of the living God. (IBIE)

How much of my body is involved in my worship?

Lord, set me free from prejudices which inhibit me from enjoying any aspect of the worship of you.

October 13   The worship of an imagination that reflects
                                                      his beauty

. . . gaze upon the beauty of the Lord.   Psalm 27:4

The book of Revelation is like a great impressionist painting of God in his glory. We cannot understand all the details but the overall impression is one of awe, wonder, glory, colour and movement which beggar imagination. If we think of praise only in terms of sound and music, we are missing a great deal. What about light, colour, form, motion, touch, flavour and fragrance? In celebrating, worshipping and praising God, we should use every imaginative, creative gift, to reflect something of his beauty.

Today, the Holy Spirit is pouring out creative gifts on his people, so that they are worshipping him not just in songs but also in dance, drama and movement, through banners and pictures, and the use of any gift which causes God's glory and beauty to shine out more clearly.

Imagination and feeling are closely linked and so the worship of renewed imaginations often goes hand in hand with the worship of renewed hearts into which God has poured his love. It's significant that in every church where there is a renewing work of the Holy Spirit, no matter what its tradition, there is also new freedom, joy, creativity and love, in worship. (YTL)

How much of my heart and imagination are involved in worship?

Help me, Lord, to gaze on your beauty and feel uplifted.

October 14   Take me

I urge you, brothers, in view of God's mercy, to offer your bodies as living sacrifices, holy and pleasing to God — which is your spiritual worship. Romans 12:1,2

A man who had no interest in Christian things was walking round an art gallery when he came across a painting of the crucifixion. As he looked at it, he realised something of the agony of Jesus, as he bore our sins. Underneath the picture he then read these words: 'All this I did for thee. What hast thou done for me?'

The man was transfixed by the painting and those words and there and then he gave his life to Jesus. His name was Count Zindendorf, and he went on to be an effective witness for Jesus, and the founder of a famous missionary movement.

A small boy really loved Jesus and longed to show it. When the collection plate began coming round, he realised he had no money, so he got a piece of paper, wrote one word on it and put it on the plate when it was passed to him. In the vestry afterwards, the people who were counting the collection came upon a crumpled piece of paper, which simply said 'myself'.

The sacrifice of our bodies symbolises the giving of ourselves. God wants the total surrender of our lives in response to the total sacrifice of his Son's life. This will mean using all we have and are for God and for the body of Christ; it will mean loving, giving, forgiving, sharing, praying, helping and other practical expressions of dedication. (AR)

Have I really offered everything I have and am to God?

Father, I want to worship you with my whole being. Take me.

October 15   **First love**

You have forsaken your first love.   **Revelation 2:4**
Fix your thoughts on Jesus.   **Hebrews 3:1**

The book of Hebrews was written to Christians going through difficult times, with worse to come, probably. Some were tempted to give up. To them was sent this letter with its central message: 'There is no one like Jesus.' He's God's last word, the heir of all things, creator of the universe, reflecting God's glory (Hebrews 1:1-3); he is the great high priest who sacrificed himself for our sins once and for all (Hebrews 3:1; 10:12), who understands us completely (Hebrews 4:14-16). We are, above all, to 'consider him' (Hebrews 12:3).

It's so easy to be taken up with other things, even Christian things, but nothing is more important than Jesus, and we need to return to our first love for him.

After fourteen years of suffering, Richard Wurmbrand wrote: 'There exists only one method of resisting brainwashing and that is heart-washing. If the heart is cleansed by the love of Jesus, if the heart loves him, you can resist all tortures.'

How do we return to our first love? We need to 'repent and do the things you did at first' (Revelation 2:4). Repenting means turning away from and confessing anything wrong in our lives, including our lack of love for Jesus.

What sort of things did the Ephesian Christians do at first? They came to the cross, were filled with the Spirit, gave serious attention to God's word, burned their books on the occult, got rid of anything that displeased him, and put him first. We need to do the same. (AR)

Somehow, Lord Jesus, bring me back to my first love for you.

Do the same for the rest of our church fellowship, too, please Lord.

Do I need to repent and do the things I did at first — that is, when I was a new(er) Christian?

October 16   Excitement in heaven

Then I looked and heard the voices of many angels, numbering thousands upon thousands, and ten thousand times ten thousand. They encircled the throne and the living creatures and the elders. In a loud voice they sang: 'Worthy is the Lamb, who was slain, to receive power and wealth and wisdom and strength and honour and glory and praise!' Revelation 5:11,12

The excitement in heaven will not be primarily over the birth of Jesus — although that was astonishing enough, since by that event God came into the world as a human being and lived among us.

Nor will the excitement focus primarily on Jesus' life — although it has been said that his character was more wonderful than the greatest miracle; or on his teaching — although that was matchless; or even on his resurrection — although that has been called the greatest fact in human history.

The greatest cause of excitement in heaven will be the death of Jesus for our sins, 'the Lamb who was slain', because that sacrifice made it possible for us to know God's love and forgiveness and to be sure that one day we would go to heaven and be with him for ever. In that place, we will be able to worship him fully for this amazing love. (K)

Lord Jesus, Lamb of God, I worship you for what you have done for me and for the world. May you be praised for ever and ever.

Am I excited about heaven?

When he comes, he will convict the world of guilt in regard to sin and righteousness and judgment.   John 16:8

I was waiting to speak to a group of university students once, when the chairman pointed someone out as the toughest girl in the place. She was part of the drug scene and she slept around. Throughout my talk, she sat with her feet up on a table, smoking and looking utterly bored. At the end of the meeting, I prayed a prayer for those wanting to accept Jesus, and then invited those who had echoed it in their hearts to come and see me. Much to my surprise, this girl came along. The cigarette was still dangling from her lips, but she told me she'd received Christ into her life. I thought, 'Time will tell.' But the next night she was there again and I would hardly have recognised her as the same girl. She told me her story, and one of the things she said was this: 'For the last six years I have felt as guilty as hell.' Yet all the time, she had been behaving as though she was tough and insensitive.

The Holy Spirit had clearly been at work in her life, convicting her of sin, despite the outward appearance of things. Unless the Holy Spirit is at work in this way, our best efforts are useless.

William Wilberforce once took William Pitt to hear a famous preacher. Throughout the meeting Wilberforce was enthralled by the wonderful preaching and thrilled that Pitt was there to hear it. But afterwards Pitt turned to him and said, 'I haven't the slightest idea as to what the preacher was talking about.' Pitt was a very clever man, but his spiritual eyes were shut, and only the Holy Spirit could have opened them. (AR)

Father, continue to show me, through the Holy Spirit, what is wrong in my life so that I might turn from it.

Is there someone in whom the Holy Spirit is working but I am unaware of this because I've been judging by appearances?

Meanwhile, Saul was still breathing out murderous threats against the Lord's disciples. . . Then the church throughout Judea, Galilee and Samaria enjoyed a time of peace.

Acts 9:1,31

The chapter opens with Saul persecuting the church but towards the end of it we read that the Christians were enjoying a time of peace. What happened in between? Saul encountered the living Christ and passed from law to grace.

Under the law, Saul was angry — filled with hate and a desire to hurt all Christians. Religious people need to beware of loveless moral indignation and anger against those who differ from them. Anger and self-righteousness often go hand in hand.

Under the law, Saul was spiritually blind and confused. For a time, he was physically blind, too. Spiritual blindness and confusion are a person's natural state as Saul realised later (1 Corinthians 2:14).

Under the law, Saul was helpless, as we all are, because the law reveals and — in a sense — encourages sin (Romans 7:7,8).

Under the law, Saul was angry, blind and helpless *but God* loved and chose him, healed him physically and spiritually and gave him new sight and life (Acts 9:15,17-19). In other words, God's amazing grace transformed his whole life.

It's the same for us, and it isn't only at conversion that we need to depend on God's grace (God's riches at Christ's expense), but throughout our lives; God's grace is sufficient for every need and every situation (2 Corinthians 12:9). (YTL)

Do I tend to fall into the trap of Galatians 3:3?

Father, help me to live not under law but under grace.

The Twelve gathered all the disciples together and said, '. . . Brothers, choose seven men among you who are known to be

full of the Spirit and wisdom.' . . . They chose Stephen, a man full of faith and of the Holy Spirit; also Philip, Procorus, Nicanor, Timon, Parmenas and Nicolas . . . They presented these men to the apostles who prayed and laid their hands on them. So the word of God spread. The number of disciples in Jerusalem increased rapidly. Acts 6:2,3,5-7

John Stott has said, 'The desperate need of the church today is the Holy Spirit. We need individual Christians filled with the Spirit. More than that, we need revival, a mighty supernatural visitation of the Holy Spirit in the community. Nothing else will save our church from its spiritual torpor or our country from lapsing into complete paganism.'

Notice that *nothing else* will do. There is feverish activity within the church concerning *everything else*: new buildings, new services, new reports, new reunion schemes, new organisations. 'If only this were altered, or that, things would be different,' people seem to be saying. They are wrong. 'Nothing else [but the Holy Spirit's revival] will save our church from its spiritual torpor.'

Our country is increasingly sick. With pornography, permissiveness, anarchy, occultism, its pagan atmosphere is increasingly obvious. What is the answer? 'Nothing else [but the Holy Spirit's revival] will save . . . our country from lapsing into complete paganism.'

We must be ready for any and every genuine move of the Holy Spirit of God. Too many Christians are nervous and suspicious about anything outside their experience. 'We dig our little trenches,' said Billy Graham, 'and we say, "O God, you are going to work this way and only this way," but God breaks out and does it his own way!' (PL)

Lord, I want to open myself up more and more to be filled with the Holy Spirit.

What barriers, if any, am I putting up against the Holy Spirit?

Be filled with the Spirit. Speak to one another with psalms, hymns and spiritual songs. Sing and make music in your heart to the Lord, always giving thanks to God the Father for every-thing, in the name of our Lord Jesus Christ.   Ephesians 5:18-20

In these verses we have four consequences of being filled with the Spirit.

First, a Spirit-filled fellowship is one where members encourage one another in worship and praise. The same note is heard in some of the psalms, for instance: 'Glorify the Lord with me; let us exalt his name together' (Psalm 34:3).

Secondly, worship will be directed to the Lord. The way we sing and even the expressions on our faces will show just how real the Lord is to us. A reporter who attended one of our communion services wrote in his paper afterwards: 'There was in the faces of the worshippers an uninhibited pleasure in the act of worship, a look that compels even a cynical observer to reach for old-fashioned words like radiance and joy.'

Thirdly, there will be thanksgiving that expresses our trust in God in every situation. Grumbling is a sign of our times. In contrast, we should be filled with real thankfulness. Some people have taken verse 20 to mean that we should thank God for evil and accidents. This, I believe, is ridiculous if not blasphemous. What we are to thank God for is his control of every situation.

Fourthly, we are to submit to one another. In other words, our relationships must be right; if they are not, our fellowship collapses, our worship is meaningless and our thanksgiving is hollow. (YTL)

Have we the characteristics of a Spirit-filled fellowship?

Father, we long to so worship you that newcomers will sense how real you are to us.

[Jesus said:] 'Whoever believes in me as the Scripture has said, streams of living water will flow from within him.' By this he meant the Spirit, whom those who believed in him were later to receive. Up to that time the Spirit had not been given, since Jesus had not yet been glorified.   John 7:38,39

The fulness of the Spirit is not an optional extra. We are commanded to be filled with the Spirit and God longs that every part of our lives should be affected.

It is not a licence for 'doing your own thing'. Some people who claim to be filled with the Spirit become very independent: 'The Lord told me. . .' But God wants us to be united in love and then he can fill us corporately; this will be far more effective than having a few Spirit-filled, independent Christians, in the same way that a whole cup can hold far more water than the sum of what the broken pieces could hold.

It is not a spiritual one-up-manship. It only happens as we humbly yield our lives in every part to Jesus as Lord.

It's not a once-for-all experience — we need constant filling or we shall dry up.

It's not a matter of feelings but of faith in God's word. Jesus promised that the Father would give the Spirit to those who asked him.

Perhaps you've never asked to be filled with the Holy Spirit, or perhaps you have been filled in the past but are now dry, or else you found the results painful and so drew back in your commitment to Christ or in your openness to other Christians. You need to be filled with those overflowing streams of living water. Two conditions: repent of anything you know is wrong, and ask in faith. (YTL)

Is there any rethinking or repenting I (we) need to do in relation to these matters?

Father, I really do want streams of living water to flow from within me to the thirsty people around, for your glory.

The angel answered, 'The Holy Spirit will come upon you, and the power of the Most High will overshadow you'. . . 'I am the Lord's servant,' Mary answered. 'May it be to me as you have said . . . My soul praises the Lord . . . for the Mighty One has done great things for me.'   **Luke 1:35,38,46,49**

Unbelief is a big barrier against the Holy Spirit filling our lives. We find it so hard to believe that God is going to work in a new way in our lives. Jesus understood this problem. Several times in one verse (Luke 11:9) he told his disciples that if they asked, they would certainly receive.

Mary is an example of faith to us all. She was promised the gift of a son. She couldn't understand how this could happen and asked, 'How can this be?' The answer was that the Holy Spirit would come upon her.

How did she respond? She surrendered her life to the Lord, risking scandal, difficulties and much future pain, and then praised God that what he had promised was already true as far as she was concerned.

Old preachers used to make the distinction between *seeking* faith and *resting* faith. Couples coming to see me before getting married are often very nervous. They perch on the edge of the chair. Gradually, as we chat, they relax and let the chair take their whole weight. You might say that they begin by showing a seeking faith — tensed up, hoping that God might act — and end up with a resting faith — a reliance on God's promise.

We need to ask for the Holy Spirit in an attitude of resting faith — an attitude which takes Jesus at his word when he says: ' "Whoever believes in me," [not he who has certain experiences, or he who speaks in tongues] "streams of living water will flow from within him." By this he meant the Spirit, whom those who believed in him were later to receive' (John 7:38,39). (AR)

Lord, help me so to believe in your promises that I can praise you even before I see the evidence.

313

Am I praying for something which God has already promised me? Do I need to start believing and praising him for it?

'For my thoughts are not your thoughts, neither are your ways my ways,' declares the Lord. 'As the heavens are higher than the earth, so are my ways higher than your ways and my thoughts than your thoughts.'   Isaiah 55:8,9

We Christians have been affected more than we realise by the scientific materialistic outlook of this age. We are inclined to believe only what we can understand or what can be explained, and to reject what we can't understand or find an explanation for. 'This I can't believe,' states an Anglican Bishop about all the key miracles of the Christian faith. Why can't he believe them? Because they are beyond the scope of his mind to understand or explain. But God's ways and thoughts are well beyond the scope of any human mind.

The trouble is, science has become the sacred cow. Everybody believes the laws of science, but many reject the laws of God, our creator and sustainer, with whom nothing is impossible.

Many Christians do not believe in divine healing for the same reason, I suspect. They can believe that God would give a person peace, because they could almost do that themselves if they had enough time, patience and love. But they cannot believe that God would heal broken bones or cancer, because they can't understand how he could do it. The same often applies to material things — God's people don't always believe in God's power in these areas. I know one church which had to find £30,000 for a new building. They didn't rush round with collecting boxes. They prayed for a whole week and the money came in four months.

> Faith, mighty faith, the promise sees,
> And looks to that alone,
> Laughs at impossibilities,
> And cries, 'It shall be done!'

It's sheer arrogance to doubt a word or promise of God simply because I don't understand it. It's reducing God to the level of my mind! (YTL)

Am I being affected by the thoughts or words of those who leave God completely out of their thinking?

Father, forgive me for ever limiting you to my own puny understanding.

October 24   The laughter of faith

Abraham fell face down; he laughed and said to himself, 'Will a son be born to a man a hundred years old? Will Sarah bear a child at the age of ninety?'
                                                    Genesis 17:17

When I first read this story I thought Abraham's laughter was the laughter of unbelief. Certainly Sarah's was: she 'laughed to herself as she thought, "After I am worn out and my master is old, will I now have this pleasure?" ' And God rebuked her for this laughter (Genesis 18:10-15).

But there is a laughter of faith and I believe Sarah experienced it later (Genesis 21:6) and Abraham experienced it here. Certainly, God didn't rebuke him. Indeed, he went further and called the promised child 'Isaac' meaning 'laughter' in memory of Abraham's laughter when he believed the Lord.

The Bible speaks in other places of this happy laughter which springs from faith. When God's people saw his salvation, their 'mouths were filled with laughter' and their 'tongues with songs of joy' (Psalm 126:2). Peter speaks of 'an inexpressible and glorious joy' (1 Peter 1:8).

Twice I have been in the company of Christians who have laughed with holy laughter in prayer because they have been so conscious of God's presence that they haven't been able to contain their joy. I believe Abraham's laughter was like that. We hear a great deal about the power of prayer. I believe the power of praise is even greater. Within a year Abraham's promised child was born. (YTL)

Do I know anything of this kind of joy or laughter?

Lord, take control even of my laughter.

October 25   The power of praise

The trumpeters and singers joined in unison, as with one voice, to give praise and thanks to the Lord. Accompanied by trumpets, cymbals and other instruments, they raised their voices in praise to the Lord and sang: 'He is good; his love endures for ever.'   **2 Chronicles 5:13**

I was present once at an international Anglican Conference for spiritual renewal. . . The final communion service, held in the choir of Canterbury Cathedral, was profoundly moving. There was a magnificent spirit of praise. . . At the time of the 'peace' we were encouraged to greet one another, and I turned to the person on my right. I discovered that he was an American tourist, drawn into the Cathedral by the sound of singing and praise. I asked him what he thought of the service. 'I have never been anywhere that is so alive,' he replied. I gently enquired, 'Do you know the One who makes us alive — Jesus Christ — or are you not sure about it?' He told me he was not at all sure, so we slipped round behind the choir stalls, and, as the praise started up again, I had to shout the gospel to him. Suddenly he grabbed me by the wrists and asked, 'Can we pray?' So I led him in a simple prayer, committing his life to Christ, shouting it phrase by phrase, with him shouting back. In that unusual way, he became a true Christian, and a few minutes later received the tokens of God's forgiveness and acceptance in the bread and the wine.

God had broken into that young man's life in a marvellous way; and it all began with the power of praise. (D)

Teach me to praise you more often and more wholeheartedly.

How much do I know of the power of praise in my life?

Dear friends, I urge you as aliens and strangers in the world, to abstain from sinful desires, which war against your soul.

1 Peter 2:11

The traditional picture of a static church, solid in its establishment, conservative in its attitudes, entrenched in familiar patterns of work and worship, is a gross distortion of the church as it is meant to be and as pictured in the Bible. The Old Testament speaks of the church in the wilderness, the New Testament of 'aliens and strangers' — members of the household of God, yes, but travelling through the desert wastes of this world and through the valley of the shadow of death until the consummation of all things in Christ, when the kingdom of the world becomes the kingdom of our Lord and of his Christ. It is therefore a people on the move, delivered from Egypt, summoned at Sinai to meet with God, and called to go with him to the land of promise. It must never become a people that settles down in the wilderness, but always alive and alert, pressing on 'towards the goal to win the prize for which God has called me heavenwards in Christ Jesus' (Philippians 3:14).

The temptation, however, is always to look back, and not to move with the cloud and fire of God's presence. (IBITC)

In our church's annual meetings, how much time is spent looking back and how much looking forward with new vision?

Father, am I too strange and alien to relate to non-Christians or they to me — or so comfortable and settled that my lifestyle is almost indistinguishable from theirs?

October 27   Commitment is costly

Anyone who does not carry his cross and follow me cannot be my disciple . . . Any of you who does not give up everything he has cannot be my disciple.   Luke 14:27,33

Jesus was pursued by crowds. What a teacher! What a healer! But then he taught the conditions of discipleship: putting Jesus first, before all other relationships, and even before one's own life; bearing one's own cross — willing to go all the way, regardless of the pain and hardship involved; renouncing all possessions and letting Jesus have control over every part of one's life, including time, money, work, leisure, friendships and ambitions.

And when they heard hard-hitting words like that, some of the crowd went away. It was more than they could stomach.

This is how a communist explained the success of his 'religion': 'Of salaries and wages we keep only what is strictly necessary, and we give up our free time and part of our holidays... How can anybody believe in the supreme value of the [Christian] gospel if you do not practise it, if you do not spread it, if you sacrifice neither time nor money for it? We believe in our communist message and we are ready to sacrifice even our life. But you people are afraid to soil your hands.'

'Give me twelve men,' Spurgeon once wrote. 'Importunate men, lovers of souls who fear nothing but sin and love nothing but God, and I will shake London from end to end.'

We should have no difficulty believing these words, for Jesus started with twelve real disciples and shook the world. (PL)

Show me, Lord, whether you really are my first love.

Is Jesus asking me to pay some price for him? What must I do?

October 28   Do we need to adopt a simpler lifestyle?

By faith Moses, when he had grown up, refused to be known as the son of Pharaoh's daughter. He chose to be ill-treated along with the people of God rather than to enjoy the pleasures of sin for a short time. He regarded disgrace for the sake of Christ as of greater value than the treasures of Egypt, because he was looking ahead to his reward.   Hebrews 11:24-26

Today in the West we are in the generation of the rich fool. Our number one sin is covetousness, which is idolatry. We worship mammon instead of God. It isn't only secular society that is committing this sin; idolatry is in the church. On the whole we do not live simply that others may simply live.

Ronald Sider wrote this in *Rich Christians in an Age of Hunger*: 'If we fail to feed the needy, we do not have God's love, no matter what we say. Regardless of what we do or say at 11 am on a Sunday morning, affluent people who neglect the poor are not the people of God.'

I once attended an international consultation on simple lifestyle in which twenty-seven countries participated. In a statement produced at the end of the consultation, the delegates said this: 'We intend to re-examine our income and expenditures in order to manage on less and give away more. We lay down no rules or regulations for either ourselves or others, yet we resolve to renounce waste and expose extravagance in personal living, clothing, housing, travel and church buildings. We also accept the distinction between necessities and luxuries, creative hobbies and empty status symbols, occasional celebrations and normal routine. We must not cease to proclaim Christ as Saviour and Lord throughout the world. The church is not yet taking seriously its commission to be witnesses to the ends of the earth, but it is impossible with integrity to proclaim Christ's salvation if he has not evidently saved us from greed, or his lordship, if we are not good stewards of our possessions.' (AR)

Lord, help me at least to be open to the possibility of simplifying my lifestyle.

Do any of my (my church's) plans need rethinking?

October 29   The place of good works

In Joppa there was a disciple named Tabitha (which, when translated, is Dorcas), who was always doing good and helping the poor.   Acts 9:36

Good works are very much played down in some church circles. This is because so many people believe that salvation can be earned by good works, whereas, as evangelicals rightly stress, it can only be received as a free gift. Two verses you could share with anyone who thinks he will be justified by good works are: 'We may be justified by faith in Jesus Christ and not by observing the law' (Galatians 2:16); 'It is by grace you have been saved, through faith . . . not by works' (Ephesians 2:8,9).

On the other hand, good works ought to be the fruit of living faith (James 2:14-26). James writes: 'I will show you my faith by what I do' (verse 18), and: 'Faith without deeds is useless' (verse 20).

Dorcas was a disciple first and good works followed because she was a disciple. We ought to praise God for every 'Dorcas'. Such helpers are just as indispensable as those with other gifts (1 Corinthians 12).

Calvin wrote, 'While it is faith alone that justifies, the faith that justifies is never alone.' It will be accompanied and shown by good works, and therefore those concerned will not be praying in effect: 'We the miserable owners of increasingly luxurious cars and ever-expanding television screens, do most humbly pray for that two-thirds of the world's population that is undernourished.' (YTL)

What is our attitude to 'helpers' — who do practical, perhaps menial, tasks?

Father, thank you for 'those able to help others' (1 Corinthians 12:28), especially. . . Help me to encourage. . .

October 30   **We need more like Barnabas**

Let us not give up meeting together, as some are in the habit of doing, but let us encourage one another — and all the more as we see the Day approaching.   **Hebrews 10:25**

We all need encouragement.

I remember having to give a series of Bible readings at a

Conference, and after the first of these, someone came up to me. Speaking very slowly, he said, 'The greatest Bible study I have ever heard. . .'

'Give me humility, Lord,' I thought, but the man had not finished, and he went on with his sentence '. . . was given by Mr X last week!' So I had a very quick answer to my prayer for humility!

Encouraging each other is one of the vital things that we do when we commit ourselves to one another. If we don't commit ourselves fully to each other, how will we be able to witness to Christ who died that we might be one not just with God but also with other Christians?

When the tide is out, we find all the shrimps in their own little pools. When the tide of the Spirit is out, Christians stay in their own little pools, as it were. But when the tide of the Spirit comes in, we all start swimming together in the one great ocean of God's love. This *agape* love is the one priceless unique gift we have to offer the world, but God will only pour it into our hearts as we commit ourselves to each other. (AR)

Lord, thank you for . . . who have encouraged me.

Who do I know who is discouraged? Is there any reason why I should not be the one to encourage that person?

October 31   **Is it reasonable to believe in God?**

In the beginning God created the heavens and the earth.
                                                    Genesis 1:1

The Bible doesn't set out to prove God's existence; it simply assumes it and sees everything else in the light of this central fact. Many of us work on the opposite principle: we assume the existence of everything else, and then see if God fits in anywhere. That's not the right way round at all!

Though we can't prove God's existence, there are four traditional arguments which give strong support to it. First, there is the argument from cause and effect. If things happen, it's likely that something or someone caused them to happen. In the Bible, God is seen as the First Cause behind all events. 'By faith we understand that the universe was formed at God's command, so that what is seen was not made out of what was visible' (Hebrews 11:3). Man can manufacture, but God can create what he wants out of nothing.

Secondly there is the argument from order and design. 'For since the creation of the world God's invisible qualities . . . have been clearly seen, being understood from what has been made' (Romans 1:20). The incredible complexity and order of the human body and all created things point to a great Designer.

Thirdly, there is the argument from conscience (Romans 2:14,15). An idea of right and wrong is very widespread indeed; even those who reject moral absolutes are often very concerned about justice.

Also widespread, and the fourth argument, is man's basic desire to worship something or someone (Acts 17:22). If there is a God who made man, then this need of his is understandable.

We cannot prove that God exists, but it's a perfectly reasonable assumption to make. (YTL)

Think through the traditional arguments in more detail, with more Bible references, so that you are able to give a reasonable answer if someone should challenge you about your belief in God.

In the beginning God. . . Hallelujah!

NOVEMBER
Life's Experiences

November 1   Peculiar or truly human?

People were overwhelmed with amazement. 'He has done everything well,' they said.   **Mark 7:37**

God wants us to be whole people, not religious people. I have recently been struck by the *sheer normality* of true spirituality. Jesus, the only perfect man who ever lived on this earth, was so 'normal' that most of his relations, friends and neighbours could not believe that he could possibly be the Messiah. He was nothing like 'religious' enough for that! He was simply the son of the local carpenter (Matthew 13:55). He was later accused of being a glutton, drunkard and friend of sinners (Matthew 11:18,19).

How easily we fall into the trap of thinking that the truly spiritual person has some special aura of holiness or mystique about him, which keeps him separate from the more ordinary wholesome things of life! How urgently we need to rediscover God as Creator as well as Redeemer. As Paul Burbridge expressed it, 'God does not have to put texts on tulips before we can wholeheartedly thank him for them.'

It was part of the gnostic heresy that spirituality meant denying, or trying to escape from, the bodily, natural aspects of our humanity and concentrating wholly on the realm of the spirit. But God wants us to be fully human as well as — indeed, because of — being filled with his Spirit. (PL)

Lord, show me where I still need to be made whole through your saving, healing touch. I offer that part of my life and personality to you now, for your healing, changing power to start working.

Am I peculiar and proud of it, if I'm honest, or am I growing in true humanity?

Bible study: How does being a Christian affect our experiences of life or our reactions to them? Should we be growing more or less human as we grow spiritually?
Starters: Luke 2:40; Mark 7:37; Luke 22:47-53; 22:63-23:49; Acts 4:19,20,5:29;7:54-60;27:1-44; 2 Corinthians 11:22-33, and see under 'life's experiences' in index.

November 2   The glory of God

Whether you eat or drink, or whatever you do, do it all for the glory of God.   **1 Corinthians 10:31**

The problem for the Christian is not how to avoid buying and selling, eating and drinking, marrying and giving in marriage — these are all integral parts of human existence. The basic problem is how to avoid being controlled by *the power behind these things,* the power of the evil one himself.

There is only one solution to this problem: as Christians we must handle these routine activities for the glory of God alone. Remember the example of Johann Sebastian Bach, who inscribed every musical score, sacred or secular, with the words *soli gloria Deo* — 'To God alone be glory.' Therefore, our activities belong either to God, if we can do them to his glory, or to Satan. Remember that in the parable of the sower, Jesus described the seed that fell among thorns like this: 'The seed that fell among thorns stands for those who hear, but as they go on their way they are choked by life's worries, riches and pleasures, and they do not mature' (Luke 8:14). In other words, ordinary things were used by Satan to spoil God's work.

'Oh,' says someone, 'I must have that dress (or record or car). I *must* have it!' Must you? Have you prayed about it? Are you buying it for God's glory? You may retort that you don't pray about such things. But you should, because when you are handling the things of this world you may well be coming under the power that controls it all.

Even with the most ordinary decisions and activities, our lives should be so centred in Christ and his glory that our choices and actions contribute to his kingdom, not Satan's. (HW)

Show me how to do ordinary everyday things for your glory, Lord.

List the things you've been doing in the past days, and think about why you did them. What things were done to or for God's glory?

November 3   No dead end

Christ has indeed been raised from the dead, the firstfruits of those who have fallen asleep. For since death came through a man, the resurrection of the dead comes also through a man. For as in Adam all die, so in Christ will all be made alive.
                                          1 Corinthians 15:20-22

My godson Andrew was born with a serious heart defect, but he enjoyed comparatively good health. Then the surgeon felt that the time had come for them to perform a difficult and delicate heart operation which had a fifty-fifty chance of success. The operation was performed successfully and Andrew's parents watched their son's strength returning. But on the day he was due to go home — he had a relapse and died. His mother and father were, naturally, heartbroken. But they were not bitter, although they might so easily have been. After all, why had God allowed this to happen? Were they not Christians? Hadn't they and hundreds of others been praying? Why hadn't God answered their prayers?

Andrew's parents still can't answer all those questions, but they soon came to see God's amazing pattern of blessing for themselves and for others as a result of Andrew's death.

At his son's funeral service, this father was able to stand up and thank God for the life they'd been privileged to enjoy for five years, for the comfort and peace they had experienced through the difficult days, and for their assurance about God's faithfulness in the future. Most of all he thanked God that Andrew was more alive than ever — with the risen and ascended Christ, enjoying something far better than anything he could have experienced in this world. Of course, they were sad for themselves, but they couldn't possibly be sad for Andrew.

Was their deep assurance merely wishful thinking? Not at all! It was based on the very solid and substantial evidence for the resurrection of Jesus Christ — and his resurrection guarantees ours. (TLR)

How does our church family support those who mourn?

Lord, stop me from giving answers where there are none — in this life, anyway. Just help me to show love and sympathy.

November 4   Pursued by goodness and love

Surely goodness and love will follow me all the days of my life, and I will dwell in the house of the Lord for ever.
                                        Psalm 23:6

This verse is really saying that goodness and mercy will hunt us down and catch up with us wherever we go. God pursues us, when we stray or are beset by problems, in order to chasten us or break down our stubbornness or speak forcefully to us about something.

Writing to Christians enduring great trials, Paul says, 'And we know that in all things God works for the good of those who love him' (Romans 8:28). So in our difficult times we need to say, 'Lord, what is the good thing you are doing in my life? Help me to recognise the goodness and love with which you are even now pursuing me.'

When we have this attitude, then we are assured that nothing can 'separate us from the love of God that is in Christ Jesus our Lord' (Romans 8:39), and that we will 'dwell in the house of the Lord for ever'. This is another way of saying that we will enjoy being in God's presence: 'You will fill me with joy in your presence, with eternal pleasures at your right hand' (Psalm 16.11).

Enoch was someone who knew how to live in God's presence all the time. He 'walked with God; then he was no more, because God took him away' (Genesis 5:24). A little girl once heard a talk on Enoch and this is how she explained his story to her mother afterwards: 'He went on walks with God. And one day he and God walked on and on and on, and God said to him, "Enoch, you've walked a long, long way from your home. Come into my home and stay with me for ever."'

Those like Enoch who have the Lord as their shepherd, will live now and always in his presence. (YTL)

Show me, Lord, in this situation . . . your goodness and love.

Think back and see whether what you thought were mishaps have proved since to be God's love and goodness.

November 5   **Why do I feel like this?**

Why are you downcast, O my soul? Why so disturbed within me? Put your hope in God, for I will yet praise him, my Saviour and my God.   **Psalm 42:11**

'Why are you downcast, O my soul?' One of the worst aspects of some depressions is that the sufferer can't answer that question. He doesn't know why he is depressed. But one thing is certain: depression is a very common experience indeed.

One group of people who may be specially liable to this form of suffering, are Christian ministers and leaders. Charles Spurgeon wrote: 'All mental work tends to weary and depress, for much study is a weariness of the flesh. But ours (i.e. the work of the Christian minister or leader) is more than mental work; it is *heart* work — the labour of the inmost soul. How often on Lord's Day evenings do we feel as if life were completely washed out of us!'

Hosts of great men have suffered from depression, including many great saints such as the writer of Psalms 42 and 43, Elijah, Paul, Henry Martin, Watchman Nee, William Cowper and Martin Luther.

The possible causes of depression are many and varied. There may be spiritual causes and one of the commonest of these are guilt feelings about the past and worries about the future. Equally, there may be physical causes, or situational causes, such as disappointment, bereavement, sickness, pain, frustration and pressures of various kinds.

The cures for depression will be as varied as the causes, but the sufferer can hold on to two unchanging truths whatever he may be feeling: the fact of God's presence — 'Never will I leave you; never will I forsake you' (Hebrews 13:5), and the fact of his care — 'How precious to me are your thoughts, O God! How vast is the sum of them' (Psalm 139:17)! (YTL)

'Lord, save me' (Matthew 14:30).

How can I simply hold on to God? Would writing out some of his promises and carrying them around with me to refer to frequently help at all?

November 6   What are you saying, Lord?

The creation waits in eager expectation for the sons of God to be revealed ... We know that the whole creation has been

groaning as in the pains of childbirth right up to the present time. Not only so, but we ourselves, who have the firstfruits of the Spirit, groan inwardly as we wait eagerly for our adoption as sons, the redemption of our bodies.

Romans 8:19,22,23

A question people ask very frequently is: 'If there's a God of love in charge of the world, why is there so much suffering?' There is no complete answer to that question — only a few pointers.

We must be clear about this however. If God is truly God, it's no surprise that to thousands of questions I may have to answer, 'I don't know.'

But one thing is observable. It's often through suffering that God speaks to people. Many of us feel self-sufficient until we find ourselves almost drowning in waves of suffering. Only then do we realise that we are not self-sufficient, that we are frail and needy. It is at this point that people often start asking the important questions about God, life and death.

And another thought is this: God didn't create the suffering. It came about through man's rebellion against God which affected the whole creation. This pain-filled world is not as God planned it to be, but he does allow things to be as they are for his own good, though often mysterious, purposes. And he can and often does bring good out of suffering.

People react to suffering in different ways and it's very clear that how they react is the vital factor. Two people experiencing the same tragedy can be affected very differently by it, depending on their attitude to the situation. Those who stop asking, 'Lord, why did you allow this?' and ask instead, 'Lord, what are you saying to me in this?' are really inviting God to show them the good that he can bring out of their situation. (CFP)

Lord, what are you saying to me in this situation?

Look for ways of showing compassion to those who are suffering.

**We also thank God continually because, when you received
the word of God, which you heard from us, you accepted it,
not as the word of men, but as it actually is, the word of God
which is at work in you who believe.   1 Thessalonians 2:13**

Two words help us to see the link between the word and the
Spirit: they are *inspiration* and *illumination.*

Something becomes the word of God only when it is
inspired by the Spirit of God. The Scriptures are God-
breathed, so they are the word of God. But the church is not
the word of God unless its members are alive in the Spirit and
showing Christ, through his Body, to the world. Similarly it's
not enough for dancers to dance well, musicians to play well,
or even preachers to preach well in order to be the word of
God. They must be Spirit-inspired, and that involves being in
touch with the Lord and in harmony with one another; otherwise what they do is simply a performance.

You can have something that is inspired, however, and find
that it fails to illuminate the people who are hearing or seeing
it. The Thessalonians received the word, accepted it and let it
work in their lives. Unless we do that, we will have the
outward shell of the word of God without the necessary
inward spiritual reality — inspiration without illumination.
(YTL)

Lord, I do pray for illumination for...

How can we have 'ears to hear and eyes to see'?

**But the day of the Lord will come like a thief. The heavens will
disappear with a roar; the elements will be destroyed by fire,
and the earth and everything in it will be laid bare.**
2 Peter 3:10

Not so long ago, people would have laughed at the idea that the world would come to an end. Not many are laughing now; they know that this is all too possible: the United States and Russia have the nuclear capacity to destroy the globe in a short space of time.

Because the prospect is so terrifying, people either bury their heads in the sand and bumble along trusting that all will be well somehow, or they are filled with despair. The Christian *must* not hide from reality and *need* not lose all hope.

Jeremiah was not faced with the prospect of nuclear war, but he was in an equally terrifying situation, faced by enormous military powers able to crush his nation at any moment, and living in the midst of a country where materialism, immorality, spiritism, drunkenness, murder, violence and corruption in church, government and palace were rife. He must have felt utterly powerless in this situation. But God showed him very clearly that he was in control. He told Jeremiah, 'I am watching to see that my word is fulfilled,' and, 'I am about to summon all the peoples. . . I will pronounce my judgments on my people' (Jeremiah 1:12,15,16).

As we look at the world today we see evil and darkness. But the eye of faith sees that, beyond and behind everything, a loving God is in control. This is not a runaway world. When God's time is right, the day of the Lord (not the day of Russia, China or America) will come, and it will be a wonderful day for those who know and love Jesus (1 Thessalonians 4:16-18). (YTL)

How would I feel if the day of the Lord were to come tomorrow?

Father, help me to face reality with the only hope there is.

November 9   Judgment — no idle threat

I spoke to you again and again, but you did not listen; I called you but you did not answer. Therefore what I did to Shiloh I

will now do to the house that bears my Name, the temple you trust in, the place I gave to you and your fathers. I will thrust you from my presence, just as I did all your brothers, the people of Ephraim.   Jeremiah 7:13-15

Jeremiah prophesied that Jerusalem would be captured and the inhabitants killed or taken captive. It wasn't a very popular message; it didn't help the 'I'm backing Jerusalem' campaign at all. But his words came true. Elsewhere in the Bible there are messages of judgment against Sodom and Gomorrah, Petra, Tyre and Sidon, Babylon and other places. Babylon had walls three hundred feet high and so wide that two chariots could ride abreast on top of them. The inhabitants laughed at the idea that Babylon would be destroyed. So did many people in the other places. But the judgments all came true; those places were utterly destroyed. Jesus, in tears, warned Jerusalem of coming judgment. The people didn't listen. They simply crucified him for disturbing the peace — but a few years later that city was brutally destroyed.

When the Bible warns of impending judgment — this is no idle threat, any more than when a mother says to her child, 'Don't run out into the road, you may get run over.'

Just as God's other pronouncements of judgment came true, so will that ultimate judgment so often spoken of in the Bible, when those who have rejected God will be eternally separated from him and from everything good. (YTL)

Lord, show me those whom you want to use me to save from your final judgment. Take me and make me your messenger of love and judgment in the power and wisdom of your Holy Spirit.

Is there someone I'm still in touch with, whom I met during a period of backsliding, and failed to witness to? Should I write to that person, telling him (her) of my failure and of my present faith and hope?

I tell you that you are Peter, and on this rock I will build my church, and the gates of Hades will not overcome it.
Matthew 16:18

When Christ said these words to Simon Peter, what did he mean by 'this rock' on which he would build his church? Some say he meant Peter's confession, or Peter's faith. This may be right. But in a way he might have meant Peter himself. As William Barclay wrote, 'Peter was the first man to discover who Jesus really was. He was the first man to make the leap of faith which saw in Jesus Christ the Son of the living God. In other words, Peter was the first member of the church and in that sense the whole church is built on him. It is as if Jesus said to Peter, "You are the first man to grasp who I am, you are therefore the first stone, the very beginning of the church which I am founding, and in ages to come everyone who makes the same discovery is another stone added to the edifice of the church of Christ." '

Clearly the words do *not* mean that the whole church was built on Peter. Other passages make this very clear. The foundation of the building which is the church is said to be 'the apostles and prophets' (Ephesians 2:19-22). Again, Jesus is the only foundation (1 Corinthians 3:11); he is 'the capstone', and all believers are the 'living stones' (1 Peter 2:5,7). Peter himself was very fallible (Matthew 4:10; 16:23); he was just the first member of the church. Everyone else who sees the same truth as he saw, and puts his trust in Jesus, is a member, too. (YTL)

Is it clear from my behaviour that my life is built on rock?

Lord, I bless you that you are my rock, my sure foundation.

Elijah went before the people and said, 'How long will you

waver between two opinions? If the Lord is God, follow him; but if Baal is God, follow him.' But the people said nothing.

1 Kings 18:21

The majority of people in Israel in Elijah's day still believed in God, but they felt that following him wholeheartedly was too demanding and restricting. Baal worship was all the rage at the time and it offered excitement and sensuality. Besides, the queen, Jezebel, favoured it. So why not have the best of both worlds? Why not God and Baal?

The same thing happened in New Testament times. Some people believed in Jesus, but they were also attracted to Greek and Roman gods and philosophies, which they found to be colourful and fascinating — offering insights into the occult, or sexual licence, and so on.

It is the same in our country today. Most people believe in God in a general way: ninety-eight per cent wish to be buried by the church, for instance. But many want God and mammon, God and sex, God and whatever else they love as much as or more than him.

Elijah saw very clearly that you can worship God or Baal but not both. 'Baal' means 'master', and whatever we worship masters us. If God is not Lord of all, he is not Lord at all. Jesus expressed it like this: 'No one can serve two masters. Either he will hate the one and love the other, or he will be devoted to the one and despise the other. You cannot serve both God and Money' (Matthew 6:24). God, in the person of Jesus, has done so much for us. Understandably, he expects us to forsake all others and cleave only unto him. This is a challenge to Christians as well as to non-Christians in this uncommitted age. (YTL)

Is there anything in my life or the life of our church which is becoming as central as Jesus?

Father, keep me and others from the temptation of trying to get the best of both worlds.

If anyone is in Christ, he is a new creation.   2 Corinthians 5:17

Christ lived in a world of violence. When he was a young boy,
the Roman soldiers crucified three thousand Jews on a hill
overlooking his home. What did the Son of God do about
that? Did he organise a march from Nazareth to Jerusalem, or
sit outside the Roman embassy? He did not. His teachings
contain scarcely any hint of solutions for the tremendous
problems at that time. There is only one basic problem — that
of human sin — and one solution — new people in Christ — and
Jesus came and lived and taught, died and rose again, to make
that possible.

A history teacher resigned from the Communist Youth
Movement, giving as her reason her Christian faith. In a letter
she wrote to the communist secretariat, she said, 'I believe that
the only way of leading men to live rightly is to lead them to
follow the teaching of Christ. If the communist faith succeeded
in creating new men before the coming of material prosperity, I
would agree, but at present I see no evidence of this. In places,
however, where Christians are in a majority, those laws about
which you communists can only dream are a practical reality.'
(YTL)

*Is there any situation in my life or the life of my church for
which a spiritual solution is needed when a material, organis-
ational or social one is being sought?*

Is Jesus continuing to shape and change my life?

November 13   God's new society

**You are no longer foreigners and aliens, but fellow-citizens
with God's people and members of God's household, built on
the foundation of the apostles and prophets, with Christ Jesus
himself as the chief cornerstone.   Ephesians 2:19,20**

There are many ways in which God's people are to be new and different, but chiefly two.

We are to have *new relationships.* Our churches often concentrate on doing the right things, but what God looks for are right relationships. The essence of Christianity is the breaking down of barriers between, and the bringing together of, man and God and man and man (Ephesians 2:13,14). In fact, people will *see* that our relationship with God is right when they observe our harmonious relationships with one another. The New Testament church demonstrated that there were no barriers of age, class, colour, race, background, or anything else, between Christians. Among the leaders who were working harmoniously together in the early church, there was an ex-Pharisee and aristocrat, a landowner, a Greek-speaking Jew and a black African (Acts 13:1). Paul had a great deal to say about the importance of relationships in his letters, so he must have considered the topic vitally important.

We are also to have *a new commitment* — both to Christ and to fellow-Christians. If we say, 'All I have is yours,' to the Lord, then we should be able to say the same to any other Christian. In these days of covetousness and self-seeking, the church that not only says this, but demonstrates it by giving, sharing and serving, will have a very powerful impact. (YTL)

When we meet to worship, do we really have this sense of belonging not just to a few close friends but to every member of the church?

Father, all I have is yours. All I have is also available for your people.

November 14   *Agape-*Love

Love your enemies and pray for those who persecute you.
                                               Matthew 5:44

Nothing, absolutely nothing, is more important than our personal love for Jesus, resulting, through the gift of the Holy

Spirit, in this godly quality of love among his disciples.

Virtually all other forms of love inevitably involve the feelings and the emotions. When a man and woman *fall in love*, it is something which happens to them. They have little or no control over the matter, although the intensity of the emotion can be encouraged or discouraged depending on the degree of contact the two of them have.

Agape, however, is much more an attitude of our *mind* which depends largely on the direction in which we set our *will*. It has nothing to do with the emotions, at least in the first instance. Michael Harper has described it in this way: 'Love is not feeling sentimental towards others. Nor is it primarily saying the right things. Nor is it to be found in giving, for, according to Paul, you can give your life and all that you possess to others, and still be bankrupt of true love. It is an *attitude*, which is never superior, and which is devoid of criticism, but which is deeply concerned about and committed to the good of the other person.'

This explains how it is that Jesus can tell us to love our enemies. Humanly speaking, that is impossible — but not with God. (IBITC)

What situation in my life, or in the life of our church, needs a good dose of agape-love *now?*

Lord, there is so much selfishness in my love. I pray that you will keep purifying it.

November 15   Depression through personal weaknesses

Elijah said: 'I have had enough, Lord. . . Take my life, I am no better than my ancestors. . . I have been very zealous for the Lord God Almighty. . . I am the only one left, and now they are trying to kill me too.'   **1 Kings 19:4,10**

'Elijah was a man just like us,' writes James (5:17); in other words, he had human frailties, just like us. I wouldn't want to over-emphasise Elijah's failings as part of the cause of his depression, but there are hints that this great man was not completely right in all his attitudes.

What he says (verse 4) suggests that he has a touch of *rebellion* in his heart. In a completely understandable outburst, he exclaims, 'I've had enough. I'm not carrying on any longer.' God's answer to that, in effect, is: 'All right, what's the problem? Tell me what this outburst is about.' So Elijah tells the Lord just how he is feeling, and God gives him a job to take his mind off himself. He may deal with us like that, too.

As well as rebellion, there seems to be a hint of *pride*: 'I am no better than my ancestors ... I have been very zealous.' What Elijah needed to learn was that without God he *was* nothing, and could *do* nothing of any real value. God doesn't choose to use people because they are better than their fathers, but because they put themselves completely into his hands. God wanted to teach Elijah this, and also, perhaps, to point out gently to him that he was not indispensable. Just as he, God, had chosen Elijah, so he now chose Elisha (verse 16).

There is also a touch of *self-pity* which exaggerates the situation. 'I'm all alone,' says Elijah. 'No you're not,' answers God. 'Seven thousand others are also true to me' (verse 18). God wanted Elijah to know about the others and presumably to join them. What we may need to do when we are depressed and full of self-pity is not to crawl away into a corner and hide, but to join a Christian fellowship, particularly a small group in which we can share and grow. (YTL)

Which of my human failings triggers off or deepens my depressions? What can I do about it?

Father, I know that I am nothing without you, but that with you the possibilities are staggering.

November 16   Unity with variety

May the God who gives endurance and encouragement give you a spirit of unity among yourselves as you follow Christ

Jesus, so that with one heart and mouth you may glorify the God and Father of our Lord Jesus Christ. Accept one another, then, just as Christ accepted you, in order to bring praise to God.   Romans 15:5-7

Christian groups and churches are notoriously negative and suspicious towards one another, fearing the worst instead of believing the best. We are often ignorant of one another; we do not listen to one another; we are quick to attack and criticise, prejudging each other's position.

For myself, I welcome the strong emphasis on the sovereignty and holiness of God stressed by some of my Calvinist brethren; I am profoundly thankful for the joyful enthusiasm of the Pentecostal churches that has made many of us look again at our doctrine and experience of the Holy Spirit; I shall always be grateful for the thorough biblical foundations given to me by evangelicals from the time of my conversion onwards; I thank God for the disturbing challenge that radical Christians give towards the church's involvement in politics and social reform; I have been enriched by the deep devotion and disciplined prayer life of many of my high church friends; and I have benefited enormously from Roman Catholics in my whole understanding of community and the corporate nature of the church. The list of acknowledgements could continue almost indefinitely. (IBITC)

How receptive am I (is my church) to other Christians who worship in a different way?

Lord, help me to be secure enough to listen to others without feeling that I'm compromising, and open enough to receive anything that is part of your truth.

November 17   The price of unity

My prayer is not for them alone. I pray also for those who will believe in me through their message, that all of them may be

339

one, Father, just as you are in me and I am in you. May they also be in us so that the world may believe that you have sent me. John 17:20,21

How can we experience what Jesus prayed that all his disciples would know? There are four things we must do as individuals and as churches.

First we must repent for having divided the Body of God's Son. We mustn't point the finger of criticism at anyone else. That church group which we judge to be doctrinally wrong may well be so because of our church's attitudes and judgments in the past or present. It takes two sides to cause a division. Don't wait for the other side — let *us* repent of our attitude to them.

Secondly, we must come to the cross. We cannot come to that place as Anglicans, Methodists, charismatics or anything else. God is not interested in our labels; it's the devil who uses labels to divide us. We can only come as sinners and when we do that God says to us, 'My beloved son, my beloved daughter.'

Thirdly, we must open our lives to the Holy Spirit and to one another. There is so much to learn from others.

Fourthly, we must become peacemakers — willing to stretch out one hand to one person or group and the other to another, to try to bring them together in Christ. We may receive no thanks, but there's a great need in the church and in the world today for people willing to pay the price of being peacemakers. (AR)

How can we, as individuals and as fellowships, all 'be one'?

Lord, draw the Christians in. . . together to worship, to serve the community and to stand out against what is wrong, so that people may see beyond our labels to our unity of purpose and spirit.

November 18 Five 'musts' in evangelism

God was reconciling the world to himself in Christ, not count-

340

ing men's sins against them. And he has committed to us the
message of reconciliation.   2 Corinthians 5:19

Paul gives us the essentials of evangelism (2 Corinthians 5).
Here are five 'musts' from that chapter.

Evangelism must take account of the *judgment* of Christ
(verse 10). If there is no future judgment, there is little point in
evangelism.

Evangelism must be motivated by the *love* of Christ (verse
14). The word *compels* has the idea of being hemmed in and
pressurised. The love of Christ should be so strong that it
sweeps us along.

Evangelism must experience the *power* of Christ (verse 17).
This power makes new men — alive in a new world.

Evangelism must be an extension of the *ministry* of Christ
(verses 18,19). Christ brought man and God together and he
passed on that ministry of reconciliation to us, his church. We
need to keep close to God and to man in order to exercise this
ministry.

Evangelism must focus on the *death* of Christ. 'God made
him who had no sin to be sin for us'; this is one of the most
devastating truths in the whole Bible, and the purpose was
'that in him we might become the righteousness of God' (verses
20,21). If it cost Jesus so much, we may be sure that carrying on
his work will cost us something too.

All five 'must's are linked with the cross of Christ. The cross
speaks of the death of Christ, of judgment, of love, of power,
and of Christ's reconciling ministry. If we keep Christ crucified
central in our thinking, we will have a truly powerful motive
for evangelism. (YTL)

How effective is our church in evangelism?

*Lord, it is not easy to be your ambassador. Surround with
your love and a sense of your close presence any ambassadors
who are suffering for you at this time, especially. . .*

God has raised this Jesus to life, and we are all witnesses of the fact.   Acts 2:32

A question people often ask is, 'How can I witness?' First, pray for two or three friends as often as possible, asking God to show himself to them as he did to you. Also pray that the Holy Spirit will guide you to see what you can do to help them see Jesus.

Secondly, invite them to 'come and see' (see John 1:39,46; 4:28). You may not be able to say much yourself, but you can invite your friends to services, or house-meetings, or introduce them to people who can explain Christian teaching clearly.

Thirdly, you can share your personal experience, telling others how you came to trust in Jesus and the difference he makes in your life. The reality of your experience will speak loudly even if you can't answer all the questions and objections which people may raise.

Fourthly, lend books, booklets or cassettes. Many explain the Christian faith clearly to seekers. It's a great joy to hear of people accepting Jesus through something one has written or said, but in virtually every case, it is other people's lives, words or prayers which have prepared the ground first (see 1 Corinthians 3:6).

Fifthly, use opportunities presented by conversations with people. To be ready for these, you will need to do your homework, which is to work out how you would explain about becoming a Christian and answer the most common objections raised by people concerning our faith. (C/LANL)

Lord, help me to want to witness for you and to be more effective as your witness.

Should I act on any of the suggestions I have just read about?

But because of his great love for us, God who is rich in mercy, made us alive with Christ, even when we were dead in transgressions — it is by grace you have been saved.

Ephesians 2:4,5

This is love: not that we loved God, but that he loved us and sent his Son as an atoning sacrifice for our sins.   1 John 4:10

There is a *Peanuts* cartoon in which Shroeder is holding up a placard saying, 'Christ is the answer!' Behind him comes Snoopy holding up another poster, saying, 'But what is the question?'

Today we can be in danger of commercialising Christ, putting him on the same level as the soap powders on TV advertisements: 'This one will wash whiter all the stains in your life! Jesus will meet all your needs!'

To approach evangelism in this way is to regard man as the centre of the universe, and to encourage him to sit in judgment on Christ: 'You first satisfy my questions before I am prepared to consider believing in you!' The whole idea is hopelessly man-centred. It is not man who calls out the questions, but God. If Pilate thought that he was judging Jesus, he had yet to learn 'that at the name of Jesus every knee should bow . . . and every tongue confess that Jesus Christ is Lord' (Philippians 2:10,11). Jesus is the sovereign Lord of the universe. He is the one who commands us to lay down our arms of rebellion and surrender to him. Any evangelism which soft-pedals the truth that God is Creator and Jesus is Lord is a poor short-sighted attempt to obtain quick results. (IBIE)

In all my praying and thinking and evangelising, help me to begin with you, Lord God — Creator and Redeemer.

Am I beginning each day with God and consulting him about each challenge, job or opportunity? How can I make sure I do this?

Fix these words of mine in your hearts and minds; tie them as symbols on your hands and bind them on your foreheads. Teach them to your children, talking about them when you sit at home and when you walk along the road, when you lie down and when you get up.   Deuteronomy 11:18,19

A church that neglects its youth is a dying church. But if a church is to be relevant for young people, it must keep on its toes. It must change, in some measure at least, as the culture changes; it must be fresh and flexible in its presentation of the gospel; it must allow room for young blood to come into positions of responsibility, leadership and ministry; it must rejoice when young people not only take over some of the positions held by older members but also do the jobs more effectively; it must release its finest leaders to give maximum time and attention to the young; it must be understanding when faced with immature zeal, misguided energy, or damage to church property; it must at all costs, 'hold unfailing love' towards young people so that they know they are really wanted within God's family. A church that is unwilling to do this is digging its own grave.

Further, the ministers and leaders of a church must learn to listen. What are the questions being asked by the young today? What problems do they find with the church? What do they feel is irrelevant? What are the issues in society and in the world that really concern them? ... And who, within the family of the church, have been given by God the gifts to relate to them at some depth? Such members ought to receive every possible encouragement to give themselves wholeheartedly to the task of building tomorrow's church. (IBIE)

Have I any part to play in teaching or encouraging the young in our church?

Lord, I pray for these young people. . . Keep them in your faith and fear through these turbulent years.

If any of you lacks wisdom, he should ask God, who gives generously to all without finding fault; and it will be given to him. James 1:5

Guidance isn't like trying to open some combination lock and thinking, 'If I'm lucky, I'll get it right some time.' Basically, guidance is following the guide, who is Jesus. But here are five 'don'ts' which you might find helpful.

Don't claim too quickly that you've received the Lord's guidance. I often hear Christians saying, 'The Lord told me to do this.' Perhaps he did, but it's easy to be presumptuous, and also, by making such a statement, a person is virtually insuring himself against any possible objection or disagreement!

Don't think that if you want to do something, it can't be God's will! Some people fear that God will always make them do whatever they most dread. I don't believe God is like that. He's a loving heavenly Father: 'Delight yourself in the Lord and he will give you the desires of your heart' (Psalm 37:4).

Don't wait till you're a hundred per cent sure before stepping forward. We are seldom totally sure beforehand: 'Whether you turn to the right or to the left, your ears will hear a voice behind you saying, "This is the way; walk in it"' (Isaiah 30:21).

Don't automatically assume you've made the wrong decision when you take a step and almost immediately encounter difficulties. When the disciples went on the lake one day there was a great storm (Mark 4:35-41). I don't think they were wrong to get into the boat that day. In fact, through things apparently going wrong, they learnt something very important. Difficulties may be tests or learning opportunities.

Don't wallow in regrets. God is a wonderful restorer (Joel 2:25); he can bring good and glory out of any situation which is surrendered to him (Romans 8:28). (CFP)

If someone asked me for the 'do's' of guidance, what would I say?

Looking back, I can see your guiding hand, Father. . . Thank you.

When I tried to understand all this, it was oppressive to me, till I entered the sanctuary of God.

Psalm 73:16,17

Have you ever felt confused because you really believed that God had guided you to a certain decision, only to find that things didn't work out as you'd hoped? You may wonder why God seemed to 'lead you up the garden path'. But did you really understand the principles of guidance, or did you act hastily on the strength of only one or two indications? Normally, with major decisions, we need to take our time and wait until several things are pointing in the same direction. Often the Bible, the counsel of wise Christian friends and an inner peace concur in leading us to a decision.

But what if we did wait for all the signs before acting, and still things don't seem to be working out? We must not assume automatically that difficulties and problems indicate a wrong decision. God may be wanting to test our faith, or humble us, or correct us, or equip us for something. He may be teaching us to trust him in the dark, hoping to hear our hearts say, 'I don't understand what you're doing in my life, Lord, but I trust you just the same.' (C/LANL)

Lord, I bring you my confusion, and I wait to receive your peace and reassurance.

Read the biography of someone who learned to trust God in the dark.

November 24   At breaking point

My soul is in anguish... Turn, O Lord, and deliver me; save me because of your unfailing love... I am worn out with groaning; all night long I flood my bed with weeping and drench my couch with tears... Away from me, all you who do evil, for the Lord has heard my weeping. The Lord has heard my cry for mercy; the Lord accepts my prayer.

Psalm 6:3,4,6,8,9

Some people think Christians should have permanent smiles on their faces. Certainly joy is a very important part of Christian experience. But in my own life there have been moments of deep depression, too.

This may happen because a relationship goes wrong and I feel rejected, or because I feel a failure after something hasn't worked out as I'd planned it should, or because I am completely exhausted.

Whatever the reason, I know moments of blackness when I soak my pillow with tears as the psalmist did.

But it is in those moments of anguish that I've discovered this: if I cry out to the Lord, he comes to where I am and leads me through the darkness and back into the light and joy. It doesn't always happen right away — but a cry from the heart to God for help never goes unanswered. (STD)

In my darkness, I turn to you. Come into my anguish and lead me out into your peace and joy, I pray.

Think about these words of a wise Christian: 'There's no telling what God can do with a broken heart, provided he gets all the pieces.'

November 25   The patience of faith

You need to persevere so that when you have done the will of God, you will receive what he has promised.   Hebrews 10:36

One night, Abraham went out of his tent and looked up at the millions of pinpricks of light scattered all over the heavens.

'Do you see all those stars, Abraham?' God asked him. 'Can you count them? Your descendants will be as many as those.'

Abraham was seventy-six years old and his wife sixty-six at

the time when God made this wonderful promise. I don't suppose Abraham slept very well that night and he must have been very excited as he broke the news to Sarah at breakfast the next morning. No doubt they both praised God together for this great gift.

However a year passed, and there was no sign of a child. Then two years went by, then three, four, five years and so on, up to ten, and still nothing had happened.

You might have been praying for years for guidance, or about a thorn in the flesh, or an illness, and received no answer at all — no sign that God is going to keep his promise.

Why did God test Abraham and Sarah and why does he test us in this way? Because he wants our faith to grow stronger and more patient and persevering, as we hold on to his word through disappointment, apparently unanswered prayer, hardship and persecution. When these come along, we show God and ourselves what kind of believers we are — either those who really believe, or those who merely believe that we believe. (YTL)

Help me to hold on to your promise . . . in this matter. . .

How patient is my faith?

November 26   The Lord — my shepherd

The Lord is my shepherd.   Psalm 23:1

We have become so familiar with the idea of God as our shepherd, that we might fail to appreciate just how striking such an idea would have been in David's time. God had revealed himself to his people by many names, but most of these emphasised his greatness and power, his majesty and holiness. 'O Lord our Lord, how majestic is your name in all the earth' (Psalm 8:1). 'Holy, holy, holy is the Lord Almighty' (Isaiah 6:3). But here David daringly describes God as 'my shepherd' — stressing a personal intimate relationship.

This was as revolutionary then as was Jesus' later teaching about God being like a father. He taught us that those who put their trust in him as Saviour and Lord, can look up into the face of Almighty God, creator of the universe and say, 'My daddy'.

That is a very startling truth, but no less startling in its time was David's triumphant outburst, 'The Lord is my shepherd.' In the six verses of this psalm, he refers to God thirteen times and to himself seventeen times — stressing the close personal relationship between them.

Notice that it is *the Lord* who is David's shepherd — and ours. I can claim Jesus as my Saviour *only* when he is also my Lord — Lord of every area of my life. So, he is not my shepherd unless he is my Lord, but if he is my Lord, he is also my shepherd. (YTL)

How has God been a good shepherd to me? Turn the answer into praise.

Thank you, my Lord and Shepherd for . . .

November 27   A time to shout

Shout! For the Lord has given you the city!   Joshua 6:16

Many times in the Bible, the people of God encouraged themselves and one another in the battle against the enemy. The psalmist wrote: 'Blessed are those who have learned to acclaim you' (Psalm 89:15). After Jehoshaphat had worshipped the Lord, 'some Levites . . . and Korahites stood up and praised the Lord, the God of Israel, with very loud voice' (2 Chronicles 20:18,19).

In the New Testament, the believers 'raised their voices together in prayer' (Acts 4.24).

A Saudi Arabian was once feeling very oppressed — conscious of being in the middle of a country where Jesus' name was not honoured. 'I got on my knees and began praying,' he said. 'After a time, I stood up and praised the Lord in a loud voice, rejoicing in the name of Jesus uttered aloud in that place. Praise and worship of the Lord, and the joy of the Holy Spirit, filled my heart and being, and within a few minutes my depression was replaced by an exultant joy. This joy increased to a higher and higher level for about an hour and a half. I praise God — I've never been so upborne.' (AR)

Have I ever been confident enough in God's word or victory to shout in triumph?

Lord, set me free to shout in triumph at the right moments.

November 28   The light still shines

Jesus . . . said, 'I am the light of the world.'   John 8:12

Some three thousand years ago the nation of Israel was going through a time of great moral and spiritual darkness. The future was bleak, depression was rife and restlessness and despair gripped many. Yet God spoke a message of hope to his people: 'The people walking in darkness have seen a great light; on those living in the land of the shadow of death a light has dawned. . . For to us a child is born, to us a son is given. . . And he will be called Wonderful Counsellor, Mighty God, Everlasting Father, Prince of Peace' (Isaiah 9:2,6).

Centuries passed and once again the situation was black — perhaps even blacker than before. The nation was oppressed, violence was rife, revolutionary groups were spreading terror. Yet God's message of hope rang out: 'The rising sun will come to us from heaven to shine on those living in darkness and in the shadow of death, to guide our feet into the path of peace' (Luke 1:78,79).

Today the gloom in the world is heavier and more wide-spread than ever before. For the first time in history man is faced with the real possibility of total human destruction. However, the light of Christ has not been and never will be extinguished. It still scatters the darkness wherever Jesus is welcomed into lives and homes. Moreover, one day he is coming in a blaze of splendour to take those who love him and belong to him to his Father's house for ever. For them, whatever the world news, the best is yet to be. (PL)

Lord, show me any darkness in my life and help me to open that area up to your light.

Those whom Jesus lights up are to be lights to others. Am I?

November 29   As now, so then

Peter declared, 'Even if I have to die with you, I will never disown you.' And all the other disciples said the same.
Matthew 26:35

Peter was looking into the future, visualising martyrdom and the glory of suffering for Jesus, but he wasn't ready for the present. Jesus had tried to bring him sharply back to reality: 'This very night, before the cock crows, you will disown me three times,' he'd said, but Peter's eyes had been firmly fixed on future glory. It was another sign of his spiritual pride at that time.

If you are thinking of being a minister or missionary or full-time worker for God — remember Bishop Taylor Smith's words: 'As now, so then.' As you *now* study the Bible, pray, witness, are reliable and thorough in your work, so you will do or be *then*.

Stuart Holden said, 'Live a moment at a time, and that moment for God. Think not of a holy life, but of a holy moment as it flies. A succession of holy moments constitutes a holy life.' (YTL)

Am I in danger of being too immersed either in the present or in the future?

Lord, I long to have foretastes of your glory, to enrich the present, and to remind me of my wonderful future.

351

And they sang a new song: 'You are worthy to take the scroll and to open the seals, because you were slain, and with your blood you purchased men for God from every tribe and language and people and nation.'   **Revelation 5:9**

The new song tells us three things about Christ's death on the cross, which is what 'the Lamb' symbolises.

First, it was a sacrificial death. 'You are worthy . . . because you were slain.' It was a sacrifice for sins: 'without the shedding of blood there is no forgiveness' (Hebrews 9:22).

Secondly, it was liberating: 'You purchased men for God.' The idea of ransom lies behind the purchasing and Peter writes that we were redeemed 'with the precious blood of Christ, a lamb without blemish or defect' (1 Peter 1:19).

Thirdly, it was powerful. It 'purchased men for God from every tribe and language and people and nation' and 'made them to be a kingdom and priests' who would 'reign on the earth' (Revelation 5:9,10).

The song will be just a part of the worship of heaven. There will be much singing in heaven but worship will involve other things too. We will serve God 'day and night in his temple' (Revelation 7:14). There will be work as well as worship, in this place of total submission to, enjoyment of, and delight in God and the Lamb, the Lord Jesus.

I hope you're enjoying worshipping God and the Lamb now, because if you're not, heaven will be hell for you, as it was for the coach party to heaven from hell in C. S. Lewis' *The Great Divorce*! (YTL)

Lord, help me to sing more of that new song day by day with every part of my being.

Do we spend enough time thinking or learning about heaven? If not, reading The Great Divorce *by C. S. Lewis would be a good starting point.*

DECEMBER
Church Fellowships

December 1 **United we stand**

How good and pleasant it is when brothers live together in unity! ... For there the Lord bestows his blessing, even life for evermore. **Psalm 133:1,3**

God deals with people as individuals: spiritual experience ought never to be stereotyped. However, one outstanding feature of the early church was the togetherness of its members. God's power is for God's *people* and so God's blessing will depend to a remarkable extent on the depth and reality of the fellowship within the church.

The first Christians saw this clearly. Any problem in the fellowship was an immediate threat, and had to be dealt with at once, as Ananias and Sapphira discovered dramatically (Acts 5:1-11). I have little doubt that if we long for more of God's power and reality among us, we must look first and foremost to ourselves and to our relationships within the fellowship. Niggling criticisms, jealousies, resentments are all too common in any church. 'They're only natural,' you say. Therefore we need God's *supernatural* love poured constantly into our hearts by the Holy Spirit. This is our greatest need. (PL)

Help me to see how important loving unity is and how much my backbiting and critical spirit grieve you, Lord.

353

What needs to be put right in my relationship with any other Christian? How shall I set about this?

Bible Study: What are the differences between Christian fellowship and the fellowship that might exist in a non-Christian club? How can our church be more truly Christian in its fellowship?
Starters: John 13:34-35; 15:1-17; Acts 2:44-47; 4:32-37; Romans 12:4-13; 15:25-27; 1 John 1:3, and see under 'church fellowships' in index.

December 2   A critical spirit

The acts of the sinful nature are obvious: sexual immorality, impurity and debauchery; idolatry and witchcraft, hatred, discord, jealousy, fits of rage, selfish ambition, dissensions, factions and envy; drunkenness, orgies and the like.

Galatians 5:19-21

Grumblings, resentments, criticism, bitterness — they can destroy God's work more quickly than almost anything else. Satan makes frequent and devastating attacks through these things.

In these verses the things which produce carping and criticisms are listed as 'acts of the sinful nature' alongside sexual immorality, drunkenness and orgies! Either these things or the Holy Spirit must go from our midst.

It is one thing to speak the truth in love and quite another to speak the truth in negative, destructive ways. Even if our criticisms are a hundred per cent right — a critical, unloving attitude is a hundred per cent wrong, and God is very concerned with our attitudes and motives.

Remember that every fellowship is a fellowship of sinners, who need constantly to forgive one another. The consequences are serious if we don't forgive (Matthew 18:21-35).

If you have a suggestion to make about what should or should not be done, take it directly to the person concerned; never discuss it negatively behind his back.

We are called to serve one another. So surely we can lay down pride, jealousy and party spirit for the sake of God's work in and through us. (PL)

Deliver me from a critical spirit, O Lord.

If I can't speak the truth in love — I must keep silent and pray about the matter.

December 3   Our words can heal each other

Let your conversation be always full of grace, seasoned with salt, so that you may know how to answer everyone.
Colossians 4:6

People who only see me speaking at meetings may be tempted to think that I am mature and well balanced all the time and have no needs. Nothing could be further from the truth. At times I have an overwhelming sense of failure and am deeply distressed. I can get critical, jealous and resentful. Often I hate or condemn myself. Once or twice I have wanted to kill myself. I confess these things simply to show that I have as many needs as you have. I am not yet a whole person, just as you may not yet be a whole person. We need each other.

When I was depressed once, someone sent me these words: 'Enjoy who you are, my child — my child who has nothing to prove but the depths of your Father's everlasting and unchanging love.' This helped to bring me relief and healing.

A woman was a patient in a mental hospital, classified as a chronic schizophrenic, as a result of being sexually abused when she was a little child. One day a pastor came to visit that woman. After talking with her, he said, 'My dear, you are full of self-pity, and self-pity is a form of pride. Until you repent of your pride, you will never be healed.' The woman was furiously angry at first. But afterwards she did repent of her pride and self-pity. Within a year, she was out of hospital — healed, and now she is a missionary for Christ.

God uses other members of the Body of Christ to meet our needs, just as he can use us to meet the needs of others. And among the things he can use, are our words — which need to be 'full of grace' or 'seasoned with salt' — as appropriate! (AR)

Am I giving and receiving this kind of healing?

Lord, show me my real needs at this moment, or the real needs of anyone whom you could use me to help.

December 4   Different kinds of service

There are different kinds of service but the same Lord.
1 Corinthians 12:5

How far am I willing to serve in the church? God will never force service on an unwilling servant, but he will try to bring him to a point where he looks up and says eagerly with all his heart, 'Lord, here am I, send me, use me, speak through me, enable me to use some gift that will be a blessing to someone else.' We are told to 'follow the way of love and eagerly desire spiritual gifts' (1 Corinthians 14:1), and Paul writes that he longs to impart some spiritual gift to the Roman Christians to encourage and be encouraged by them (Romans 1:11,12). When we really long to be used by God, perhaps even in ordinary, practical ways, then we can expect God to use the gifts we already have and give us others.

These gifts are for two purposes: to glorify Christ and to edify Christ's body, the church. In the parable of the talents, the talents belonged to the master and were to be used for him (Matthew 25:14-30). Remember what he said to the servant who did *not* use his talent: 'You wicked, lazy servant!' Then he ordered the talent to be taken from him. Similarly, if God gives me a gift and I do not use it, not only do I make God sad and perhaps angry, but also I am robbing others of the blessing that God longs to bring them through me. (YTL)

Am I robbing Christ or his church through sitting on my talent?

Father, make us willing to serve in any way just as long as we are glorifying Jesus and helping others.

December 5   The basis of fellowship

Peter replied, 'Repent and be baptised, every one of you, in the name of Jesus Christ, so that your sins may be forgiven. And you will receive the gift of the Holy Spirit.'   **Acts 2:38**

Putting twenty or so Christians together isn't necessarily creating a Christian fellowship. In fact, people have come into Christian gatherings and gone away saying or thinking, 'I can find more fellowship in my pub or club!' So what is the basis on which true Christian fellowship can grow? In this verse we are given our part and God's part in laying the foundations of genuine Christian fellowship.

On our part, there must be, first of all, repentance. This is more than remorse; it involves three elements: a realisation that there has been wrong in the past, real sorrow for that wrong, and a decision to about-turn and change things in the future. The quality of repentance determines the quality of Christian fellowship within a group.

Peter tells his hearers to repent and be baptised; in other words, he tells them to publicly confess their faith in Jesus. 'For it is with your heart that you believe and are justified, and it is with your mouth that you confess and are saved' (Romans 10:10).

On God's side there is forgiveness and the gift of the Holy Spirit. Remember what happened when the Spirit came down on 120 disciples; they were filled with the love of Jesus. And this is what still happens when the gift of the Holy Spirit is given.

You will only find a deep Christian fellowship where there is a deep sense of forgiveness, through true repentance and a deep work of the Holy Spirit. (YTL)

Is our fellowship on the right basis?

Father, may we be willing, if this is necessary, to dig deeper foundations in order that our fellowship may be stronger.

December 6   Three-way submission

Submit yourselves . . . to God.   **James 4:7**
Obey your leaders and submit to their authority.
Hebrews 13:17
Submit to one another out of reverence for Christ.
Ephesians 5:21

When I was in the army I had to do all kinds of seemingly annoying and unnecessary things — as part of my training in submission and obedience. This habit of obedience has to be so ingrained that in the heat of the battle, one would do, instantly and unquestioningly, whatever one's commanding officer ordered. In the spiritual battle, I believe God can wonderfully use and bless those soldiers who will obey instantly and unquestioningly. Read the story of the centurion (Luke 7:1-10) to see the good that Jesus was able to do for a man who thoroughly understood the principle of authority and obedience, in the Roman army. In God's army we need to submit completely to Christ — taking 'captive every thought to make it obedient to Christ' (2 Corinthians 10:5).

As Christians we are also commanded to submit to our leaders, whether or not we agree with them, and to one another. At times I have had to submit to people even when I have honestly believed them to be in the wrong. Because the point has not been a fundamental one, I have submitted, after a struggle, and in every case, God has blessed as a result. For years I submitted all my invitations to speak or lead missions to the rest of the elders. I went nowhere without their full approval. This did not make me feel limited, but safe and protected. I know I can so easily be wrong when making decisions on my own.

Our three-way submission isn't to make us into slaves, but to surround us with the love and protection which we all need in our fight against the world, the flesh and the devil. (YTL)

Do we need to learn anything about submission in our church fellowship? Where are we weakest in this matter?

Father, help me to be strong enough in your strength to submit in love where I need to, today.

December 7   Reviewing the situation

The Spirit sent him [Jesus] out into the desert.   Mark 1:12
The Spirit gives life.   John 6:63
Where the Spirit of the Lord is, there is freedom.
**   2 Corinthians 3:17**

The Spirit of God is a Spirit of movement. He will never allow us to become static, or to fossilise into patterns and meetings which no doubt were a blessing in the past.

For the sake of effective evangelism, the leadership of any church should review, at least once a year, the whole pattern of services, meetings and organisations. Ruthless questions need to be asked in an attitude of prayer and submission to God, who alone is head of the church. Are the meetings achieving anything *today*? Are they the best use of time and money *today*? Are they helping to build up the Body of Christ *today*? Are they assisting the church in evangelism *today*? Their value yesterday is not the important point.

Christian work is constantly crippled by clinging to blessings and traditions of the past. God is not the God of yesterday. He is the God of today. Heaven forbid that we should go on playing religious games in one corner when the cloud and fire of God's presence have moved to another.

359

Sometimes I speak at rallies or conventions which doubtless were times when God gloriously displayed his power yesterday. But today the word 'Ichabod' is manifestly written over the whole affair: 'The glory of God has departed.' (IBIE)

Do I cling to blessings and traditions of the past?

Lord, if our church is too static, may your Spirit move like wind among us, stirring and moving us into vitality and openness to new ideas.

December 8   Facing opposition

The priests and the captain of the temple guard and the Sadducees came up to Peter and John while they were speaking to the people. They were greatly disturbed because the apostles were teaching the people and proclaiming in Jesus the resurrection of the dead.   Acts 4:1,2

Tragically, these religious leaders weren't interested in the fact that God's power had been evident and that a man who had been a cripple for forty years had been healed. They were only concerned that what had happened was unorthodox — outside their official channels! It's still sadly true today that there is opposition from *religious* circles when God's power is shown outside orthodox demarcations. Instead of rejoicing, there is jealousy that God is blessing others.

There is also opposition from *worldly* circles. People hated Jesus because his life exposed their sinfulness (John 15:18,19,22) and, although we are far from perfect, if we are leading godly Christian lives, we will show up the world's sin, emptiness and foolishness, and this will not make us popular, either.

If we are effective witnesses for Jesus we must expect opposition — but how should we react to it?

Our natural reaction will probably be one of anger or wanting to hurt back. But this was not Jesus' way (1 Peter

360

2:23). The best thing to do is to pause, pray and ponder before saying anything at all. An experienced evangelist has written: 'Whenever in conversation someone makes a blatant, perhaps ignorant and untruthful, criticism of the Christian way of life, I pause before replying and pray for grace to enable me to discover what lies behind the remark.' (YTL)

What is the right attitude to opposition? Should we deliberately provoke it, avoid it at all costs, or what?

Lord Jesus, only your Spirit can cause me to love those in opposition while not loving their deeds.

December 9   Expect rejection

Come to him, the living Stone — rejected by men but chosen by God and precious to him. . . See I lay a stone in Zion, a chosen and precious cornerstone, and the one who trusts in him will never be put to shame.   1 Peter 2:4,6

In every church there should be those who are on the fringe, thinking about the Christian gospel, tasting something of the love of the Lord Jesus before making a real commitment to him. No church should organise itself exclusively for those who are already 'in'. However, it is only those who have committed themselves to Jesus, who really belong to the church, the Body of Christ.

Today, in an increasingly pagan society, it's not always easy to show a clear, unashamed commitment to Jesus where we live and work. 'The living Stone' was 'rejected by men', and Jesus himself warned us that this would happen to his disciples. In many parts of the world today, belonging to Christ means risking fierce persecution. An Orthodox believer in Russia, brought to faith by his grandmother, was sentenced to twenty years in prison for his faith, in addition to the ten years he had already served. For a time he was put into a psychiatric asylum. At forty, he had lost all his teeth and hair and could scarcely stand, but he still had to do slave labour. There are hundreds and thousands of Christians suffering like that man.

For us it's much easier, but even so in school, college, business, there will be some mockery, rejection or loss of popularity, and we must expect it (John 15:18,19). Bonhoeffer said that suffering should be the badge of every Christian. We must be willing to be identified with Christ, who suffered and was rejected, before we can belong to his church. (YTL)

Father, help me never to remain silent out of fear of rejection when I should speak, for the sake of Jesus who was rejected for my sake.

Does our church lay too much or not enough emphasis on the cost of commitment to Jesus?

December 10   **The persecuted church**

**Who shall separate us from the love of Christ? Shall...
persecution?**   **Romans 8:35**

In a radio broadcast about Christian dissidents in the Soviet Union on June 9th 1977, an Orthodox priest said this: 'We are at the front line. In the front line. And this front line is all around us because the enemy has surrounded us on all sides. We are surrounded by the godless. There is not a single place which is free from attack — the press, art, the theatre, schools, official institutions, everything is occupied by the godless. The laws are designed to suffocate religion. We've been at the front for a long time: many of us have been taken prisoner. One might almost say that the whole front has been captured. Anyone who can hear us, respond. Do not believe those who try to dismiss the danger. The aim of the enemy is to destroy us. He has no other aims. But having destroyed us, he will destroy you as well. Listen, listen all those who can hear: we are alive, after all the terrible attacks, after all the awful bombardments, we are *still* alive. But we need help. Help us in every way you can.' (IBITC)

Do I and does our church spend time praying for the persecuted church? How much time?

Father, I pray for those suffering for the sake of your truth. I ask you to hear this prayer on behalf of one person who is at this moment at the end of his tether in the face of persecution. Deliver that person in or from his trial and make him aware overwhelmingly of your presence with him.

December 11   Love on its knees

Remember those who are in prison as if you were their fellow-prisoners, and those who are ill-treated as if you yourselves were suffering.   **Hebrews 13:3**

We may sometimes think that our failure in prayer is due to 'lack of faith'. Often that may be true. But perhaps more often, we fail through lack of sympathy or compassion. Jesus was repeatedly moved with compassion when he saw the enormous needs of sinful, suffering men and women. Such compassion naturally led to prayer and practical help. Richard Foster in *Celebration of Discipline* writes: 'If we have God-given compassion and concern for others, our faith will grow for them far more as we pray. In fact, if we genuinely love people, we desire for them far more than it is within our power to give, and that will cause us to pray.'

Compassion means 'suffering with' someone — trying to enter into his pains and problems... In *Prayer without Pretending* Anne Townsend writes: 'If I can imagine what it must be like to be the one for whom I am praying, then I can begin to intercede for that person. My imagination leads me on to want to be more deeply involved with him in his own life. This involvement leads to caring; caring to love; and love to intercession. I may never meet the one for whom I pray; but I may come to love him enough to offer him one of the most precious gifts one person can offer another — that of intercession, "love on its knees".' (D)

Father, please show me how I can use my imagination in praying for others.

Perhaps it's time to abandon, for good or temporarily, my 'shopping list' of people whom I simply name before God — and concentrate on the few who really need loving and time-consuming prayer right now.

December 12   See how these Christians love one another!

Love must be sincere.   **Romans 12:9**

Love is *sincere*; it has an open heart and an open hand; it knows nothing of corruption and deceit. It is *generous* (2 Corinthians 8:24; 1 John 4:11), marked by sacrificial giving of time, money, energy and gifts to those in any form of need. It is *active* (Hebrews 6:10; 1 John 3:18), backing expressions of love with acts of service.

It is *forbearing* and *forgiving* (Ephesians 4:3; Colossians 3:12-14), turning a blind eye and a deaf ear to the faults and failings of others, and quickly releasing them from the sins that have hurt us.

It is *uniting* (Ephesians 4:3; Philippians 2:2; Colossians 2:2), seeking always to make peace and to heal the divisions within Christian homes and churches.

It is *positive* (1 Corinthians 13:4-7), believing the best about others, not fearing the worst.

It is *sensitive* (Romans 14:15; Galatians 5:13), taking care not to say or do anything that will cause another brother to stumble.

It is *upbuilding* (Ephesians 4:15; 2 Timothy 2:22-26), so that even when the truth that is spoken must sometimes hurt, always it aims to build up that person into Christ.

It is the *summary* of the entire Christian faith (Romans 13:10; Colossians 3:14; 1 Corinthians 13:1; 14:1), the fulfilling of the law, and it must be the Christian's first and foremost aim.

If that portrait of love leaves us somewhat breathless, it is meant to. God does not require us to strive for such qualities in our own strength. (D)

Lord, I confess that I lack love. I long to open myself up to your limitless supply. Show me how to, I pray.

How can we show our love for those outside as well as within our church fellowship?

December 13   In the doldrums of doubt

Why did you doubt?   Matthew 14:31

A few weeks after committing my life to Christ, I wrote in a small diary: 'Is it all true, or am I making it up?' Almost every Christian, especially perhaps after his 'spiritual honeymoon', will struggle with doubts. There are several possible causes of these doubts.

First, it is part of the devil's work to try to sow doubts in the minds of Christians. One of his oldest and commonest tricks is to shake our confidence in the word of God (see Genesis 3:1). Is Christ really with me? Does he truly love me? Has he really forgiven me? Like Jesus, we can counter the devil's temptations to doubt God's word by claiming God's promises and holding on to what he has said.

Secondly, doubt can arise through disobedience. God's presence can seem unreal because of our wrongdoing (see Isaiah 59:2). Once we are God's children, that relationship is fixed, but the joy of that fact can fade and die, as a result of going our own way.

Thirdly, we can doubt God through ignorance about him. As we know and learn more of the truth, we are set free from ignorant doubts (see John 8:32).

Fourthly, living as an isolated Christian when we should be enjoying Christian fellowship can cause us to grow doubtful about our faith. We need the encouragement of other Christians (see Hebrews 3:13; 10:25).

Fifthly, inactivity can be a breeding ground for doubt, especially if we spend the time brooding on our problems. Taking an active and determined interest in the needs and problems of others can be a good corrective to this tendency. It was when Job started praying for his friends that God began to bless him with good things. (C/LANL)

Lord, I long to see you more clearly, love you more dearly, and follow you more nearly, day by day.

If someone were to come to me with their doubts, how would I help him? Would I know, for instance, where to turn to in the Bible for help?

December 14   Depression through exhaustion

Then he, Elijah, lay down under a tree and fell asleep. All at once an angel touched him and said, 'Get up and eat.' He looked around, and there by his head was a cake of bread baked over hot coals, and a jar of water. He ate and drank and then lay down again.   1 Kings 19:5,6

Elijah had had a long spiritual crisis and battle. Then he'd run thirty miles to Jezreel and prayed very intensely. He'd been without food for days, probably, and the final straw was Jezebel swearing to kill him. When he heard that, all he wanted to do was to get right away, so he went 120 miles to Beersheba. No wonder he was physically exhausted! His body, mind and emotions could take no more strain and pressure.

What was God's solution? He didn't at this stage send him spiritual counsel or rebuke his pride, rebellion and self-pity. He sent him two long refreshing periods of sleep, two nourishing meals and six weeks complete rest and change!

Many Christians today are depressed partly or wholly from sheer physical exhaustion. A man I know who counsels people with breakdowns said that ninety per cent of the Christians he sees have had inadequate rest in their lives. It is essential, especially for those very busy in Christian service, to have sufficient rest, change and relaxation.

Jesus says to us, as to his disciples long ago, 'Come with me by yourselves to a quiet place and get some rest' (Mark 6:31). (YTL)

Am I having enough physical, mental and emotional rest and refreshment?

Jesus, I want to go with you to a quiet place for rest. Show me how, when and where to do this.

December 15   Poor old me

I remember my affliction and my wandering, the bitterness and the gall. I well remember them, and my soul is downcast within me.   **Lamentations 3:19,20**

Self-pity is a real trap we can fall into. The devil uses this to turn our thoughts right away from the Lord so that we concentrate upon ourselves, our problems, our pains, our battles, our difficulties and our wretchedness. Self-pity is like a little grub that eats away at the plant of faith until that plant shrivels and dies.

As a deliberate act of our will, we need to turn away from ourselves and begin to call to mind the many expressions of God's love to us. Jeremiah knew what it was to be overcome by self-pity, as we see from the verses above. But he goes on, 'Yet this I call to mind [as a deliberate act of the will] and therefore I have hope: Because of the Lord's great love we are not consumed, for his compassions never fail. They are new every morning; great is your faithfulness' (verses 21-23).

Martin Luther, when he walked through the woods, used to raise his hat to the birds and say, 'Good morning, theologians! You wake and sing. But I, old fool, know less than you and worry over everything, instead of simply trusting in the Heavenly Father's care.' (IAT)

Father, I turn from self to you, and call to mind your faithfulness. . .

How can I help myself or another to keep looking upward and outward today?

December 16   Rooted in God

I do not trust in my bow, my sword does not bring me victory; but you give us victory over our enemies, and you put our adversaries to shame. In God we make our boast all day long, and we will praise your name for ever.   Psalm 44:6-8
But this happened that we might not rely on ourselves, but on God, who raises the dead.   2 Corinthians 1:9

Where do you really place your trust? As Christians, we know the right answer in theory: 'We trust in God!' But in practice, *do we*? When facing troubles, do we look to God for *his* way through, or do we manipulate things a little using *our* wisdom and skill? When wanting guidance, do we wait till the Lord makes *his* will clear, or do we ask him to bless *our* decisions, perhaps made after consulting only other Christians likely to agree with us? When tested, do we confidently look to God, or do we become negative and defeatist, knowing our own weakness?

The Bible makes it clear that God sometimes allows trials and temptations to teach us to depend wholly on himself. Self-reliance can be spiritually counter-productive. So can relying *too* heavily on others. Fellowship is vital, but it is possible to depend too much on other Christians and not enough on Jesus alone.

Every now and then God takes away our props — and then we find out whether we are rooted firmly enough in him. This rock-like stability can always be trusted. He will never, never let you down. Try him and see! (PL)

Lord, if you take away my props, help me not to be afraid, but to learn to take root more and more firmly in you.

Am I growing in dependence on God — even in ordinary, daily situations? Do I really believe Jesus' words: 'Apart from me you can do nothing' (John 15:5)?

December 17   One day at a time

Give us each day our daily bread.   **Luke 11:3**
Do not worry about tomorrow, for tomorrow will worry about itself. Each day has enough trouble of its own.
                                                  Matthew 6:34
Your strength will equal your days.   **Deuteronomy 33:25**

So often we put today's sun under tomorrow's cloud. We not only take upon our shoulders today's worries, but tomorrow's as well. And God doesn't promise us enough grace for *that* load. He promises a day's strength for a day's needs. We can exhaust ourselves thinking about what might happen when most of what we dread will probably never materialise.

Robert Louis Stevenson wrote: 'Anyone can carry his burden, however hard, until nightfall. Anyone can do his work, however hard, for one day. Anyone can live sweetly, patiently, lovingly, purely until the sun goes down.'

Living a day at a time is what life is about — especially in times of depression and difficulty. Worrying about our future robs us of some of the energy we need for today. Someone has put it more strongly: 'Worry on the part of God's children is unconscious blasphemy.' We may not realise this, but when we fret about the days ahead, we are in effect saying, 'God, you are not in control, you can't help me, you're not all-powerful.'

Martin Luther once met a peasant who was very depressed because fire had destroyed his home and goods.

'Do you know the Apostles' Creed?' Luther asked the man.

'Of course,' was the reply.

'Then say it,' said Luther.

'I believe in God the Father Almighty. . .' the man recited.

When he'd finished, Luther asked him to say it again. The man did so.

'Now,' said Luther, 'if you really believe what you have just said, surely you cannot doubt that your loving, almighty God will look after your needs?' (YTL)

God, the Father Almighty, I bring to you my needs for this day. . .

What action will I take every time a worry rears its ugly head?

December 18   If my people

If my people, who are called by my name, will humble themselves and pray and seek my face and turn from their wicked ways, then will I hear from heaven and will forgive their sin and will heal their land.   **2 Chronicles 7:14**

In the Old Testament, the year of Jubilee wasn't a jamboree; it was a time for national repentance and restoration. Our country has much to repent of, and so have we, as Christians. We have failed our nation because of our failure to preach the full gospel of the power of the Holy Spirit; to present the world with a living God and a relevant message; to move with the Holy Spirit and keep spiritually alive and renewed; to love each other as Christ loves us and commanded us to love each other; to live as Jesus lived; to take action against the things that are ruining our country.

Someone has worked out a recipe for a country's ruin, and here are a few ingredients from it:

Affirm man's animal origin, nature and functions to the exclusion of everything else and ridicule all reference to his spiritual qualities.

Inculcate general disrespect for any kind of authority by urging people to obey their own impulses in the name of freedom.

Soft-pedal all discussion of loyalty, responsibility, patriotism, duty and sacrifice in order that freedom of dissent may be established.

Discourage the practice of prayer and Bible reading by forbidding it in schools.

Indoctrinate the public into believing that Jesus Christ is a myth, Christianity a byword for ancient superstitions, and the church an institution that mankind has outgrown.

A recipe for a country's healing is contained in the verse for today. (YTL)

Where does national repentance begin?

Father, I repent of. . .

December 19   **Real repentance**

David said to Nathan, 'I have sinned against the Lord.'
**   2 Samuel 12:13**

For the background to this verse read the whole story (2 Samuel 11; 12:1-25). David had not been able to hide his guilty secret from one man at least — Nathan, the perceptive prophet. No doubt through prayer, this man received God's guidance as to what he was to say and do to make David face the truth.

When Nathan went in to David, he told a moving story about a rich man who had robbed a poor man of his one ewe lamb. David's reaction was immediate and violent. Red in the face with rage, he shouted, 'The rich man deserves to die, and he must pay for that lamb four times over!' Now the law stated that a man should give back four times as much as he had taken, but it didn't demand the death penalty in such cases. David was over-reacting because of his own guilty conscience. If we find ourselves quick to offer strong criticisms of or harsh judgments about someone, we had better beware! Perhaps we are saying, 'Look at him!' because we want to make quite sure no one is focusing attention on us!

David very quickly had to look at himself because Nathan faithfully said, 'You are the man!' and proceeded to spell out what David had done and the consequences of his actions.

Face to face with his sin, the king blurted out, 'I have sinned against the Lord.' No doubt, like Simon Peter, he then went out and wept bitterly, as he really repented (Psalm 51). He saw that he had wronged not only Bathsheba but also God. As he became aware of how utterly sinful he was, he cried out in agony for cleansing and forgiveness.

The sin was removed, but not its consequences (2 Samuel 12:18), because David needed to learn that God is not mocked (Galatians 6:7; Numbers 32:23). But neither does he bear grudges, and David and Bathsheba had another son whom 'the Lord loved' (2 Samuel 12:24,25).

If there is anything on your conscience, put it right before you next go to communion. (YTL)

If I have sinned against the Lord in some matter — am I prepared to pray my way through Psalm 51?

Lord, as I understand more of your sufferings on the cross, may my repentance go deeper and the joy that follows it be greater.

December 20   **The church— God's work**

Be shepherds of the flock of God, which he bought with his own blood.
                                                    Acts 20:28

The church belongs to God, comes from God and cannot live without God.

It's a *comfort* to remember this when results seem disappointing. Of course, if that is so, we should ask ourselves searching questions, but we can also remind ourselves that it is God's work and leave it in his hands. Equally, when people are critical of us, we can hand the matter over to God. Incidentally, if you do want to say something critical about a sermon or service, it's wise to wait twenty-four hours. However positively you intend your comments, they can be very deflating if delivered immediately after the event, when the person concerned is likely to be tense or tired or both.

Knowing that the church is God's work is also a good *corrective* when things go well. When there's blessing, it's the Lord's doing. So when God works through you, just praise him for what he has done, however foolish, weak, lowly, despised and 'nothing' you may feel yourself to be (1 Corinthians 1:27-29)!

The truth that the work is God's work brings a *challenge*. Are we really trusting in God and not in people or personalities (1 Corinthians 3)? We should be. 'What, after all, is Apollos? And what is Paul? Only servants, through whom you came to believe — as the Lord has assigned to each his task' (1 Corinthians 3:5). Besides, that the church has survived, let alone thrives, must be due to God's grace, will and activity — in view of all the terrible things that have been done down the ages by some of its members. (YTL)

What practical steps can we take this week to be the church of God rather than the church of ... (whatever the name of our church or minister is)?

Father, thank you for the people who have helped me, but may I not rely on them too heavily or put them on pedestals.

December 21   The Lord told me . . .

While they were worshipping the Lord and fasting, the Holy Spirit said, 'Set apart for me Barnabas and Saul for the work to which I have called them.' So after they had fasted and prayed, they placed their hands on them and sent them off.

Acts 13:2,3

Today people seek guidance on all sorts of matters from all kinds of sources. Some are prepared to become involved with occult practices, for the sake of receiving supernatural guidance on some matter or other. But the Holy Spirit will not guide through these means, nor will he guide you to the next Derby winner, or any other thing which you seek for your own personal advantage. Evil spirits *do* guide people along these lines, but their purpose is to deceive people and keep them from Jesus. Guidance from the Holy Spirit will be true and will always glorify Jesus.

I found at least thirteen instances of direct guidance in the Acts and, in every case, the purpose was the glory of Christ and the advance of his kingdom; also, in every case, some form of hardship, usually persecution, was involved for the Christians. As then, so now — Jesus is often glorified through circumstances which we may find disturbing or hard.

Guidance *can* come in the form of a direct word from the Lord, but this seems to be quite rare. More often it comes to Christians through circumstances, the advice of other Christians, prayer, perhaps with fasting, the Bible, and a deep inner peace or conviction.

The essential quality is humility; we need to be free of our own ideas of importance, and to wait quietly before God. Unfortunately, this is sometimes the last thing we do. (YTL)

Am I too quick to claim that the Lord has told me this or that?

Father, may I be willing to listen to the advice of other Christians.

December 22 **What does being led by the Spirit mean?**

If you are led by the Spirit, you are not under law.

Galatians 5:18

Being led by the Spirit certainly means acting in accordance with the Scriptures. So if you were to tell me that you felt led to marry a non-Christian I would have to tell you that the Holy Spirit had *not* so led you, because the Scriptures say, 'Do not be yoked together with unbelievers' (2 Corinthians 6:14). The same would be true if you were to say that you felt led to have sex before marriage or to do anything else which is contrary to Scripture.

Being led by the Spirit normally means travelling along 'Spirit Street', having turned away from 'Flesh Way'. The characteristics of those who are being led by the Spirit along 'Spirit Street' are listed, as are the characteristics of those following 'Flesh Way' (Galatians 5:19-22; Romans 8:5-7).

Sometimes, but not often, the leading of the Spirit is more specific, as when Paul was given a revelation (Galatians 2:2). But nearly always this kind of guidance is in the context of suffering or hardship; where the Spirit is clearly active, so is the enemy. So we shouldn't be surprised if the Spirit leads us into painful, testing situations.

This specific guidance should always be checked — with the Scriptures, with leaders, by circumstances and with other Christians. It should also be marked by a deep inner peace (Colossians 3:15).

Of course we will make mistakes, but God will gently call us back (Isaiah 30:21), and if we surrender our mistakes to him, he will even use them to increase the beauty of his pattern for our lives. (YTL)

Father, it's wonderful to be led by your Holy Spirit. Thank you.

Is there any leading I need to check with anyone today?

December 23   Test questions

Let us throw off everything that hinders.   **Hebrews 12:1**
Be careful ... that the exercise of your freedom does not become a stumbling block to the weak.   **1 Corinthians 8:9**

If a Christian has doubts or questions about how to discern right and wrong in relation to the daily necessities of living in this world, here are three practical principles that have often helped me.

First, will what I want to do help or hinder my relationship with Jesus?

Then, will it help or hinder someone else's relationship with Jesus?

Above all, finally, will it glorify God (1 Corinthians 10:31)?

Our warfare is against the world, the flesh and the devil. The world, this earth on which we live, is the scene of the battle because it is temporarily dominated by the controlling power of that diabolical invader, Satan. But his destiny is total defeat and oblivion. That is why he is so desperately trying to demonstrate his powers in the short time he has left. (HW)

Help me to remember that I am in the middle of a battle — and to keep looking at the One who is in command of the army to which I belong.

Ask the three questions about something I am thinking of doing.

December 24   Greater than Solomon

The Queen of the South will rise at the judgment with the men of this generation and condemn them, for she came from the ends of the earth to listen to Solomon's wisdom, and now one greater than Solomon is here.   Luke 11:31

King Solomon was perhaps the greatest king who ever lived. His wealth and wisdom were unique. He was a builder, planter, promoter of the arts, peacemaker, and many other things. But it was chiefly his amazing God-given wisdom that was known to all. The Queen of Sheba came to test it and was left speechless (1 Kings 10:1-13). With all that in mind, think about the words of a carpenter's son spoken at a little place called Nazareth: 'One greater than Solomon is here.' To those listening to Jesus these words must have been shocking to say the least. How could Jesus claim to be greater than Solomon?

First, he was a hundred per cent obedient to God. 'I always do what pleases him [God],' Jesus said (John 8:29). It was no easy option. He knew pain, depression, rejection, loneliness and anguish. Once he sweated drops of blood, as 'he learned obedience from what he suffered' (Hebrews 5:8). That was one reason why he was far, far greater than Solomon although he had no worldly advantages.

Secondly, his power was far, far greater than Solomon's. The religious leaders could not deny his power, since people were healed and demons cast out, so they tried to deny that God was the source of it (Luke 11:15).

Thirdly his wisdom was greater than Solomon's (Luke 2:40). He was filled with wisdom — and power and grace, truth and glory (John 1:1-18), because he was full of God.

Jesus is not just the greatest. He is the one and only — the man Christ Jesus. (YTL)

Lord, our nation deserves to be condemned for largely rejecting the one who is greater than Solomon and greater than Jonah, but we pray that Christians will so repent and live out the truth that our land will also repent and turn and live.

How much are we praying for our country?

December 25   **The man from heaven**

The Word became flesh and lived for a while among us. We have seen his glory, the glory of the one and only Son, who came from the Father, full of grace and truth.   John 1:14

'We have seen his glory': five words with staggering implications. What is God like? How can an infinite and holy God reveal himself to finite and sinful man? The greatest thinkers of the world have been grappling with questions like these for over three thousand years without reaching any final conclusions.

The Old Testament prophets spoke about what God was like, but when Jesus came down from heaven and was made man, he revealed God so perfectly that he is described as 'the image of the invisible God' (Colossians 1:15), 'the radiance of God's glory and the exact representation of his being' (Hebrews 1:3). When the disciples wanted to be quite sure about God, Philip said to the Lord, 'Show us the Father and that will be enough for us' (John 14:8), and Jesus replied, 'Anyone who has seen me has seen the Father' (John 14:9).

We hear so much about communication problems these days. God solved the problem perfectly. What could be more meaningful than the birth of a baby — growing into boyhood and manhood, sharing love and compassion, knowing loneliness and hatred, suffering pain and agony — and finally death? In Luther's famous words: 'He ate, drank, slept, walked: was weary, sorrowful, rejoicing; he wept and he laughed; he knew hunger and thirst and sweat; he talked, he toiled, he prayed . . . so that there was no difference between him and other men, save only this, that he was God and had no sin.'

Since God revealed himself so plainly, it's tragic that the Christian church is guilty of theological jargon and confused thinking. (PL)

Lord, I pray that those who will be preaching the Christmas message in our church at this time will think clearly and speak simply and relevantly to all who come to listen.

Do I have a 'communication problem' with someone? Have I ever opened my heart and shared my true self with that person?

December 26   Why did he come?

Christ Jesus . . . made himself nothing, taking the very nature of a servant, being made in human likeness.

Philippians 2:5,7

What was the purpose of Jesus' coming into the world? First, he *came to save* — not to judge. He lived in this sinful, lost world for as long as we allowed him to. In the end, it was not that he rejected us because of all our faults and failings, but that we rejected him. He suffered and served — and that's what his followers are called to do. So if you are tempted to pull out of your church situation, because you find the faults and failings of others hard to bear — remember Jesus Christ.

Secondly, Jesus *came as a wonderful counsellor*, perfectly fulfilling the name given to him hundreds of years before (Isaiah 9:6). And when he left the earth physically, he promised that another counsellor would come and be with his people for ever (John 14:16).

Thirdly, Jesus *became poor for us* — desperately poor — 'so that you through his poverty might become rich' (2 Corinthians 8:9) — rich in faith and love, joy and peace, and all those priceless qualities which money cannot buy. Truly to follow Jesus means accepting his lifestyle so that others might live.

Fourthly, Jesus *came as the Prince of Peace*. In God's eyes the quality of our relationships is more important than the rightness of our particular convictions. As Christians, we are often bad at learning how to disagree; but we do need to remain in harmony. 'Make every effort to keep the unity of the Spirit through the bond of peace' (Ephesians 4:3). If we cannot experience and demonstrate the reality of this in Christ, what have we to offer to the rest of society, with its fractured relationships? We are to be peacemakers rather than peacelovers and this is a painful calling, but it's what we should be involved in if we are true followers of Jesus. (PL)

Father, all through this day keep me remembering the example of your son.

Am I serving others in this way? How can I?

December 27

Rejoice in the Lord always.

Let us fix our eyes on Jesus.

Look at Jesus

Philippians 4:4

Hebrews 12:2

C. S. Lewis once wrote: 'Look for yourself and you will find in the long run only hatred, loneliness, despair, rage, ruin and decay. But look for Christ, and you will find him, and with him also everything else thrown in.'

What we all need to do increasingly is — look to Christ. When we look at ourselves or at other Christians we may be tempted to focus on faults and failings, and reap a harvest of despair. Or we may be tempted to congratulate ourselves on our spiritual progress. But what we are told to do is to look to Christ and rejoice in him.

A church fellowship may be profoundly aware of its own problems, while visitors to it are touched by the love and joy of Jesus so evident there. Every church fellowship must accept that at best it is a fellowship of sinners — forgiven sinners, but sinners just the same — and that joy and satisfaction will result from looking not at one another but at Jesus.

It may be comforting to remember that all God's saints have been increasingly aware of their sinfulness and of their need for and experience of God's grace. It may also be comforting to remind ourselves of Jesus' problems with the men among whom he lived and worked for three years. How slow they were to believe! How self-centred they were! How badly they let him down at his moment of greatest need!

The apostle Paul didn't find it easy to help his converts grow into mature Christians. He experienced 'the pains of childbirth until Christ is formed in you' (Galatians 4:19).

So it has always been. May our confidence and joy, therefore, always rest in Jesus Christ who alone is worthy of all praise. (PL)

Lord, help me to keep taking my eyes off myself and others, and keep looking upwards to you as my example, my helper and my source of inner strength and delight.

Is there someone I know who is bogged down because of his own or the church's failure, and who needs to be gently encouraged to look at Jesus? What can I do about it?

For you died, and your life is hidden with Christ in God.
                                                    Colossians 3:3

The treasure of the Christian is this: 'Christ in you, the hope of glory' (Colossians 1:27); Paul is not just speaking here of the future or life *after* death, but of the present glory which Christians enjoy, or life *before* death. Now, in the present, we enjoy Christ's presence in us.

If we grasped even a little of that staggering truth, we would be 'overflowing with thankfulness' (Colossians 2:7). Sometimes Christians seem to indulge in a kind of one-up-man-ship by being one-down on everyone else! We are always more tired, more pressurised than anyone else! If we were overflowing with thankfulness, we would not find the Christian life such a drag and we wouldn't have time for self-pity. Jean Darnell was once ill in bed. She had lost her voice and was feeling miserable. A friend came in and said, 'Christ in you, the hope of glory,' twice, and then left.

Do we really grasp the stupendous implications of the truth that Christ is in us now? If so, we would surely be more joyful and more victorious.

Jean Darnell was left meditating on those words. Not only did she experience Christ's joy and victory, but also his complete and instant healing.

If Christ is in us, then we are already, in one sense, raised with him; therefore we need to set our minds on things above (Colossians 3:2). Paul isn't urging us to opt out of our responsibilities at all; he wants us to see the whole of life from our new vantage point — the position of triumph and victory won for us through Jesus' death and resurrection. (YTL)

Lord, please show me what difference your presence in and with me can make to my needs and problems today.

Finish the sentence: Because Christ is in me, I have ...

The Spirit of the Sovereign Lord is on me, because the Lord has anointed me to preach good news to the poor.   Isaiah 61:1

There are more non-Christians in the world today than there were at the turn of the century. Many churches have become redundant or have dwindling congregations, while false cults and other groups are winning adherents at an alarming rate. We must evangelise. Churches which lose their evangelistic edge grow weak, often through members being critical of one another, instead or working together in outreach.

What is evangelism? Essentially it is sharing the good news of Jesus, calling people to respond to him as Saviour and Lord in repentance and faith, and bringing them into his Body, the church, for service in the world.

Preaching an evangelistic sermon from the pulpit is only *one* aspect of evangelism, and it will have very little effect if the gospel is not being both proclaimed and demonstrated by the church in question. Throughout the New Testament the word was preached and demonstrated through actions of one sort or another, or through signs and wonders (e.g. Mark 1; Luke 7 and 8; Acts 8 and 10). When Peter went into Cornelius' house (Acts 10:25) he was demonstrating the gospel even before he said a single word: a Jew entering a Gentile home in peace and love was in itself good news.

In one church where I led a mission, large numbers were converted in one day. Why? Because in that church the word of the gospel was given a very rich context: the members knew something of the gifts of the Spirit, there was a wonderful atmosphere of love and caring, and people were involved in the community and in house-groups. Preaching there was like sowing the seed in very fertile ground. (YTL)

Is the word preached in our church, and if so how rich is its context?

Jesus, you lived what you spoke. Help me to do the same, more and more.

The word of the Lord came to me saying, 'Before I formed you in the womb I knew you, before you were born I set you apart; I appointed you as a prophet to the nations.'

Jeremiah 1:4,5

When the people of God were in a desperate situation, God's answer was a nervous, inexperienced young man — a country lad from a poor village, with no startling gifts, very conscious of his weakness and desperately in need of love and understanding. Surely God had picked the wrong man. The man in question thought so anyway.

'Ah, Sovereign Lord,' he said, 'I do not know how to speak; I am only a child.' But God answered, 'I am with you and will rescue you. . . . I have put my words in your mouth' (Jeremiah 1:8,9).

Why did God choose Jeremiah? It was for one reason only — because he was willing to obey. If a person is willing to obey God, weakness, inexperience, youth and lack of ability do not matter because God's Spirit within that person is more than enough for every situation.

Throughout the history of the church, God has taken young, inexperienced men and equipped them by his Spirit for great work. Think of David, Samuel, Daniel, John the Baptist and Timothy. Calvin wrote his Institutes at the age of twenty-four, Wesley founded Methodism at twenty-five and McCheyne, who shook Scotland by his preaching, died at twenty-nine.

Another young man heard someone remark, 'The world has yet to see what God will do with a man fully consecrated to him,' and his reply was, 'By the Holy Spirit, I'll be that man.' His name was D. L. Moody and thousands turned to Christ through his ministry.

In these critical days, God is calling out and looking for more Jeremiahs. (YTL)

Nothing, Lord, I am nothing;
Anything, Lord, anything for thee;

Anywhere, Lord, to any service,
No matter how lonely it may be.

Am I willing to say that prayer and mean it?

December 31   Love story

Your Maker is your husband.   Isaiah 54:5

Nowhere is the warmth, passion and tenderness of the relationship between God and his people more clearly seen than in two Old Testament passages, originally conceived as secular poems about human love (Psalm 45 and the Song of Songs). The church that has become cold, hard, efficient (perhaps!), and moralistic, could do no better than to spend time meditating on these poems. What an astonishing thing for the heavenly Bridegroom to say to us, his earthly and faithless bride: 'You have stolen my heart, my sister, my bride; you have stolen my heart with one glance of your eyes, with one jewel of your necklace. How delightful is your love, my sister, my bride' (Song of Songs 4:9,10)!

The marriage analogy used so frequently for Israel is an important theme for the nature of the church. When Jesus was asked by John's disciples about fasting, he replied, 'How can the guests of the bridegroom fast while he is with them' (Mark 2:19)? Later, speaking of the wise and foolish virgins waiting for the coming of the bridegroom, he described the kingdom of heaven as a marriage banquet for the king's son. Paul likewise thought of the church as the bride of Christ on a number of occasions. And in the Revelation of John, the summit of praise in heaven is when 'the wedding of the Lamb has come, and his bride has made herself ready' (Revelation 19:7). (IBITC)

Am I afraid of dwelling on this picture of God's love? If so why?

Father, help me to see the relationship between you and your people as the greatest love story of all time.

INDEX
of themes

Bible characters
Dates
July 16; *Abel* — Mar. 13; *Abraham* — Apr. 29; June 8, 10; Oct. 4, 24; Nov. 25; *David* — Jan. 8, 27; Mar. 14, 25; July 17, 24; Sep. 22; Dec. 19; *Elijah* — Mar. 15; Sep. 8; Nov. 11; *Enoch* — Sep. 13; *Habakkuk* — July 13; *Jeremiah* — Feb. 18; Dec. 30; *Peter* — July 18; Aug. 15; *Philip* — Sep. 3; *Prodigal's brother* — Feb. 16; *Rahab* — June 19; *Saul* — Apr. 3.

Christian basics
Dates
Feb. 13, 16; Mar. 16; Apr. 1—7, 8, 9; July 30; Aug. 8, 9, 12; Sep. 26; Oct. 8; Nov. 10, 12, 28; Dec. 5, 24—26.

Church fellowships (Christians together)
Dates
Jan. 30; Feb. 19, 20, 26; Mar. 10, 11, 23, 24; Apr. 24, 25; May 16, 20, 26; June 7, 12, 16; July 10, 12; Aug. 16, 19—22, 24, 26, 30; Sep. 19; Oct. 8; Nov. 13, 21; Dec. 1—7, 27.

Church worldwide
Dates
Jan. 30; Feb. 22; Mar. 9; May 19; June 12, 28; July 1—7; Aug. 18; Oct. 26; Nov. 13; Dec. 20, 31.

Committed discipleship
Dates
Feb. 15; Mar. 16, 18; May 1—7, 12, 16, 25; June 22; Aug. 1, 12, 15, 17; Oct. 14, 15, 27—29; Nov. 11, 29; Dec. 9.

Cross
Dates
Jan. 17; Apr. 2, 13, 14, 20, 21; Sep. 28, 29; Oct. 14; Nov. 18, 30.

Evil
Dates
Jan. 9, 26; Feb. 14, 18; Mar. 9, 15; July 20—23; Aug. 2; Nov. 28; Dec. 18.

Faith
Dates
Feb. 11; Mar. 13; Apr. 19; June 19, 20; July 13, 16, 27; Aug. 8, 9; Sep. 13, 20; Oct. 22—24, 31; Nov. 25, 27; Dec. 16, 17.

God (character & activity)
Dates
Jan. 8, 26, 27; Feb. 12; Mar. 23;
Apr. 1, 29; June 10, 11, 14, 27, 29;
July 3, 8, 15, 23; Aug. 14, 28; Sep.
8, 11, 14, 15, 17; Oct. 23, 31;
Nov. 4, 8; Dec. 18, 20.

God's word
Dates
Jan. 21, 25, 27–29; Feb. 27; Mar.
19; May 8, 27–29; June 17, 18;
Sep. 18; Nov. 7.

Gospel
Dates
Jan. 10, 11; May 13; June 27;
Sep. 7.

Guidance
Dates
May 8, 9, 23, 28; July 26; Aug.
27; Nov. 22, 23, 26; Dec. 21–23.

Healing
Dates
Jan. 15; Mar. 28; June 6; Aug. 28;
Sep. 20, 24; Oct. 23; Dec. 3.

Heaven
Dates
June 27, 29, 30; July 1, 31; Oct.
16; Nov. 30.

Holy Spirit (character & activity)
Dates
Jan. 13, 19; Feb. 2, 12, 23–25;
Mar. 22, 26; Apr. 7, 24–28; May
22, 25; June 2–5; Aug. 13, 26, 27;
Sep. 16, 19; Oct. 9, 17, 19–21;
Dec. 7, 22.

Jesus
Dates
Jan. 16; Feb. 13; Mar. 17; Apr. 5,
6, 8–12, 15–19, 23; May 12;
June 25; July 31; Aug. 9, 13, 31;
Sep. 9, 12, 24; Oct. 15, 16; Nov.
10, 20, 26, 28; Dec. 24–28.

Joy
Dates
Apr. 15, 17; July 28–30; Oct. 25.

Judgment
Dates
Mar. 30, 31; June 24; Sep. 26, 27;
Nov. 8, 9.

Love
Dates
Jan. 31; Feb. 21; Apr. 21; May 14;
June 13, 16; July 14; Aug. 10;
Sep. 25, 26; Oct. 15; Nov. 4, 14;
Dec. 11, 12, 31.

Life's experiences
Dates
Feb. 1, 17; Mar. 14, 29, 30; Apr.
12, 18; May 17, 18; June 20, 23;
July 24, 25; Aug. 14; Sep. 11, 12;
Nov. 1–7, 24; Dec. 8, 13, 14, 17.

Mission (telling & showing others the good news)
Dates
Jan. 23, 25; Feb. 25–29; Mar. 21,
22, 24; Apr. 22, 23; June 23, 24,
26; Aug. 16–18, 31; Sep. 1–7;
Oct. 9–12; Nov. 18–21; Dec.
29, 30.

New birth — new life
Dates
Feb. 1–7; May 5; July 8; Aug. 11;
Oct. 18; Nov. 12.

Obedience
Dates
Jan. 24; Mar. 1, 5, 7, 10, 13; May
1, 11, 15; June 11, 14, 15; July 11;
Aug. 10; Oct. 29; Dec. 6, 30.

Peace
Dates
Apr. 4; June 25; Sep. 10.

Prayer
Dates
Jan. 18—20; Feb. 8, 9, 17; Mar. 8; Apr. 26, 29; May 10; June 8, 9; Oct. 1—7; Dec. 11.

Relationships between Christians
Dates
Mar. 11, 12, 28; Apr. 28; May 6, 14, 26; June 9, 13; July 11, 14; Aug. 21, 24; Sep. 29; Oct. 30; Nov. 13, 17; Dec. 2, 4.

Renewal
Dates
Feb. 23, 24; Apr. 24, 26, 28; May 22, 25; June 1—7; Aug. 15, 23; Sep. 17, 23; Oct. 11, 19—21; Dec. 28.

Scriptures
Dates
Jan. 21, 22, 24, 29; Feb. 8; Mar. 1—7; June 17, 18; Sep. 18, 21.

Sin & forgiveness
Dates
Jan. 9, 12, 14, 15, 17, 28; Feb. 3, 6, 7; Mar. 11, 12, 25—28; Apr. 2, 29; May 24; July 17, 18; Aug. 25, 29; Sep. 16, 22, 30; Oct. 17; Nov. 15, 29; Dec. 18, 19.

Spiritual war
Dates
Feb. 29; Mar. 31; May 30, 31; June 21; July 19, 20; Aug. 1—7; Sep. 9, 24, 28; Nov. 2; Dec. 13, 15, 23.

Suffering
Dates
Feb. 17; Mar. 14, 29; Apr. 10, 18; May 2, 7; June 1, 20, 22, 23; July 9, 24, 25; Aug. 27; Sep. 8, 12, 23; Nov. 3, 5, 6, 15, 23, 24; Dec. 8—10, 14—16.

Truth
Dates
Mar. 3; May 21, 30; Aug. 25; Sep. 21.

Unity
Dates
May 19, 26; June 28; July 7; Aug. 23, 24; Sep. 29; Oct. 5, 6; Nov. 16, 17; Dec. 1.

Worship & praise
Dates
Jan. 1—7; Feb. 10; Mar. 20; Apr. 11; May 17, 18; June 26, 29; July 28, 29; Sep. 14, 15; Oct. 12—14, 25; Nov. 27, 30.

SOURCES

The readings have been taken from the following sources — suitably edited or paraphrased. The dates in the text are indicated:

Anchor Recordings
Dates
Jan. 5, 13, 14, 16, 19, 24, 25; Feb. 1, 2, 6, 12, 16, 24, 26; Mar. 17, 18, 28, 29, 31; Apr. 1, 9, 11, 15; May 15, 24, 25; June 1, 13, 20, 21, 28; July 10, 11; Aug. 6, 8, 23, 24; Sep. 4; Oct. 14, 15, 17, 22, 28, 30; Nov. 17, 27; Dec. 3.

Christian Foundation Publications (Cassettes)
Dates
Feb. 17, 21; Mar. 2, 12, 21; Apr. 13, 18, 24; May 9, 16; June 4; July 27; Aug. 3; Nov. 6, 22.

Key Cassettes, Scripture Union
Dates
Apr. 2, 5, 28; May 7; Sep. 28; Oct. 16.

Live a New Life, David Watson (Cassette)
Dates
Jan. 22; Feb. 4; May 6, 14; Oct. 2; Nov. 19, 23; Dec. 15.

Start the Day Cassettes, Scripture Union
Date
Nov. 24.

York Tape Library
Dates
Jan. 3, 6—8, 10, 11, 15, 17, 21, 23, 26—31; Feb. 3, 5, 9, 11, 13, 18—20, 22, 25; Mar. 9, 13—15, 23—25, 27, 30; Apr. 3, 4, 6—8, 10, 12, 17, 19, 22, 25—27, 29, 30; May 4, 5, 8, 10, 11, 13, 17, 19, 21—23, 28, 29; June 2, 3, 5—8, 10, 12, 17—19, 24, 25, 27, 29, 30; July 3—5, 8, 9, 12—15, 17, 18, 20, 23, 24, 30, 31; Aug. 5, 7, 9—11, 13, 16, 18, 22, 26—29; Sep. 2, 3, 6, 8—16, 18—20, 22—24, 26, 27; Oct. 4, 6, 9—11, 13, 18, 20, 21, 23, 24, 29, 31; Nov. 4, 5, 7—13, 15, 18, 25, 26, 29, 30; Dec. 4—6, 8, 9, 14, 17—22, 24, 28—30.

Bible Reading Notes, Scripture Union
Date
Mar. 5.

Discipleship, Hodder

Dates

Jan. 18, 20; Feb. 8, 15, 23; Mar. 1, 4, 6, 16, 26; Apr. 20; May 1, 12, 20, 27, 30; June 9, 22; July 21; Aug. 2, 17, 25; Sep. 25, 29; Oct. 3, 5, 7, 25; Dec. 11, 12.

Hidden Warfare, STL

Dates

May 31; July 19; Aug. 12; Nov. 2; Dec. 23.

I Believe in the Church, Hodder

Dates

Feb. 27, 28; Mar. 3, 7, 10; May 18; June 14—16; July 1, 2, 6, 7, 28; Aug. 1, 4, 20, 30; Sep. 1, 21; Oct. 26; Nov. 14, 16; Dec. 10, 31.

I Believe in Evangelism, Hodder

Dates

Jan. 12; Feb. 14, 29; Mar. 19, 20, 22; Apr. 21; May 2; June 23, 26; July 26, 29; Aug. 14, 19, 31; Sep. 5, 7; Oct. 12; Nov. 20, 21; Dec. 7.

In Search of God, Falcon

Dates

June 11; July 25

Is Anyone There? Hodder

Dates

Apr. 14; Dec. 15.

Live a New Life, IVP

Dates

Mar. 8; Apr. 23; Aug. 21.

My God is Real, Falcon

Date

Jan. 9

One in the Spirit, Hodder

Dates

Jan 2; Feb. 10; May 26.

Pastoral Letters

Dates

Jan. 1, 4; Feb. 7; Mar. 11; Apr. 16; May 3; July 16, 22; Aug. 15; Sep. 17, 30; Oct. 1, 8, 19, 27; Nov. 1, 28; Dec. 1, 2, 16, 25—27.

Talk for Local Radio (Bristol)

Date

Nov. 3.

SCRIPTURE INDEX

YOU ARE MY GOD

David Watson

David Watson was internationally renowned and loved as an evangelist and teacher. His autobiography makes enthralling reading, telling of his spiritual pilgrimage, the growth of his marriage and the transformation of St Michael-le-Belfrey, York, into a pioneering church.

'A story of a triumph, told without a trace of triumphalism.'

Church Times

'Read this book. It will move and stir you.'

Buzz

'A truly brave and candid account.'

Church of England Newspaper

'Invigorating reading.'

Renewal

'Should be compulsory reading for all who are interested in Christian leadership, church growth and evangelism today.'

Redemption Tidings

'Excellent and moving.'

Life and Work

'David Watson was one of the best known and loved Christian leaders of modern times ... he had an impact as evangelist and teacher second only to Billy Graham.'

Michael Green

I BELIEVE IN EVANGELISM

David Watson

The passionate convictions that motivated David Watson's ministry are revealed in this important book which explores what evangelism is and how it can be carried out by both Church and individual.

'It is rooted in experience. It is grounded in a remarkable grasp of the New Testament. It is alive with the freshness and power of the Holy Spirit.'

Michael Green

'Fresh, lively and enjoyable ... solid thinking and practical application.'

Baptist Times

The late David Watson is author of many books, including *Discipleship, Fear No Evil, I Believe in the Church* and *You Are My God.*

ONE IN THE SPIRIT

David Watson

'For centuries,' writes David Watson, 'the Holy Spirit has been effectively subordinated to the Bible or to the Church. The Pentecostal explosion has largely been a reaction to this, with a fresh recognition of the Third Person of the Trinity and a deep longing for the same wind of the Spirit that energised believers both in the first century and in all the revivals of the Church down the years.'

ONE IN THE SPIRIT provides a sensitive and penetrating account of the glorious complexity of the work of the Holy Spirit, calling Christians to be daily filled afresh with the Spirit. 'Above everything else,' asserts David, 'we need to be united in love, One in the Spirit and One in the Lord.'

I BELIEVE IN THE CHURCH

David Watson

David Watson was known, loved and respected worldwide as a gifted teacher and Christian communicator. His dynamic ministry lives on through his writing, and *I Believe in the Church* has become a classic. It draws on the years of leadership and learning at St Michael-le-Belfrey, York, to give a crucial message to the Church of the twentieth century.

'You will be staggered at the revolutionary impact of a Christianity which is radical enough to get back to the New Testament, and courageous enough to apply it in practice.'

Michael Green

'Who could not be genuinely moved, profoundly challenged and positively inspired by so prophetic a book?'

Church of England Newspaper

'Spiritual power.'

Church Times

'Passionate belief is stamped upon every page.'

Christian Herald